By
Agnes Arany-Makkai, M.A.
Former Lecturer, Hong Kong Baptist University
President, Association for Translation, Literature
and New Talent Instigation Studies—*Atlantis-Centaur, Inc.*

BARRON'S

All inquiries should be addressed to:
Barron's Educational Series, Inc.
250 Wireless Boulevard
Hauppauge, New York 11788

International Standard Book Number 0-8120-9436-0

Library of Congress Catalog Card Number 96-84562

Printed in the United States of America

987654321

Contents

Acknowledgments

I wish to express my gratitude to the following individuals who have helped me a great deal during the preparation of this dictionary. They are, first and foremost, Dr. Raisa Gerasimovna Grinkot, and Mr. Maks Moyseyevich Vaysberg, who have generously donated their time and energy throughout the entire process of writing this dictionary. I am also grateful to Dr. Prof. Larissa Aleksandrovna Mashkova of Moscow State University, Visiting Professor at the University of Illinois at Chicago, for her helpful observations.

Foreword

One of the most striking characteristics of languages is that standard, average sentence constructions and word combinations such as *the boy kissed the girl* and *the boy didn't kiss the girl* also abound in expressions such as *the cowboy kicked the bucket, the room was at sixes and sevens.* If someone, who doesn't know that these are idioms, rushes unsuspectingly to the dictionary and looks up each word, he or she will get strange paraphrases that don't make any sense, such as 'the cowboy's foot came into collision with a pail'; 'the room was [probably arranged according to the numbers] six and seven.'

But these sentences do not have these meanings. As most Americans know, they mean 'to die' and 'to be very messy,' respectively. These meanings, however, are by no means obvious to a foreigner.

The same is true of Russian idioms for speakers of English. Russians take their idioms just as much for granted as Americans do theirs. These frozen speech forms reveal their strange imagery when one tries to understand them for the first time without previous familiarity.

Idioms are semantic entities whose constituent words do not, as a rule, suggest the actual meaning, or do so misleadingly and only up to a certain extent.

Yet to know a language really well, as an "insider," one must master the idiomatic expressions of a language. Lacking this skill, the speaker of the language in question sounds like a lifeless grammar book for beginners.

Both Russian and English are Indo-European languages — English is West Germanic, Russian is Eastern Balto-Slavic. Once, in the distant past of several millennia ago, they sprang from the same source, known as Proto Indo-European.

A few cognates still exist, of course — think of Russian *мать* versus English *mother*, both meaning 'female parent'; or one may also think of Russian *брат* 'brother' or *сестра* 'sister.' Such cases are rare, and any English speaker wishing to learn Russian must acquire a great deal of new vocabulary.

Recent events on the international scene have dramatically increased the traffic between the Russian-speaking world and the United States. There are thousands of recent Russian-speaking arrivals; American business people go to Russia in increasing numbers and learn the language. The more genuine Russian idioms they can understand and use, the better it will be for their human relations and for their businesses.

In this dictionary a great effort has been made to match the most common and most important Russian idioms with their American English counterparts. In many instances there is a match, but very often there isn't. Thus for instance the Russian idiom *добрыми намерениями вымощена дорога в ад* corresponds exactly to the English *the road to hell is paved with good intentions.* The same is true of *делить шкуру неубитого медведя*, which literally means 'to divide the hide of a bear that hasn't been killed yet.' This corresponds to the sense — not to the words! — of *don't count your chickens before they're hatched.* However, another frequent version in Russian has *цыплят по осени считают,* in which both 'chicken' and 'counting' are mentioned, making this a very close relative of the English proverbial idiom.

Some of the most typical Russian idioms have no English counterparts — these had to be translated only as to their sense. Examples include *бесструнная балалайка*, meaning 'a chatterbox' from a literal 'stringless balalaika.' The balalaika is a famous Russian musical instrument, which is normally stringed. If it lacks a string, it cannot be played or it will sound foul or unnatural. Here the Russians use an image from their folk culture for which there is no exact English equivalent; this idiom is glossed, then, as 'chatterbox,' which is the unpredictable meaning it developed in Russian.

The Russian idiom *жить как на вулкане* literally means 'to live as if on a volcano,' that is, 'in peril, in an explosive situation.' In English one says *to sit on a powder keg.* A powder keg is not a volcano, but they are both explosive. Compilers of idiom dictionaries must walk a fine line between trying to find the nearest English equivalent, or give a short and concise definition. Whenever two idioms match almost exactly — as in the example *the road to hell is paved with good intentions* — we are dealing with commonly inherited proverbial wisdom which has evolved across national boundaries.

The task of an idiom dictionary is not to teach elementary Russian. This does not mean that beginners cannot make use of this dictionary; it simply means that to profit from this dictionary, they would have to look up the literal meanings of the Russian words in a regular Russian-English dictionary.

As in other idiom dictionaries, entries are alphabetically arranged according to the first basic or key word in the given expression or sentence. This is followed by the Russian idiom in which the leading word appears; then the closest English paraphrase is given. The leading or "strong word" is often a noun; it can also be a verb, an adjective or an adverb. If a noun is involved, we use the most frequent verbs of spoken Russian to go with them; needless to say, others are also possible in most cases. This is followed by a typical sentence from modern colloquial Russian, which then is translated into English.

During the creation of this book I have consulted the following references:

Англо-русский синонимический словарь [English-Russian Dictionary of Synonyms], А.И. Розенман, Ю.Д. Апресян, «Русский язык,» Москва, 1988.

Англо-русский фразеологический словарь [English-Russian Phraseological Dictionary], А.В. Кунин, «Русский язык,» Москва, 1984.

Dictionary of American Idioms [3rd revised and updated edition] by Adam Makkai, Maxine T. Boatner and Edward J. Gates, Barron's Educational Series, Hauppauge, N.Y., 1995.

Dictionary of Russian Idioms and Colloquialisms, by Wasyl Jaszczun and Szymon Krynski, University of Pittsburgh Press, 1967.

Фразеологический словарь русского языка [A Phraseological Dictionary of the Russian Language], «Советская энциклопедия,» А.И. Молотков, Москва, 1967.

Russian-English Dictionary of Idioms, by Sophia Lubensky, Random House, New York, 1995.

Russicizmusok [Set Russian Expressions] by Erno Keszthelyi, Terra, Budapest, 1993.

The Great Russian-English Dictionary of Idioms and Set Expressions, by Piotr Borkowski. Published by P. Borkowski, London, 1973.

The Oxford Russian Dictionary, Oxford University Press, Oxford, New York, 1995.

It is my sincere hope that both Russian immigrants to the United States and American students of Russian will find this dictionary useful and interesting.

Agnes Arany-Makkai

Идиомы русского языка (Russian Idioms)

А

А—*(бу́ква) "А"*

от А до Я—*from A to Z; from beginning to end; inside out*

Пётр изучи́л фи́зику от А до Я. *Peter learned his physics inside out.*

аво́сь—*maybe; perhaps*

аво́сь да небо́сь (да ка́к-нибудь)—*it will work out somehow; something will happen*

Когда́ вре́мя тяжёлое, то́лько тем и живём, что аво́сь да небо́сь. *When times are hard, you can only endure it thinking that something will work out.*

на аво́сь—*on the off-chance; at random*

В авиа́ции ничего́ не должно́ быть на аво́сь. *Nothing must be left to chance in the flying of an airplane.*

ад—*hell*

До́брыми наме́рениями вы́мощена доро́га в ад—*The road to hell is paved with good intentions.*

Жела́я спасти́ меня́, Ива́н испо́ртил мне жизнь. Да, до́брыми наме́рениями вы́мощена доро́га в ад. *Ivan wanted to save me, but he actually ruined my life. Well, the road to hell is paved with good intentions.*

ад кроме́шный—*unbearable suffering; hell on earth; nightmare*

Это мучи́тельно тяжёлая рабо́та, настоя́щий ад кроме́шный. *This painfully difficult work is hell on earth.*

Ада́м—*Adam*

от Ада́ма—*from day one; from the very beginning; from Adam and Eve*

Когда́ Па́вел что-то расска́зывал, то начина́л от Ада́ма. *Whenever Pavel told a story, he always started from the very beginning.*

а́дрес—*address*

не по а́дресу—*isn't meant for someone; to the wrong person; bark up the wrong tree*

Извини́те, я это сказа́л не по ва́шему а́дресу. *Excuse me, I wasn't referring to you.*

Ва́ше замеча́ние напра́влено не по а́дресу. *With your remark you are barking up the wrong tree.*

ажу́р—*open-work*

в по́лном ажу́ре—*tip-top; A-OK*

Пётр счастли́вый: у него́ до́ма и на рабо́те всё в ажу́ре. *Peter is lucky—both his home and his work are A-OK.*

аз—*(Slavonic name of the letter A)*

с азо́в начина́ть—*start from the very beginning* (or *from scratch* or *from square one)*

Наводне́ние разру́шило наш дом, и нам пришло́сь начина́ть с азо́в. *The flood ruined our house and we had to start over from scratch.*

а́кция—*share*

па́дают а́кции—*things are looking bleak for someone; one's odds are getting worse*

С перехо́дом эконо́мики на ры́ночную осно́ву, а́кции Оле́га, как специали́ста социалисти́ческой эконо́мики, упа́ли. *With the change-over to a market economy, Oleg's chances, as a specialist of socialist economics, are getting bleak.*

повыша́ются а́кции—*one's prospects are getting brighter*

По́сле того́, как А́нна заняла́ пе́рвое ме́сто на ко́нкурсе красоты́, её а́кции повы́сились. *After Anna won first prize at the beauty contest, her prospects are getting brighter.*

áльфа—*alpha*

от áльфы до омéги—SEE: от **А до Я**

Амéрика—*America*

открывáть Амéрику—*reinvent the wheel*

Изобретáть печáтание в нáшем вéке, это как открывáть Амéрику зáново. *To invent printing nowadays amounts to reinventing the wheel.*

антимóния

разводи́ть антимóнии—*shoot the breeze; chew the fat; beat one's gums*

Мужчи́ны за крýжкой пи́ва разводи́ли антимóнии. *The men were shooting the breeze over a mug of beer.*

аншлáг—*notice*

пройти́ с аншлáгом—*be a great hit*

Нóвая пьéса прошлá с аншлáгом. *The new play was a great hit.*

аппети́т—*appetite*

аппети́т прихóдит во врéмя еды́—*appetite comes with eating; get into the swing*

Бори́с неохо́тно на́чал де́ло, но аппети́т прихо́дит во вре́мя еды́. *Boris was reluctant to start working, but then he got into the swing of it.*

во́лчий аппети́т—*ravenous appetite*
И́горь съе́л у́жин с во́лчьим аппети́том. *Igor ate his supper with a ravenous appetite.*

дразни́ть аппети́т—*whet the appetite*
За́пах пирога́ дра́знит мой аппети́т. *The smell of the pie is whetting my appetite.*

прия́тного аппети́та!—*enjoy your meal!*
Мы се́ли за стол, и мать пожела́ла нам прия́тного аппети́та. *Mother wished us a good appetite once we had sat down at the table.*

раздража́ть аппети́т—*make one's mouth water*
Вид пече́нья всегда́ раздража́ет мне аппети́т. *The sight of cake always makes my mouth water.*

апре́ль—*April*

поздравля́ть с пе́рвым апре́ля—*play April fools on someone*
Па́вел осме́лился поздра́вить да́же дире́ктора с пе́рвым апре́ля. *Pavel had the guts to play April fools even on the director.*

апте́ка—*drugstore*

как в апте́ке—*exactly; to the drop* (or *ounce)*
Ингредие́нты на пиро́г у А́нны рассчи́тываются как в апте́ке. *Ann measures the ingredients for the pie to the ounce.*

ара́п—*swindler*

на ара́па—*bluff one's way through something*
Мой брат, не подгото́вившись, всегда́ сдаёт экза́мены на ара́па. *My brother, who doesn't study for his exams, always bluffs his way through.*

архи́в—*archives*

сдава́ть в архи́в—*leave out of account; be sent to the glue factory; be written off*

«В совреме́нной обстано́вке я пло́хо ориенти́руюсь, пора́ меня́ сдать в архи́в»—сказа́ла ба́бушка. *In today's circumstances I am at a loss, it's time to send me to the glue factory.*

арши́н—*arshin* (= 28 inches)

бу́дто (*or* **как** *or* **сло́вно** *or* **то́чно**) **арши́н проглоти́л**—*straight as a ramrod*

А́нна сиде́ла сло́вно арши́н проглоти́ла. *Ann sat there straight as a ramrod.*

ви́деть на два арши́на под землёй—be nobody's fool

Ива́на не обма́нешь, он ви́дит на два арши́на под землёй. You can't trick Ivan, he's nobody's fool.

ме́рить на сво́й арши́н; ме́рить свое́й ме́ркой—*judge by one's own standard; measure another's corn by one's own bushel; measure others by one's own yardstick*

Почему́ ты всех ме́ришь на сво́й арши́н? Why do you judge everyone by your own standards?

атмосфе́ра—*atmosphere*

разряди́ть атмосфе́ру—*ease tension; cool things off*

Ната́ша пришла́ во вре́мя на́шей ссо́ры, и её прихо́д разряди́л атмосфе́ру. *Natasha arrived just when we were quarreling, and her arrival eased the tensions.*

аттеста́т—*diploma*

аттеста́т зре́лости—*high school diploma*

На́ша дочь получи́ла аттеста́т зре́лости. *Our daughter received her high school diploma.*

а́укнуться—*haloo to each other*

как а́укнется, так и откли́кнется—*as the call, so the echo; as you sow, so shall you reap*

«Как аýкнется, так и отклúкнется»—подýмал я и укрáл часы́ у вóра. *"As the call, so the echo," I thought, and stole the thief's watch.*

афёра—*shady transaction(s)*

пустúться в афёры—*get mixed up in the wrong deal*

Он пустúлся в афёры úз-за отсýтствия дéнег. *Because he was broke, he got mixed up in the wrong deal.*

Б

бáба—*(peasant) woman*

бой-бáба—*tough lady*

Моя́ тётя бой-бáба. *My auntie is a real tough lady.*

нé было у бáбы хлопóт, купúла порося́—*trouble comes to him who seeks it*

Борúс купúл стáрый автомобúль, котóрый пришлóсь чáсто сдавáть в ремóнт. Вот нé было у бáбы хлопóт, купúла порося́. *Boris bought an old car that needed repair all the time—trouble comes to him who seeks it.*

бáбушка—*grandmother*

бáбушка нáдвое сказáла—*there is no telling just yet; it remains to be seen*

Мы надéемся, что у дóчери бýдут дéти, да бáбушка нáдвое сказáла. *We hope, that our daughter will have children, but there is no telling just yet.*

вот тебé, бáбушка, и Ю́рьев день!—*that's a fine kettle of fish! What a pickle we're in!*

Когдá нáша лóдка сéла на мель, мы сказáли: «Вот тебé, бáбушка, и Ю́рьев день!» *When our boat ran aground, we exclaimed: "What a pickle we're in!"*

расскажú(те) э́то своéй бáбушке—*I wasn't born yesterday!*

Я ни сло́ву не ве́рю. Расскажи́ э́то свое́й ба́бушке! *I don't believe a word of it. I wasn't born yesterday!*

баклу́ши

бить баклу́ши—*loiter away; twiddle one's thumbs*

От ску́ки Пётр весь день бьёт баклу́ши. *Peter has got nothing to do—he twiddles his thumbs all day.*

бал—*ball*

ко́нчен бал—*the game* (or *the party) is over*

«Ко́нчен бал»—сказа́ли лю́ди, когда́ во́ра взя́ли под аре́ст. *"That's the end of that," the people said, when the thief got arrested.*

балала́йка—*balalaika (*Russian stringed musical instrument*)*

бесстру́нная балала́йка—*chatterbox; a wordy person; one who can't shut up*

Мой дя́дя бесстру́нная балала́йка. *My uncle is a chatterbox.*

ба́ня—*baths; bath-house*

зада́ть ба́ню—*give someone hell; make it hot for one*

Е́сли у нача́льника настрое́ние плохо́е, он нам задаёт ба́ню. *When the boss is in a bad mood he gives us hell.*

бара́н—*ram*

смотре́ть (or **уста́виться) как бара́н на но́вые воро́та**—*give a blank stare*

Са́ша смотре́л на меня́, как бара́н на но́вые воро́та. *Sasha was staring at me with a blank stare.*

как бара́н упере́ться—*be pigheaded; be stubborn as a mule*

От Бори́са ничего́ не жди́—он упёрся, как бара́н. *Expect nothing of Boris—he is stubborn as a mule.*

ба́рин—*nobleman; landowner*

жить ба́рином—*live the life of Riley*

Жени́вшись на бога́той он живёт ба́рином. *Since he married a rich woman, he lives the life of Riley.*

башма́к—*shoe*

быть под башмако́м—*be under someone's thumb*

Алексе́й вла́стный челове́к, и все у него́ под башмако́м. *Aleksey is a powerful man, he keeps everyone under his thumb.*

быть под башмако́м у жены́—*be a hen-pecked husband*

И́горь бо́льше не хоте́л быть под башмако́м у жены́ и оста́вил её. *Igor left his wife, because he no longer wanted to be a hen-pecked husband.*

бе

не зна́ть (or **понима́ть**) **ни бе ни ме** (**ни кукаре́ку**)—*not to know the first thing about*

Па́вел в э́том де́ле не зна́ет ни бе ни ме. *Pavel doesn't know the first thing about the matter at hand.*

бег—*run; running*

быть в бега́х—*be on the run; be in hiding*

Никола́й убежа́л из тюрьмы́ и до́лгое вре́мя был в бега́х. *Nikolay escaped from jail and was on the run for a long time.*

бедá—*misfortune*

бедá бедý родит—*trouble begets trouble; one damn thing after another*

Сперва́ я потеря́л ключи́, а потóм кошелёк—бедá бедý роди́т. *First I lost my key, then my wallet—one damn thing after another.*

лихá бедá начáло—*beginnings are always difficult*

Сергéй пéрвый день за рулём óчень волновáлся, а потóм вождéние стáло для негó удовóльствием. Лихá бедá начáло. *Sergey was very nervous behind the steering wheel on the first day, but later driving became a pleasure for him. Beginnings are always difficult.*

что за бедá?—*what does it matter?*

Я потеря́л пýговицу. Ну, что за бедá? *I lost a button, but what does it matter?*

без—*without*

без никаки́х!—*and no arguments!; no two ways about it; that's it!*

Ты дóлжен э́то сдéлать и без никаки́х! *You've got to do it and that's it!*

безобрáзие—*outrage*

что за безобрáзие!—*it's scandalous!*

Что за безобрáзие! Мнóго невинóвных людéй арестовáли. *It's scandalous how many innocent people were arrested.*

безры́бье

на безры́бье и рак ры́ба—*in the kingdom of the blind the one-eyed is a king*

Зня́я мáло слов на англи́йском я дóлжен был сдéлать перевóд, поскóльку други́х перевóдчиков нé было. На безры́бье и рак ры́ба. *I knew but little English, yet I had to do the translating, since there weren't any other translators; in the kingdom of the blind the one-eyed is a king.*

безу́мие—*folly*

люби́ть до безу́мия—*love to distraction*

Он лю́бит жену́ сосе́да до безу́мия. *He loves the neighbor's wife to distraction.*

белена́—*henbane*

белены́ объе́лся—*be off one's rocker; go nuts* (or *bananas*)

Ты тако́е говори́шь, сло́вно белены́ объе́лся. *You're talking nonsense, you must have gone bananas.*

бе́лка—*squirrel*

верте́ться (or **кружи́ться**) **как бе́лка в колесе́**—*be like a squirrel* (or *hamster*) *on a treadmill*

Моя́ жена́ весь день с детьми́ ве́ртится, как бе́лка в колесе́. *My wife is busy all day with the kids—she's like a hamster on a treadmill.*

белу́га—*white sturgeon*

реве́ть белу́гой—*scream like a banshee*

От бо́ли Ли́за реве́ла белу́гой. *The pain made Lisa scream like a banshee.*

бе́лый—*white*

принима́ть бе́лое за чёрное—*call even a snowflake a spade*

Са́ша никому́ не ве́рит и принима́ет бе́лое за чёрное. *Sasha doesn't believe anyone, and calls even a snowflake a spade.*

говори́т бело́, а де́лает черно́—*he doesn't practice what he preaches*

Нече́стные лю́ди говоря́т бело́, а де́лают черно́. *Dishonest people don't practice what they preach.*

бельё—*underwear; linen*

копа́ться (or **ры́ться**) **в гря́зном белье́**—*stick one's nose into someone else's personal affairs; dig up dirt on someone*

Ники́та ро́ется в гря́зном белье́, что́бы причини́ть неприя́тности пре́жней подру́ге. *Nikita digs up dirt in order to cause his former girlfriend trouble.*

бельме́с

ни бельме́са не зна́ет (or **не понима́ет**)—SEE: **ни бе ни ме (ни кукаре́ку)**

бельмо́—*walleye; cataract*

как бельмо́ на глазу́—*an eyesore; thorn in someone's side*

В спо́рте он всегда́ ли́дер, и э́то мне как бельмо́ на глазу́. *When it comes to sports, he always has to lead, and that's a thorn in my side.*

бес—*devil*

бе́са лы́сого—*hell, no!*

Что моя́ зарпла́та высо́кая? Бе́са лы́сого! *What? My salary is high? Hell, no!*

рассыпа́ться (or **верте́ться**) **ме́лким бе́сом** (or **би́сером**)—*shine up to someone; flatter someone*

Что́бы ему́ повы́сили зарпла́ту он рассыпа́лся ме́лким бе́сом пе́ред дире́ктором. *He kept shining up to the director in order to get a salary increase.*

беспоко́йство—*anxiety; nervousness; trouble*

прости́(те) за беспоко́йство—*I'm sorry to trouble you*

Прости́те за беспоко́йство, вы не зна́ете кото́рый час? *I'm sorry to trouble you, could you please tell me what time it is?*

бессты́дство—*shamelessness*

хвати́ло бессты́дства—*have the cheek* (or *gall)*

У него́ хвати́ло бессты́дства повто́рно проси́ть у меня́ де́ньги. *He had the gall to ask me for another loan.*

бесце́нок

купи́ть (or **прода́ть) за бесце́нок**—*buy (*or *sell) for a song (*or *a mere trifle* or *next to nothing)*

Ле́тнее пла́тье зимо́й она́ купи́ла за бесце́нок. *She bought summer clothes in the winter for a song.*

Мы прода́ли автомоби́ль по́сле ава́рии за бесце́нок. *After the accident we sold our car for next to nothing.*

бе́шенство—*fury; rage*

доводи́ть до бе́шенства—*drive one nuts (*or *wild* or *mad); drive one to a frenzy*

Шум строи́тельства дово́дит меня́ до бе́шенства. *The construction noise is driving me nuts.*

приходи́ть в бе́шенство—*see red; get mad; fly into a rage*

Уви́дев любо́вника жены́, Ива́н пришёл в бе́шенство. *Ivan flew into a rage, when he caught sight of his wife's lover.*

биле́т—*ticket*

биле́т в оди́н коне́ц—*one-way ticket*

Я купи́л биле́т в оди́н коне́ц, так как возвраща́лся на автомоби́ле дру́га. *I only bought a one-way ticket, since I got a ride home from my friend.*

би́сер—*(glass) beads*

мета́ть би́сер пе́ред сви́ньями—*cast pearls before swine*

Ему́ объясня́ть об иску́сстве—сло́вно мета́ть би́сер пе́ред сви́ньями. *Talking to him about the arts is casting pearls before swine.*

рассыпа́ться ме́лким би́сером—SEE: **рассыпа́ться ме́лким бе́сом**

би́тый—*striken, hit*

би́тый-переби́тый—*run into the ground; has been talked to death*

Переста́нь! Э́та те́ма уже́ би́тая-переби́тая. *Stop it! This subject has been run into the ground.*

бла́го—*blessing; good*

всех благ—*all the best; take care; best of luck*

Мы пожела́ли ему́ всех благ, и он отпра́вился в доро́гу. *We wished him all the best and he set out on his way.*

ни за каки́е бла́га (в ми́ре)—*not for the world; not for all the tea in China*

Ни за каки́е бла́га я за него́ за́муж не вы́йду. *I won't marry him for all the tea in China.*

блат—*connections*

по бла́ту—*by pulling strings; through one's connections*

Са́ша нашёл себе́ рабо́ту по бла́ту. *Sasha found work for himself through his connections.*

блю́дечко—*saucer*

как на блю́дечке (or **блю́де**)—*be in plain sight; be in full view*

С высоты́ пти́чьего полёта наш го́род был ви́ден, как на блю́дечке. *From a bird's eye perspective we had a full view of our town.*

на блю́дечке с голубо́й каёмочкой—*on a silver platter*

Я зави́дую лю́дям, кото́рым судьба́ всё прино́сит на блю́дечке с голубо́й каёмочкой. *I envy people who get everything handed to them on a silver platter.*

блю́до—*platter; dish*

дежу́рное блю́до—*today's special*

Сего́дня в рестора́не дежу́рное блю́до—борщ. *Today's special at the restaurant is borscht.*

боб—*bean*

бобы́ разводи́ть—*beating around the bush*

Никола́й весь ве́чер разводи́л бобы́ вме́сто конкре́тного разгово́ра. *Nikolay kept beating around the bush all evening instead of saying anything concrete.*

остáться (or **сидéть**) **на бобáх**—*be left holding the bag; be left out in the cold; be left empty-handed*

Миллионéр отдáл всё женé, а расчётливая любóвница остáлась на бобáх. *The millionaire left everything to his wife, and his scheming mistress was left holding the bag.*

бог, бóже—*God*

бережёного и бог бережёт—*better safe than sorry*

Мы подýмали, что бережёного и бог бережёт, поэ́тому пéред óтпуском сдáли все драгоцéнности в ломбáрд. *"Better safe than sorry," we thought, and put all our jewelry in the safe before we took our holiday trip.*

бóже мой!—*Heavens!; good God!*

«Бóже мой, как ты вы́рос за э́ти дéсять лет!»—сказáла Ли́за своемý племя́ннику. *"Heavens! how you've grown during these past ten years!" Lisa said to her nephew.*

дай бог нóги—*run for one's life; take to one's heels*

Алексéй услы́шал стрельбý—и дай бог нóги! Бóльше мы егó не ви́дели. *Aleksey heard shooting and ran for his life. We didn't see him any more.*

как бог свят—*I swear!*

Я э́то вы́полню как бог свят. *I'll do this, I swear!*

как бог нá душу полóжит—*let matters take their course*

Мáша живёт как ей бог нá душу полóжит. *Masha lives letting matters take their course.*

на бóга надéйся, а сам не плошáй—*trust in God and keep the gunpowder dry*

Я всегдá руковóдствуюсь прáвилом: на бóга надéйся, а сам не плошáй. *I always follow the principle: trust in God and keep the gunpowder dry.*

не дай бог—*God forbid*

Не дай бог испытáть мне такóе гóре! *God forbid that I should experience such a sorrow!*

ни бóгу свéчка, ни чёрту кочергá—*neither one thing nor the other; neither fish nor fowl*

Сáша такóй человéк, что ни бóгу свéчка, ни чёрту кочергá—*Sasha is the kind of person who's neither fish nor fowl.*

одномý бóгу извéстно—*God only knows*

Одномý бóгу извéстно, что за э́той закры́той двéрью дéлается. *God only knows what's happening behind this closed door.*

рáди бóга—*I beg you!; for Heaven's sake!*

Рáди бóга, не обижáйтесь за мои́ словá! *For Heaven's sake, don't be offended by what I said.*

с бóгом—*good luck to you; God bless you*

«С бóгом!»—сказáла мать, провожáя сы́на в áрмию. *"God bless you!" the mother said as she bade farewell to her son joining the army.*

убéй меня́ бог—*honest to God; may I be struck dead; may God strike me dead*

Убéй меня́ бог, éсли я э́то сказáл. *May I be struck dead if I said such a thing.*

богáтый—*rich*

чем богáты, тем и рáды—*you are welcome to whatever we have*

Неожи́данно приéхавшим гостя́м хозя́йка сказáла: «Чем богáты, тем и рáды.» *"You are welcome to whatever we have," the hostess said to the unexpected guests.*

бок—*side*

бок ó бок—*side by side*

Мы всю жизнь проработали бок ó бок. *All our lives we've been working side by side.*

быть (or **находи́ться**) **под бóком**—*be near by; be round the corner; be only a hop, skip and a jump away*

Шкóла у нас нахóдится под бóком. *The school is from us only a hop, skip and a jump away.*

наломáть (or **обломáть** or **намя́ть**) **бокá**—*tan someone's hide*

Е́сли ты не сде́лаешь то, что я тре́бую, я налома́ю тебе́ бока́. *If you won't do what I demand, I'll tan your hide.*

подходи́ть с друго́го бо́ку—*look at something from a different angle* (or *point of view)*

Нача́льник реши́л подойти́ к пробле́ме опозда́ния сотру́дников с друго́го бо́ку, и с понеде́льника была́ введена́ систе́ма штра́фов. *The boss decided to look at the colleagues' tardiness from a different point of view and so they introduced the penalty system starting with Monday.*

пора́ на бокову́ю—*it's time to hit the sack; it's time to turn in*

Уже́ по́здно. Пора́ на бокову́ю. *It's late already—time to hit the sack.*

борода́—*beard*

смея́ться в бо́роду—*laugh in one's sleeve*

Оте́ц грози́л де́тям, а сам смея́лся в бо́роду. *Dad bawled out the kids, but he himself laughed in his sleeve.*

борт—*edge*

оста́вить за борто́м—*leave one out in the cold; be thrown out*

Я бою́сь, что она́ меня́ оста́вит за борто́м. *I'm afraid that she'll leave me out in the cold.*

бо́чка—*barrel*

как бездо́нная бо́чка—*like a bottomless pit*

Его́ тру́дно насы́тить, он как бездо́нная бо́чка. *It is hard to satisfy his appetite—he is like a bottomless pit.*

пить как бо́чка—*drink like a fish*

И́горь пил, как бо́чка. *Igor drank like a fish.*

брат—*brother*

на бра́та—*1. per person 2. for each*

1. Биле́т на по́езд сто́ит со́рок до́лларов на бра́та. *The train ticket costs $40 per person.*
2. Он дал по до́ллару на бра́та. *He gave each a dollar.*

родно́й брат—*(full) brother* (as opposed to half brother)
Ива́н—мой родно́й брат. *Ivan and I are (full) brothers.*

брать—*take*

на́ша берёт (or **взяла́**)—*we're the winners*
На соревнова́ниях по пла́ванию мы пе́рвыми пришли́ к фи́нишу—на́ша взяла́. *We ended up first at the swimming contest—we are the winners.*

бровь—*eyebrow*

(попа́сть) не в бровь, а (пря́мо) в глаз—*hit the nail right on the head*
Свои́м вопро́сом он попа́л не в бровь, а пря́мо в глаз. *With his question he hit the nail right on the head.*

брудерша́фт—*fraternity*

вы́пить (на) брудерша́фт—*go on first-name terms; pledge fraternity*
По́сле пяти́ лет совме́стной рабо́ты мы вы́пили на брудерша́фт. *After five years of being colleagues we became first-name friends (and sealed it with a drink).*

бу́ка—*boogy man*

смотре́ть бу́кой (or **бу́ка-бу́кой**)—*look unfriendly; look morose* (or *sullen*)
Он был тако́й нелюди́мый, всегда́ смотре́л бу́кой. *He was so withdrawn, he always looked morose.*

бу́ква—*letter*

бу́ква в бу́кву—*word for word; to the letter*
Он всегда́ всё выполня́л бу́ква в бу́кву. *He always fulfilled everything to the letter.*

букси́р—*tow-boat*

брать на букси́р—*take one in tow; give one a leg up; give one a hand*

По математике мой друг всегдá берёт меня на буксир. *My friend always gives me a hand when it comes to math.*

бум-бум—*ding-dong*

не знать (or **не понимáть**) **ни бум-бум**—SEE: **не знать** (or **не понимáть**) **ни бе ни ме**

бýря—*storm*

бýря в стакáне воды́—*storm* (or *tempest) in a teacup*

Из сáмой простóй ситуáции он создавáл бýрю в стакáне воды́. *He turned the simplest affair into a tempest in a teacup.*

бýхты-барáхты

с бýхты-барáхты—*out of the blue*

Он всегдá являлся к нам с бýхты-барáхты. *He always showed up at our place out of the blue.*

бывáть—*be; happen*

исчезáть как не бывáло—*vanish into thin air; vanish without a trace*

Он умéл исчезáть как не бывáло, на видý у всех. *He was able to vanish into thin air with everyone looking on.*

бык—*bull*

брать быка́ за рога́—*seize the bull by the horn*

Он ча́сто берёт быка́ за рога́. *He frequently seizes the bull by the horn.*

здоро́в как бык—*fit as a fiddle*

Бори́с никогда́ не боле́ет, он здоро́в как бык. *Boris is never sick—he is always fit as a fiddle.*

как бык упрётся—SEE: **как бара́н упрётся**

бы́льё—*grass*

бы́льём поросло́—*faded into oblivion; buried in oblivion; all gone and forgotten*

Са́ша вспо́мнил исто́рию, кото́рая бы́льём поросла́. *Sasha remembered a story, faded into oblivion.*

быт—*life*

войти́ в быт—*come into use*

При Петре́ I в быт вошли́ куре́ние, карто́шка и дли́нные парики́. *During Peter the Great, smoking, potatoes and long wigs came into use.*

быть—*be*

бу́дет мне за э́то—*I'll get my comeuppance*

Я зна́л, что е́сли я ва́зу разобью́, бу́дет мне за э́то. *I knew that if I broke the vase, I'd get my comeuppance.*

была́ не была́—*come what may*

Он ду́мал де́лать или не де́лать, а была́ не была́, сде́лал. *He was thinking whether he should do it or not, and then he decided come what may and did it.*

быть мо́жет; мо́жет быть—*maybe; probably*

И быть мо́жет, вы пра́вы. *Maybe you are right.*

(и) был тако́в—*be off in a flash*; *vanish instantly*

Бори́с то́лько что был здесь, и был тако́в. *Boris dropped in for a minute and instantly vanished.*

что бу́дет, то бу́дет—*come hell or high water; what will be, will be*

Я ему́ скажу́ своё мне́ние, что бу́дет, то бу́дет. *I'll tell him my opinion come hell or high water.*

я не я бу́ду, е́сли—*my name will be mud if*

Я не я бу́ду, е́сли не зако́нчу перево́д до утра́. *My name will be mud if I don't finish the translation by morning.*

В

ва́жность—*importance*

велика́ (or **э́ка**) **ва́жность**—*big deal!; so what?*

«Я ночно́й сто́рож всеми́рно изве́стной фи́рмы»—горди́лся Ники́та. «Велика́ ва́жность!»—Оле́г сказа́л. *"I'm a night watchman at a world-famous firm," said Nikita proudly. "Big deal!" Oleg answered.*

ва́лом—*heaped up, piled up*

ва́лом вали́ть—*come* (or *flow* or *swell*) *in huge crowds; flock*

На стадио́н наро́д ва́лом вали́л. *The people flowed into the stadium in huge crowds.*

Ва́ська—*Vaska*

а Ва́ська слу́шает да ест—*turn a deaf ear*

Я прошу́ его́ помо́чь мне, а Ва́ська слу́шает да ест. *I ask him to help me, but he turns a deaf ear.*

вдоль—*along*

вдоль и попере́к—*1. far and wide; up and down 2. thoroughly; inside out*

1. Мы изъе́здили Аме́рику вдоль и попере́к. *We traveled all over America far and wide.*
2. Я зна́ю го́род вдоль и попере́к. *I know the city inside out.*

вдре́безги—*into smithereens*

пьян вдре́безги—*dead drunk*

Ива́н лежи́т на полу́ вдре́безги пьян. *Ivan is lying on the floor dead drunk.*

ведро́—*bucket; pail*

льёт как из ведра́—*it's coming down in sheets, it is raining cats and dogs*

Во вре́мя ле́тней грозы́ дождь льёт как из ведра́. *During the summer storms it rains cats and dogs.*

век—*century*

в ко́и ве́ки—*once in a blue moon*

Наш друг в ко́и ве́ки нас навеща́л. *Every once in a blue moon our friend would visit us.*

испоко́н ве́ка; от ве́ка; от ве́ка веко́в; споко́н ве́ка—*since time immemorial*

Испоко́н ве́ка земля́ кру́тится вокру́г со́лнца. *The earth has been orbiting the sun since time immemorial.*

ко́нчить век—*die*

Михаи́л неожи́данно зако́нчил свой век. *Mikhail died suddenly.*

мы́каться век—*struggle to get by; live in misery*

О́льга мы́калась весь век без де́нег. *Olga lived in misery for lack of money.*

на ве́ки ве́чные- *-for all ages to come; for ever and ever*

Стихи́ Пу́шкина остаю́тся нам на ве́ки ве́чные. *Pushkin's poetry will endure for all ages to come.*

величина́—*size*

ду́тая величина́—*one's reputation is overblown*

Когда́ у профе́ссора потре́бовали бо́лее подро́бный отчёт, вы́яснилось, что он ду́тая величина́. *When the professor was asked to hand in a more detailed resume, it became clear that his reputation was overblown.*

верёвка—*string*

вить верёвки—*twist someone around one's little finger*

Муж люби́л свою́ жену́, а она́ из него́ верёвки ви́ла. *The husband loved his wife very much, but she kept twisting him around her little finger.*

верте́ться—*turn; revolve*

как не верти́сь—*no matter what you (may) do*

Как не верти́сь, а жизнь не изме́нится. *No matter what you may do, life won't change.*

верх; верху́шка—*top*

быть на верху́ блаже́нства—*be in seventh heaven; be on cloud nine*

Пётр влюби́лся и был на верху́ блаже́нства. *Peter fell in love and was in seventh heaven.*

с ве́рхом нали́ть (or **напо́лнить**)—*fill to the brim*

На столе́ стоя́л кувши́н, с ве́рхом напо́лненный пи́вом. *On the table there stood a pitcher, filled with beer to the brim.*

весь—*whole*

весь в—*be a dead ringer for someone; be the very image of someone*

Наш сын весь в отцá. *Our son is a dead ringer for his father.*

вот и всё—*that's it*

Они́ разошли́сь, вот и всё. *They got a divorce and that was it.*

всё ещё—*yet*

И́горь óчень гря́зный, но принимáть душ всё ещё не хóчет. *Igor is filthy, yet he won't take a shower.*

всё равнó—*not to make any difference; be all the same*

Мой муж мóжет со мнóй не согласи́ться, но я всё равнó принимáю э́ту нóвую рабóту. *My husband might disagree but I'll take on the new job all the same.*

на всех не угоди́шь—*you can't please everyone*

Как не старáйся, на всех не угоди́шь. *No matter how hard you may try, you can't please everyone.*

вéтер—*wind*

вéтер в головé—*be empty-headed*

Старики́ чáсто говоря́т, что у молоды́х вéтер в головé. *Old people often say that young people are empty-headed.*

взад—*backwards*

взад и вперёд—*up and down; to and fro; backwards and forwards*

Мы ходи́ли по аллéе взад и вперёд. *We kept walking to and fro under the trees.*

ни взад, ни вперёд—*not to budge an inch; neither backwards nor forwards*

В автóбусе стóлько нарóду, что ни взад, ни вперёд. *The bus is so crowded that no one can budge an inch.*

вещь—*thing*

называ́ть ве́щи свои́ми (or **со́бственными** or **настоя́щими**) **имена́ми**—*call a spade a spade*

Говори́ конкре́тно, называ́й ве́щи свои́ми имена́ми! *Talk concretely—call a spade a spade!*

взгляд—*glance*

куда ни ки́нешь взгля́д(ом)—*wherever you turn; wherever you look*

В Пари́же куда́ ни ки́нешь взгля́дом, краси́вая архитекту́ра. *In Paris, no matter where you turn, the buildings are pretty.*

лови́ть на себе́ взгляд—*catch someone's glance*

Во вре́мя та́нца она́ лови́ла на себе́ его́ взгляд. *During the dance she caught his glance.*

на мой взгляд—*by my book; in my view; in my opinion*

Я ему́ сказа́л, что на мой взгляд он был непра́в. *I told him that by my book he wasn't right.*

обежа́ть взгля́дом—*scan*

Я не прочита́л кни́гу, а обежа́л её взгля́дом. *I didn't read the book, I just scanned it.*

с пе́рвого взгля́да—*right away; at first glance; from the very start*

Я его́ оцени́л с пе́рвого взгля́да. *I appreciated him from the very start.*

вздор—*nonsense*

говори́ть (or **моло́ть** or **нести́** or **поро́ть**) **вздор**—*talk nonsense; talk foolishness*

Переста́нь поро́ть вздор! *Stop talking nonsense!*

вздýмать—*take it into one's head*

не вздýмай(те)—*don't even think of*

Не вздýмай оде́ть шу́бу ле́том. *Don't even think of wearing a fur coat during the summer.*

взор—*look*

оскорбúть взор—*be an eyesore*

Мýсор на ýлице оскорбляéт взор. *Garbage in the streets is an eyesore.*

вид—*sight*

видáть вúды—*one has seen all sorts of things; one has been around*

Старúк мнóго расскáзывал. Бы́ло я́сно, что он видáл вúды. *The old man told us so much, it became obvious that he had been around.*

дéлать вид—*act as if; make believe; pretend*

Пётр тóлько дéлал вид, что меня́ понимáет. *Peter just acted as if he understood me.*

для вúда—*for the sake of appearances*

Сáша поругáл сы́на для вúда, но в душé он был с ним соглáсен. *Sasha scolded his son for the sake of appearances, but he agreed with him in his heart.*

имéть в видý—*keep in mind*

Éсли захóчется купúть вещь, имéй в видý, у нас нет дéнег. *When you want to go shopping, keep in mind that we have no money.*

имéть вúды—*count on; have design on one*

В решéнии э́той проблéмы он имéл вúды на негó. *He counted on him in solving this problem.*

ни под какúм вúдом—*not under any circumstances; by no means*

Пётр не признавáлся в своём преступлéнии ни под какúм вúдом. *Peter wouldn't confess under any circumstances.*

видáть—*see*

видáли однý такýю!—*we have seen a thing or two!*

Не дýмáй, что тебé всё удáстся. Видáли однý такýю! *Don't think you'll always succeed—we have seen a thing or two!*

ви́деть—*see*

то́лько и ви́дели—*be gone in a flash; vanish without a trace*

Вор укра́л кошелёк и то́лько его́ и ви́дели. *The thief stole the purse and vanished without a trace.*

виногра́д—*vine; grapes*

зе́лен виногра́д—*the grapes are sour*

Бу́дучи бе́дным, он пренебрежи́тельно говори́л о деньга́х, но мы чу́вствовали, что «зе́лен виногра́д.» *Since he is poor, he spoke contemptuously about money, but we felt that it was a case of "sour grapes."*

ви́нтик—*screw*

ви́нтика (or **ви́нтиков**) **не хвата́ет (в голове́)**—*have a screw loose; lose some of one's marbles*

По его́ расска́зу я по́нял, что у него́ ви́нтиков не хвата́ет. *The way he talked made me realize that he had a screw loose.*

вкопа́ть—*dig in*

как (or **сло́вно** or **то́чно**) **вко́панный**—*freeze on the spot; as if rooted in the ground*

Когда́ И́горь встре́тил медве́дя в лесу́, он стал как вко́панный. *When Igor saw the bear in the woods, he froze on the spot.*

вкус—*taste*

по вку́су—*be appealing to someone*

Моё замеча́ние о его́ жене́ пришло́сь Алексе́ю не по вку́су. *My remark about his wife went against Aleksey's grain.*

владе́ть—*own; be able to use*

владе́ть собо́й—*control oneself*

В любо́й ситуа́ции Па́вел уме́л владе́ть собо́й. *Pavel was able to control himself in all situations.*

власть—*power*

прийти́ к вла́сти—*come into power; take office*

Но́вый президе́нт прийдёт к вла́сти че́рез две неде́ли. *The new president will take office in two weeks.*

теря́ть власть над собо́й—*lose one's temper* (or *self-control*)
Когда́ Са́ша обижа́л меня́, я теря́л власть над собо́й. *I lost my temper when Sasha offended me.*

влезть—*climb in; get into*

не вле́зешь в кого́-ли́бо—*you can't read someone else's mind*
Как зна́ть, говори́т ли Никола́й пра́вду—как говори́тся, в него́ не вле́зешь. *How can we know if Nikolay is telling the truth—as they say, you can't read someone else's mind.*

внима́ние—*attention; consideration*

оста́вить без внима́ния—*take no notice of; disregard*
Дире́ктор остави́л мою́ кри́тику без внима́ния. *The director disregarded my criticism.*

принима́ть во внима́ние—*take into account* (or *consideration*)
При вынесе́нии пригово́ра судья́ при́нял во внима́ние тру́дное де́тство престу́пника. *When pronouncing the sentence, the judge took into consideration the criminal's difficult childhood.*

внутри́—*inside*

оборва́ться внутри́—*one's heart sinks; one's heart almost stops*
Когда́ я слы́шала об уби́йстве, у меня́ внутри́ оборвало́сь. *When I heard about the murder, my heart almost stopped.*

вода́—*water*

в му́тной воде́ ры́бу лови́ть—*fish in troubled waters*
Нече́стные лю́ди ча́сто ло́вят ры́бу в му́тной воде́. *Dishonest folks like to fish in troubled waters.*

водо́й не розольёшь—*be inseparable; be as thick as thieves*
Оле́г и И́горь таки́е бли́зкие друзья́, что их водо́й не разольёшь. *Oleg and Igor are such close buddies that they are inseparable.*

вози́ть во́ду на—*make one chop wood all day*

Ивáн такóй безрóпотный, что на нём мóжно вóду возúть. *Ivan is so submissive, that you can make him chop wood all day.*

вы́йти сухи́м из воды́—*get off scot-free*

В любóй ситуáции он умéл вы́йти сухи́м из воды́. *He was able to escape from any situation scot-free.*

лить вóду на чьё-либо **мéльницу**—*play into someone's hands*

Ты свои́ми словáми льёшь вóду на мéльницу конкурéнта. *You're playing into the competition's hands with your words.*

мнóго (or **немáло** or **стóлько**) **воды́ утеклó**—*a lot of water has flowed under the bridge*

Дéтство мы провели́ вмéсте, но с тех пор немáло воды́ утеклó. *We spent our childhood together, but since then a lot of water has flowed under the bridge.*

седьмáя (or **деся́тая**) **водá на киселé**—*be a kissing cousin; a cousin seven* (or *ten*) *times removed*

Какóй он мне рóдственник? Седьмáя водá на киселé. *What relation is he to me? We're but kissing cousins.*

чи́стой (or **чистéйшей**) **воды́**—*pure, unadulterated; genuine*

Э́то была́ пра́вда чисте́йшей воды́. *This was the pure, unadulterated truth.*

во́дка—*vodka*

дать на во́дку—*give a tip*

Гру́зчики жда́ли, что хозя́ин даст им на во́дку. *The movers were waiting for the landlord to give them a tip.*

во́здух—*air*

на во́льном (or **откры́том** or **све́жем**) **во́здухе**—*out of doors*

По воскресе́ньям мы прово́дим вре́мя на откры́том во́здухе. *We spend our Sundays out of doors.*

возмо́жность—*possibility; opportunity; chance*

по возмо́жности; по ме́ре возмо́жности—*as far as possible; to the extent one is able to*

Помоги́ мне по ме́ре возмо́жности! *Please help me as you can.*

при пе́рвой возмо́жности—*1. as soon as possible 2. at the first opportunity*

1. Пожа́луйста, позвони́ мне при пе́рвой возмо́жности. *Please call me as soon as possible.*
2. При пе́рвой возмо́жности я поступи́л в университе́т. *I entered the university at the first opportunity.*

возня́—*fuss; bustle*

мыши́ная возня́—*petty cares* (or *concerns); be of a trifling nature*

Её жа́лобы явля́лись в су́щности мыши́ной возне́й. *Her complaints were basically of a trifling nature.*

во́зраст—*age*

вы́йти из во́зраста—*be past the age limit; be too old for someting*

Ната́ша ещё не вы́шла из того́ во́зраста, когда́ уже́ не игра́ют в ку́клы. *Natasha is not yet too old for playing with dolls.*

в вóзрасте—*be of advanced age; be getting on in years*

Ири́на уже́ в вóзрасте и рéдко выхóдит из дóма однá. *Irina is getting on in years—she seldom leaves the house by herself.*

не по вóзрасту—*beyond one's age*

Серьёзное мнéние о жи́зни у мáльчика бы́ло я́вно не по вóзрасту. *The boy was serious about life beyond his years.*

вокру́г—*around*

вокру́г да óколо—*be beating around the bush*

Бори́с всё ходи́л вокру́г да óколо, а прямо не говори́л. *Boris kept beating around the bush, and never talked straight.*

вол—*ox*

рабóтать как вол—*work like a dog* (or *a horse)*

Отéц восьмеры́х детéй дóлжен рабóтать как вол. *A father of eight has to work like a dog.*

волк—*wolf*

вóлком смотрéть—*look daggers; look cross at someone*

Пётр был нелюди́м и вóлком смотрéл на всех. *Peter was a loner and looked cross at everybody.*

С волкáми жить, по-вóлчьи выть.—*When in Rome, do as the Romans (do).*

Ты дóлжен приспосóбиться к нóвой ситуáции на завóде. С волкáми жить, по-вóлчьи выть. *You have to comply with the new situation at the factory—when in Rome, do as the Romans!*

вóлос—*hair*

вóлосы стáли ды́бом—*one's hair stands on end*

Когдá я уви́дел горя́щий дом, у меня́ вóлосы стáли ды́бом. *When I saw the burning house, my hair stood on end.*

дожи́ть до седы́х волóс—*live to a ripe old age*

Ивáн дожи́л до седы́х волóс и всё-таки дéлал глу́пости. *Ivan lived to a ripe old age, yet he kept doing foolish things.*

ни на вóлос—*not a bit; not in the least*

Дéсять лет прошлó, но онá не изменúлась ни на вóлос. *Ten years have passed, yet she hasn't changed in the least.*

волосóк—*hair*

быть на волоскé от чегó-лúбо—*be on the brink* (or *on the verge) of something*

Во врéмя войны́ я чáсто был на волоскé от смéрти. *During the war, more than once I was on the brink of death.*

держáться (or **висéть) на волоскé**—*hang by a hair* (or *thread)*

Во врéмя осáды моя́ жизнь висéла на волоскé. *During the siege my life hung by a thread.*

вóля—*will; liberty*

вóлей-невóлей—*like it or not; willy-nilly*

Вóлей-невóлей емý пришлóсь взя́ться за рабóту. *Like it or not he had to get down to work.*

вóля вáша (or **твоя́)**—*it's up to you; do as you like*

Я предложúл Натáше поéхать со мной в Еврóпу, но, замéтив её колебáния, я сказáл: вóля твоя́. *I suggested to Natasha that she come with me to Europe, but seeing her hesitation, I said, "It's up to you."*

дать вóлю языкý—*let it all hang out; give full reign to one's tongue*

Никúта дóлго молчáл, а потóм дал вóлю своемý языкý. *Nikita kept silent for a long time, but then he let it all hang out.*

давáть вóлю кулакáм—*use one's fists*

Когдá Сáша выпивáл, он давáл вóлю своúм кулакáм. *Whenever Sasha got drunk, he would use his fists.*

по дóброй вóле—*voluntarily; on one's own accord* (or *free will)*

По дóброй вóле он пошёл на войнý. *He joined the war effort voluntarily.*

вон—*out*

пошёл вон!—*get out of here!*

Бори́с мне так надое́л, что я вы́нужден был ему́ сказа́ть: пошёл вон! *I was so fed up with Boris that I had to tell him, "Get out of here!"*

вопро́с—*question*

больно́й вопро́с—*touchy issue* (or *question*)

Жени́тьба для ста́рого холостяка́—больно́й вопро́с. *Marriage is a touchy issue for a certified bachelor.*

засы́пать вопро́сами—*overwhelm someone with questions*

Репортёры засы́пали актёра вопро́сами. *The reporters overwhelmed the actor with questions.*

под вопро́сом—*in doubt; up in the air*

На́ше путеше́ствие ещё под вопро́сом. *Our trip is still up in the air.*

поста́вить вопро́с ребро́м—*put a question point-blank*

Что́бы узна́ть пра́вду, я поста́вил вопро́с ребро́м. *In order to find out the truth, I put the question point-blank.*

что за вопро́с!—*What a question!*

«Хо́чешь моро́женое?»—«Что за вопро́с!» *"Do you want some ice-cream?"—"What a question!"*

вор—*thief*

не по́йман—не вор—*innocent until proven guilty*

Мы предполага́ли, что секре́тные докуме́нты Оле́г переда́л иностра́нной разве́дке, но пока́ не по́йман—не вор. *We suspected that Oleg handed the secret documents to foreign intelligence, but he's innocent until proven guilty.*

на во́ре ша́пка гори́т—*one's guilty conscience is speaking*

Па́влу ещё не предъяви́ли обвине́ния, а он уже́ опра́вдывается—на во́ре ша́пка гори́т. *Pavel was not yet reprimanded, but he's already making excuses—his guilty conscience is speaking.*

воробе́й—*sparrow*

ста́рый (or **стре́ляный) воробе́й**—*know all the tricks; be an old hand at something; be a wise old bird*

Его́ уже́ ничего́ не удиви́т—он ста́рый воробе́й. *Nothing can surprise him anymore, he knows all the tricks.*

во́рон—*raven*

куда́ во́рон косте́й не занесёт—*to the middle of nowhere; to a godforsaken place*

И́горь стреми́лся туда́, куда́ во́рон косте́й не занесёт. *Igor was headed for a godforsaken place.*

воро́на—*crow*

бе́лая воро́на—*rare bird; odd fish; stuck out like a sore thumb*

Со свои́ми необыкнове́нными сво́йствами он был как бе́лая воро́на. *With his odd habits he stuck out like a sore thumb.*

счита́ть воро́н—*twiddle one's thumb*

От безде́лья он весь день счита́ет воро́н. *He's got nothing to do; he is twiddling his thumbs all day.*

восто́рг—*delight*

администрати́вный восто́рг—*bureaucratic zeal*

Мой нача́льник в администрати́вном восто́рге забы́л о потре́бностях люде́й. *My boss forgot about the needs of the people in his bureaucratic zeal.*

быть в восто́рге—*be enthusiastic about*

Зри́тели бы́ли в восто́рге от но́вого фи́льма. *The audience was enthusiastic about the new movie.*

приходи́ть в ди́кий (or **теля́чий**) **восто́рг**—*get foolishly enthusiasic*

Ма́ша пришла́ в ди́кий восто́рг от на́шего предложе́ния. *Masha got foolishly enthusiastic when she got our offer.*

вот—*here's*

вот-вот—*at any minute*

Наш гость вот-вот придёт. *Our guest will be here any minute now.*

вот ещё!—*well, really!; What a question!*

«Ты пойдешь к нему́?»—«Вот ещё!» *"Will you go see him?"—"What a question!"*

вот и всё—*and that's that; that's all there is to it*

Ему́ в Москве́ не нра́вилось и он уе́хал в Аме́рику. Вот и всё. *He didn't like life in Moscow, so he left for the States—that's all there is to it.*

вот и́менно!—*exactly!*

Вот и́менно! Он всегда́ прав. *Exactly! He's always right.*

вре́мя—*time*

вне вре́мени и простра́нства—*in a fool's paradise; suspended in time and space*

И́горь жил сло́вно вне вре́мени и простра́нства. *Igor lived in a fool's paradise.*

во времена́—*in the days of*

Во времена́ Пу́шкина поэ́зия о́чень влия́ла на чита́телей. *In the days of Pushkin poetry deeply affected the readership.*

в одно́ прекра́сное вре́мя (or **у́тро**)—*once; one fair day*

В одно́ прекра́сное вре́мя я решил уе́хать в Париж. *One fair day I decided to go to Paris.*

вре́мени в обре́з—*be short of time; have no time for something*

У меня́ вре́мени в обре́з для тако́й рабо́ты. *I've got no time for that kind of work.*

вре́мя от вре́мени; времена́ми—*now and then; from time to time; at times*

Вре́мя от вре́мени он присыла́л мне письмо́. *Every now and then he would write me a letter.*

вре́мя рабо́тает на кого́-ли́бо—*time is on one's side*

Мы жда́ли и не волнова́лись зна́я, что вре́мя рабо́тает на нас. *We waited undisturbed, because we knew that time was on our side.*

всему́ своё вре́мя—*all in its own good time*

О́чень тру́дно де́тям внуши́ть му́дрость, что всему́ своё вре́мя. *It's very difficult to teach children the wisdom of "all in its own good time."*

в ско́ром вре́мени—*soon; before long; in the not-too-distant future*

В ско́ром вре́мени всё изме́нится. *Things will change in the not-too-distant future.*

до сего́ вре́мени—*up till now; to the present day*

Я отпрáвил письмó, но до сегó врéмени отвéта нет. *I sent a letter, but no answer up till now.*

на врéмя—*for the time being*

На врéмя мы остáнемся в э́том гóроде, а потóм подýмаем, что дéлать дáльше. *For the time being we'll stay in this town, then we'll decide later what to do.*

на пéрвое врéмя—*for starters; to start with*

На пéрвое врéмя нам хвáтит ты́сячи дóлларов на жизнь. *A thousand dollars will cover expenses for starters.*

всегó—*altogether*

всегó-нáвсего—*no more than*

Мои́ покýпки сегóдня стóили всегó-нáвсего двáдцать дóлларов. *My shopping today came to no more than $20.*

всегó ничегó—*almost nothing; next to nothing*

Из моегó расскáза он пóнял всегó ничегó. *He understood next to nothing of my whole story.*

тóлько и всегó—*all; nothing more than*

О моéй жи́зни он тóлько и всегó знал, что я учýсь. *He knew nothing more about me than that I was a student.*

всеуслы́шание—*public hearing*

заяви́ть (or **объяви́ть** or **сказáть**) **во всеуслы́шание**—*for all the world to hear; within earshot of everyone*

О свои́х проблéмах Пётр сказáл во всеуслы́шание. *Peter discussed his personal problems within earshot of everyone.*

вставáть—*get up*

не вставáя—*uninterruptedly; in one stretch; nonstop*

Ники́та рабóтал с утрá до вéчера не вставáя. *Nikita worked from morning till night in one stretch.*

вулка́н—*volcano*

жить как на вулка́не—*sit on a powder keg; sit on a time bomb*

Среди́ враго́в мы́ живём как на вулка́не. *Caught between enemies we live as if sitting on a powder keg.*

выводи́ть—*take out*

выводи́ть из себя́—*rile; drive one out of one's wits*

Крик дете́й меня́ всегда́ выво́дит из себя́. *The crying of the children always drives me out of my wits.*

вы́йти—*go out; appear; transpire; happen; turn out*

вы́йти за́муж—*get married (*said about women only*)*

Ната́ша вы́шла за́муж за врача́. *Natasha married a physician.*

вы́шло совсе́м не так—*it happened* (or *turned out) entirely differently*

Мы соста́вили подро́бные пла́ны, но всё вы́шло совсе́м не так. *We made detailed plans, but things turned out differently.*

выраже́ние—*expression*

с выраже́нием—*with feeling; with emotion*

Ири́на всегдá читáла стихи́ с выражéнием. *Irina always recited poetry with feeling.*

высотá—*height*

быть на высотé (положéния)—*rise to the occasion; be in control of the situation*

Врач всегдá был на высотé положéния, когдá нýжно бы́ло сдéлать срóчную операцию. *The doctor always rose to the occasion during an emergency operation.*

с высоты́ пти́чьего полёта—*bird's eye view*

Стóя на верши́не горы́, мы ви́дели гóрод с высоты́ пти́чьего полёта. *From the mountain top we saw the city from a bird's eye view.*

Г

газ—*gas*

дать гáзу—*step on it*

Я сел в маши́ну и дал гáзу. *I got into my car and stepped on it.*

на пóлном газý—*at full speed*

Автóбус шёл на пóлном газý. *The bus was running at full speed.*

гвоздь—*nail*

гвоздём засéсть (or **сидéть**)—*fixed idea; be unable to get something out of one's head*

Мысль о развóде гвоздём засéла в моéй головé. *I wasn't able to get the thought of divorce out of my head.*

гвоздь сезóна—*hit of the season*

Пéсня о любви́ былá гвоздём сезóна. *A love song was the hit of the season.*

где—*where*

где бы то ни́ было—*wherever one may be*

Где бы то ни́ было, Никола́й никогда́ не расстава́лся со свое́й гита́рой. *Wherever Nikolay may have been he never parted with his guitar.*

геро́й—*hero*

геро́й не моего́ рома́на—*not to be one's type (of hero)*

Алексе́й мне сде́лал предложе́ние, но он геро́й не моего́ рома́на. *Aleksey proposed marriage to me, but he isn't my type.*

гла́вный геро́й—*main character*

Гла́вным геро́ем рома́на «Отцы́ и де́ти» явля́ется База́ров. *Bazarov is the main character of the novel "Fathers and Sons."*

глаз—*eye*

броса́ться в глаза́—*strike one; be noticeable*

Её красота́ пря́мо броса́ется в глаза́. *Her beauty is very striking.*

в глаза́х двои́тся—*see double*

Уви́дев двойня́шек, я поду́мал, что у меня́ в глаза́х двои́тся. *I thought I saw double when I saw the twins.*

в чьих глаза́х—*in one's opinion*

В мои́х глаза́х му́зыка Ба́ха краси́вее всего́. *Bach's music is the most beautiful in my opinion.*

глаза́ на мо́кром ме́сте—*be (always) on the verge of tears*

С тех пор как ребёнок заболе́л, у Ната́ши глаза́ на мо́кром ме́сте. *Ever since her child got ill, Natasha is always on the verge of tears.*

глаз да глаз ну́жен—*one must have a close eye on someone; one must be closely watched*

Ма́льчик о́чень подви́жный—за ним ну́жен глаз да глаз. *The boy is very vivacious, he has to be closely watched.*

говори́ть (пря́мо) в глаза́—*say right to someone's face*

Михаи́л своё мне́ние говори́л пря́мо в глаза́ дире́ктору. *Mikhail told his opinion right to the director's face.*

говори́ть за глаза́—*talk behind one's back*

То́лько нече́стные лю́ди говоря́т за глаза́ о други́х. *Only dishonest folk talk behind one's back.*

закры́ть глаза́ на что́-либо—*turn a blind eye to something*
Дире́ктор закры́л глаза́ на недоста́тки секрета́рши. *The director turned a blind eye to his secretary's shortcomings.*

покупа́ть за глаза́—*buy something sight unseen; pig in a poke*
Са́ша купи́л компью́тер за глаза́, заказа́в по телефо́ну. *Sasha bought a computer over the phone, sight unseen.*

с глаз доло́й из се́рдца вон—*out of sight, out of mind*
С тех пор как Петро́вы уе́хали в друго́й го́род, мы ничего́ о них не зна́ем—как говори́тся, с глаз доло́й из се́рдца вон. *Since the Petrovs left for another town, we know nothing about them. As they say: "out of sight, out of mind."*

с гла́зу на глаз—*in private; entre nous*
Я хочу́ с ним поговори́ть с гла́зу на глаз. *I want to talk to him in private.*

смея́ться в глаза́—*laugh in one's face*
Вме́сто отве́та она́ наха́льно смея́лась мне в глаза́. *Instead of answering she impudently laughed in my face.*

гло́тка—*throat*

крича́ть во всю гло́тку—*scream one's head off; shout at the top of one's voice*
От гне́ва Никола́й крича́л во всю́ гло́тку. *In his anger Nikolay was shouting at the top of his voice.*

глубина́—*depth*

в глубине́ души́ (or **се́рдца**)—*at the bottom of one's heart; deep down where it really counts; in one's heart of hearts*
Хотя́ Пётр не вы́сказал э́того, но в глубине́ души́ он знал, что А́нна права́. *Although Peter didn't say so, deep down where it really counts, he knew that Anna was right.*

из глубины́ веко́в—*from the remote past; from ancient times*

Э́то предáние дошлó до нас из глубины́ векóв. *This legend has been handed down to us from the remote past.*

от глубины́ душú—*with all one's heart*

С собóй в дорóгу онá далá нам цéлый мешóк я́блок, как говорúтся, от глубины́ душú. *She gave us a whole bag of apples to go, as they say, with all her heart.*

глядéть—*look*

глядéть нé на что—*it is hardly worth looking at* (or *mentioning it)*

Велосипéд моегó брáта настóлько стáрый, что глядéть нé на что. *My brother's old bike is hardly worth looking at.*

тогó и глядú—*any minute now*

Тепéрь, тогó и глядú, начнётся бýря. *The storm can hit any minute now.*

гнéв—*anger*

лóпнуть от гнéва—*explode with anger*

Ѝгорь лóпнет от гнéва, éсли не вы́скажется. *If Igor can't speak his mind, he'll explode with anger.*

не пóмнит себя́ от гнéва—*be beside oneself with rage*

О́льга довелá Николáя до тогó, что он не пóмнил себя́ от гнéва. *Olga pushed Nikolay to the point where he was beside himself with rage.*

гнуть—*to bend*

кудá он гнёт?—*what is he driving at?*

Ах, ужé поня́тно, кудá вы гнёте! *Oh, I can finally see what you're driving at!*

говорúть—*speak*

вообщé говоря́—*generally speaking*

Ну, вообщé говоря́, Чикáго совсéм спокóйный гóрод. *Well, generally speaking, Chicago is a relatively peaceful city.*

говори́ть на ты—*be on first name terms with someone*
Мы с сосéдом говори́м на ты. *My neighbor and I are on first name terms.*

инáче говоря́—*in other words*
Инáче говоря́, вы не хоти́те бóльше сотрýдничать со мнóй? *In other words you don't want to work with me anymore?*

и не говори́(те)—*that's for sure; goes without saying; you bet!*
Я тебé во всём помогáю.—И не говори́! *It goes without saying that I'll help you with everything.*

корóче говоря́—*to make a long story short*
Корóче говоря́, они́ приéхали в Амéрику и откры́ли рестора́н. *To make a long story short, they arrived in the States and opened a restaurant.*

не говоря́—*aside from; let alone; not to mention*
Не говоря́ о её красотé, онá óчень талáнтлива. *Aside from her beauty, she is also very talented*

пóпросту говоря́—*put it plainly* (or *simply)*
Пóпросту говоря́, Ники́та соверши́л глýпость. *To put it simply, Nikita acted foolishly.*

сóбственно говоря́—*as a matter of fact*
Сóбственно говоря́, егó трéбования раздражáют меня́. *His demands make me nervous, as a matter of fact.*

э́то говори́т самó за себя́—*it speaks for itself*
Фáкты говоря́т сáми за себя́. *The facts speak for themselves.*

гóголь—*golden-eye* (bird)

ходи́ть гóголем—*strut about; walk with a pompous gait*
Ивáн был гóрдым и ходи́л гóголем. *Ivan felt very proud of himself and strutted like a peacock.*

год—*year*

без гóду недéля—*only a few days; next to no time; a short while*

Без го́ду неде́ля в Аме́рике, а уже́ говори́т по-англи́йски. *He's only arrived in the States a short while ago, but he can speak English already.*

быть в года́х—*be no spring chicken* (or *youngster)*

Он уже́ был в года́х, когда пе́рвый раз жени́лся. *He was no spring chicken, when he got married for the first time.*

в мои́ го́ды—*in the old days*

«В мои́ го́ды электри́чества ещё не́ было»—говори́л стари́к. *"In the old days there was no electricity," the old man said.*

год от го́да—*year after year; from year to year*

Год от го́да он занима́ется той же рабо́той. *He does the same kind of work, year after year.*

из го́да в год—*from year to year; year in and year out*

Из го́да в год це́ны повыша́ются. *The prices keep going up from year to year.*

кру́глый год—*all year round*

Кру́глый год у нас пого́ды не́ было. *All year round the weather was bad here.*

не по года́м—*beyond one's years*

Она́ была́ серьёзная не по года́м. *She was serious beyond her years.*

годи́ться—*be good*

никуда́ не годи́тся—*it's no good; it's not good at all; it won't do*

Э́то ста́рое пла́тье уже́ никуда́ не годи́тся, ну́жно покупа́ть но́вое. *This old dress won't do anymore—I've got to buy a new one.*

го́дный—*fit*

никуда́ не го́дный—*useless; good for nothing*

Па́вел хоро́ший инжене́р, но му́жем он оказа́лся никуда́ не го́дным. *Pavel is a good engineer, but as a husband he is good for nothing.*

голова́—*head*

верте́ться в голове́—*be on the tip of one's tongue*

Его́ фами́лия ве́ртится у меня́ в голове́. *His family name is on the tip of my tongue.*

вооружённый с головы́ до ног—*armed to the teeth*

Чле́ны ма́фии бы́ли вооружены́ с головы́ до ног. *The members of the Mafia were armed to their teeth.*

голова́ в го́лову—*shoulder to shoulder*

Солда́ты шли голова́ в го́лову. *The soldiers were marching shoulder to shoulder.*

голова́ трещи́т—*have a splitting headache*

У него́ голова́ ча́сто трещи́т. *He often has a splitting headache.*

име́ть го́лову на плеча́х; он с голово́й—*have brains; be brainy; have a good head on one's shoulders*

Ма́ша не то́лько краси́вая, но и име́ет го́лову на плеча́х. *Masha is not only pretty, but has brains as well.*

лома́ть себе́ го́лову—*rack one's brains*

Пётр весь день лома́л себе́ го́лову, но вы́хода из тупика́ не нашёл. *All day long Peter was racking his brains, but was unable to get out of the jam.*

моро́чить го́лову—*play games with someone*

При ка́ждой встре́че он мне моро́чит го́лову. *Whenever we meet, he keeps playing games with me.*

не идёт в го́лову—*one cannot grasp* (or *comprehend) something*

Бы́ло жа́рко, и матема́тика совсе́м не шла в го́лову. *It was very hot and I just couldn't grasp the math.*

сам себе́ голова́—*be one's own boss* (or *master)*

Бори́с откры́л апте́ку, и тепе́рь он сам себе́ голова́. *Boris opened a pharmacy and he is now his own boss.*

своя́ голова́ на плеча́х—*be able to think for oneself; be able to decide on one's own*

«Не учи́те меня́, у меня́ своя́ голова́ на плеча́х»—сказа́л сын родителям. *"Don't lecture me, I am able to think for myself," the son said to his parents.*

го́лод—*famine*

мори́ть го́лодом—*starve someone to death*

Пле́нных мори́ли го́лодом. *The prisoners of war were starved to death.*

умира́ть от го́лода (or **с го́лода** or **с го́лоду**)—*starve to death*

Е́сли ужи́на ско́ро не бу́дет, я умру́ от го́лода. *I'll starve to death, if we don't have dinner pretty soon.*

го́лос—*voice*

в оди́н го́лос—*in unison; unanimously; in chorus*

«Доло́й ма́фию!»—закрича́ли все в оди́н го́лос. *"Down with the Mafia!"—everyone cried unanimously.*

говори́ть (or **петь**) **с чужо́го го́лоса**—*parrot someone else's words; echo someone else's opinion*

Слу́шая его́, я по́нял, что он говори́т с чужо́го го́лоса. *Listening to him I realized that he was echoing someone else's opinion.*

крича́ть во весь го́лос—SEE: **крича́ть во всю́ гло́тку**

гора́—*mountain*

гора́ на душе́ (or **на се́рдце**) **лежи́т**—*load on one's mind*

Невы́полненная рабо́та лежи́т у меня́, как гора́ на душе́. *My unfinished work is a (huge) load on my mind.*

гора́ с плеч (свали́лась)—*load off one's mind*

Ива́н сдал экза́мен, и гора́ с плеч. *Passing the exam was a (huge) load off Ivan's mind.*

за гора́ми, за дола́ми—SEE: **куда́ во́рон косте́й не занесёт**

идти́ в го́ру—*come up in the world*

Мне ка́жется, что ты пошёл в го́ру. *It seems you've come up in the world!*

не за гора́ми (а за плеча́ми)—*not far off; at hand; around the corner*

Пра́здники уже́ не за гора́ми. *The holidays are just around the corner.*

обеща́ть (or **сули́ть**) **золоты́е го́ры**—*promise the moon (and the stars)*

Пе́ред сва́дьбой он обеща́л ей золоты́е го́ры. *Before the wedding he promised her the moon.*

горб—*hump*

добыва́ть (or **зараба́тывать**) **свои́м (со́бственным) горбо́м**—*earn by the sweat of one's brow*

Он всю жизнь зараба́тывал де́ньги свои́м горбо́м. *All his life, he earned his living by the sweat of his brow.*

испыта́ть на своём (со́бственном) горбу́—*learn by one's own experience; learn the hard way*

Са́ша на своём горбу́ испы́тывал тя́жесть жи́зни. *Sasha learned the hardships of life by his own experience.*

го́ре—*grief; sorrow*

залива́ть го́ре—*drown one's sorrows in drink*

Ива́н всегда́ го́ре залива́ет во́дкой. *Ivan always drowns his sorrows in vodka.*

и го́ря ма́ло—*not to give a hoot* (or *damn)*

Мы все страда́ем от нача́льника, а ему́ и го́ря ма́ло. *We're all suffering from the boss, but he doesn't give a damn.*

хлебну́ть го́ря—*experience a great deal of sorrow; go through a lot*

Во вре́мя войны́ он хлебну́л го́ря. *He went through a lot during the time of the war.*

горе́ть—*burn*

не гори́т—*there is no need to hurry* (or *rush); there is no big hurry*

Ты мо́жешь отложи́ть рабо́ту, это не гори́т. *You can give the work a rest, there's no rush.*

го́рло—*throat*

по го́рло в рабо́те—*up to the chin* (or *neck) in work*

С ним сейча́с не говори́те, он по го́рло в рабо́те. *You can't talk to him now, he's up to his neck in work.*

сы́т(ый) по го́рло—*1. be full; be stuffed 2. be fed up*

1. Ники́та отказа́лся от обе́да, объясни́в, что он сыт по го́рло. *Nikita didn't want to eat dinner, as he was full.*
2. Я уже́ сыт по го́рло его́ обеща́ниями. *I'm all fed up with his promises.*

го́род—*city*

раструби́ть (or **трезво́нить**) **по всему́ го́роду**—*spread something all over town*

Пётр раструби́л о свое́й но́вой жени́тьбе по всему́ го́роду. *Peter spread the news of his new marriage all over town.*

горя́чка—*fever*

поро́ть горя́чку—*do things pell-mell; in a rush*

В ва́жном де́ле нельзя́ поро́ть горя́чку. *Don't do important things in a rush.*

господи́н—*mister*

быть господи́ном своего́ сло́ва (or **своему́ сло́ву**)—*be a man of one's word*

Мы ему́ ве́рим; он господи́н своему́ сло́ву. *We believe him—he's a man of his word.*

сам себе́ господи́н—SEE: **сам себе́ голова́**

Го́споди—*God*

не дай Го́споди!—*God forbid!*

Не дай Го́споди повтори́тся война́! *God forbid that the war should break out all over again.*

гость—*guest*

быть в гостя́х—*be on a visit*

Мы бы́ли в гостя́х у сестры́. *We went to visit my sister.*

в гостя́х хорошо́, а до́ма лу́чше—*there's no place like home*

Приезжа́я из о́тпуска домо́й, ка́ждый раз мы ду́мали, что в гостя́х хорошо́, а до́ма лу́чше. *Every time we arrived back from our vacation we thought that there is no place like home.*

ждать в го́сти—*expect guests*

Я жду́ бра́та в го́сти. *I'm expecting my brother to come visit me.*

гра́дус—*degree*

быть (or **находи́ться**) **под гра́дусом**—*be tipsy; have one too many*

По вечера́м он ча́сто нахо́дится под гра́дусом. *He's often tipsy in the evening.*

гражда́нство—*citizenship*

принима́ть гражда́нство—*be naturalized; become a citizen*

Па́вел при́нял гражда́нство США год тому́ наза́д. *A year ago Pavel became a U.S. citizen.*

гра́мота—*reading and writing*

кита́йская гра́мота—*it's (all) Greek to me*

Техни́ческие кни́ги для меня́ кита́йская гра́мота. *Technological books are all Greek to me.*

гран—*grain*

нет ни гра́на—*not a grain* (or *shred)*

В его́ расска́зе нет ни гра́на и́стины. *There's not a shred of truth in his story.*

грани́ца—*border; frontier; limit*

вы́йти из грани́ц—*overstep the mark; go too far*

Их спор вы́шел из грани́ц прили́чия. *They went too far in their quarrelling.*

за грани́цей—*1. foreign country 2. out of the country*

1. А́нна учи́лась за грани́цей. *Ann studied in a foreign country.*
2. Ива́н никогда́ не был за грани́цей. *Ivan has never been out of the country.*

за грани́цу—*to foreign countries; abroad*

Бори́са посла́ли за грани́цу. *Boris was sent to foreign countries.*

и́з-за грани́цы—*from abroad*

Оте́ц привёз нам мно́го пода́рков и́з-за грани́цы. *Father brought us lots of presents from abroad.*

грех—*sin*

грех сказа́ть—*it would be unfair to say*

Грех сказа́ть, что он нече́стный челове́к. *It would be unfair to say that he isn't an honest person.*

до́лго ли до греха́? недо́лго и до греха́?—*something bad may happen*

Éсли Йгорь попадёт в плохýю компáнию, дóлго ли до грехá? *Something bad may happen, if Igor falls in with the wrong crowd.*

как на грех—*as bad luck would have it*

Мне нýжно бы́ло вы́звать скóрую пóмощь, а телефóн, как на грех, не рабóтал. *I had to call an ambulance, but just then, as bad luck would have it, the phone died on me.*

мой грех—*my fault*

Прости́те, мой грех!—*I'm sorry, it is my fault!*

нéчего (or **чегó**) **(и) грехá таи́ть**—*it must be confessed; why deny it that...*

Расстáться с женихóм бы́ло Ни́не нелегкó, нéчего грехá таи́ть. *Why deny the fact that it was difficult for Nina to break up with her fiance.*

с грехóм пополáм—*with difficulty; barely manage to do something*

Бори́с мог тóлько с грехóм пополáм объясня́ться по-англи́йски. *Boris could only express himself in English with difficulty.*

гриб—*mushroom*

расти́ как грибы́ (пóсле дождя́)—*to mushroom; pop up all over*

Высóкие домá в гóроде росли́ как грибы́. *The high-rises are mushrooming all over town.*

гроб—*coffin*

в гроб вогнáть (or **вколоти́ть** or **свести́**)—*drive someone to the grave*

Свои́ми скандáлами он её вогнáл в гроб. *He drove her to the grave with his scandalous affairs.*

гром—*thunder*

(как) гром среди́ я́сного нéба—*like a bolt out of the clear blue sky*

Э́то извéстие для нас бы́ло, как гром среди́ я́сного нéба. *The news reached us like a bolt out of the clear blue sky.*

покá гром не гря́нет—*get too hot for one*

Мы отклáдывали рабóту, покá гром не гря́нул. *We kept putting our work off, until it got too hot for us.*

грош—*penny*

грошá лóманого (or **мéдного) не стóит**—*not to be worth a red cent*

Авари́йный автомоби́ль грошá лóманого не стóит. *A car that has been in an accident isn't worth a red cent.*

грошá нет; ни грошá нет; (ни) грошá за душóй нет—*not a cent* (or *penny) to one's name*

У меня́ нет ни грошá за душóй. *I haven't got a red cent to my name.*

купи́ть за гроши́—*buy for a song (*or *for next to nothing* or *dirt cheap)*

Мы купи́ли за гроши́ ужé бы́вшую в употреблéнии маши́ну. *We bought a used car for next to nothing.*

продавáть за гроши́—*sell for a song*

Мы прóдали за гроши́ свой стáрый холоди́льник. *We sold our old refrigerator for a song.*

грязь—*dirt*

обливáть гря́зью—*besmirch one's reputation; denigrate someone*

Коллéги без вся́кого основáния обли́ли гря́зью егó и́мя. *His fellow workers denigrated his character quite groundlessly.*

принимáть гря́зи—*undergo a hot mud pack cure*

По совéту врачá Елéна принимáла гря́зи. *Following her doctor's orders, Elena underwent a hot mud pack cure.*

губá—*lip*

губá не ду́ра—*have common sense; not to have bad taste; be no dummy*

Сухо́му хле́бу Ната́ша предпочла́ кусо́чек то́рта. Губа́ не ду́ра. *Natasha preferred a piece of cake to dry bread. She's no dummy.*

губи́тель—*destroyer*

губи́тель серде́ц—*lady-killer*

Всем бы́ло изве́стно, что Ива́н—губи́тель серде́ц. *Everybody knew that Ivan was a lady-killer.*

гу-гу́

ни гу-гу́—*mum's the word!*

О расска́занном я никому ни гу-гу́! *About what you said, I promise mum's the word.*

гуля́ть—*do walking*

гуля́ть с ке́м-либо—*go with someone*

Он с ней гуля́ет уже́ два го́да. *He's been going with her for the past two years.*

гусь—*goose*

гусь ла́пчатый—*a savvy character; sly old fox*

Пётр дру́жит и с ма́фией, и мили́цией—вот гусь ла́пчатый! *Peter is good friends both with the Mafia and the police—there's a sly old fox!*

Д

да—*yes*

ах, да—*by the way*

Ах да, чуть не забы́л, Мари́я посыла́ет вам приве́т. *By the way, I almost forgot that Mary sends her greetings.*

да здра́вствует—*long live*

Да здра́вствует Междунаро́дный же́нский день! *Long live International Women's Day!*

да и то́лько—*1. constantly; all the time 2. and that's all*

1. Са́ша ходи́л в кино́, да и то́лько. *Sasha kept going to the movies all the time.*
2. Он хоте́л игра́ть в ша́хматы, да и то́лько. *He just wanted to play chess, that's all.*

и да и нет—*both yes and no; to equivocate*

Она́ хо́чет вы́йти за́муж? И да, и нет. *She equivocates about getting married.*

дава́ть—*give; let*

дава́ть взаймы́—*lend*

Я ча́сто дава́л ему́ взаймы́ сто до́лларов. *I would often lend him $100.*

дава́ть поня́ть—*to hint at; to cue someone*

В рестора́не Па́вел мне дал поня́ть, что у него́ ни копе́йки нет. *When we were in the restaurant, Pavel hinted at the fact that he didn't have a penny on him.*

давно́—*long time*

давно́ бы так!—*at long last; none too soon*

«Твою́ про́сьбу я вы́полнил.»—«Давно́ бы так!» *"I did what you wanted."—"None too soon!"*

давны́м-давно́—*in a long time; for ages; very long ago*

Мы давны́м-давно́ не ви́делись. *We haven't seen each other for ages.*

далеко́—*far*

далеко́ не—*far from being*

Он далеко́ не тако́й тала́нтливый, как он ду́мает. *He's far from being quite as talented as he thinks.*

далеко́ пойти́ (or **уйти́**)—*succeed; come out on top; go far*

Зна́я компью́тер, мо́жно далеко́ пойти́. *If one knows computers, one can come out on top.*

да́льше—*farther away*

да́льше (е́хать) не́куда—*that's the limit*

Когда́ Ива́н на́чал груби́ть, его́ оте́ц залепи́л ему́ пощёчину и закрича́л—«Да́льше е́хать не́куда!» *When Ivan began to sass his father he gave him a slap in the face and yelled, "That's the limit!"*

да́ма—*lady*

да́ма се́рдца—*sweetheart*

Его́ да́ма се́рдца—высо́кая блонди́нка. *His sweetheart is a tall blonde.*

дар—*gift; donation*

да́ром не пойдёт!—*one won't get away with; one has to pay for something*

Э́то ему́ да́ром не пойдёт!—*He won't get away with this!*

два—*two*

ни два ни полтора́—*neither fish, nor fowl; neither this, nor that*

Э́тот костю́м ни два ни полтора́; его́ цвет, фасо́н меня́ не удовлетворя́ют. *This costume is neither fish nor fowl—its color and cut don't work for me.*

два́жды—*two times*

как два́жды два (четы́ре)—*as plain as the nose on your face; as plain as two times two is four*

Её пра́вда была́ ясна́ как два́жды два четы́ре. *It was plain as the nose on your face that she was right.*

дверь—*door*

дверь в дверь—*next-door*

Я с подру́гой живу́ дверь в дверь. *My girlfriend and I live next-door to each other.*

ломи́ться в откры́тую дверь—*belabor the obvious*

Я с твоúм решéнием давнó соглáсен, а ты лóмишься в открытую дверь. *I've agreed with you some time ago—you are belaboring the obvious.*

у дверéй—SEE: **не за горáми**

двор—*courtyard*

быть не ко дворý—*be ill-suited; undesirable; unwelcome*

По приéзде я замéтил, что был не ко дворý. *No sooner had I arrived than I noticed that I was unwelcome.*

на дворé—*outside; out-of-doors*

Одéнь калóши, снег лежúт на дворé. *Take your galoshes, it's snowy outside.*

чёрный двор—*backyard*

На чёрном дворé мы пострóили гарáж. *We built a garage in our backyard.*

декорáция—*decoration*

декорáции переменúлись—*situation has changed; it's a different ball game*

С нóвым руковóдством и декорáции переменúлись. *With the new management it's a whole different ball game.*

дéло—*matter*

блúже к дéлу!—*stick to the point!*

«Блúже к дéлу!»—кричáли слýшатели орáтору. *"Stick to the point," the audience shouted at the speaker.*

вáше дéло—*that's your business; up to you*

Уéдете úли остáнетесь здесь—э́то вáше дéло. *It's up to you whether you stay or leave.*

в сáмом дéле—*really; indeed; actually; in fact*

Ты в сáмом дéле сдал экзáмен? *Have you, in fact, passed your exam?*

в чём дéло?—*What's the matter?*

В чём дéло? Почемý вы не рабóтаете? *What's the matter? Why aren't you working?*

говорúть дéло—*have a point; talk sense*

Васúлий немногослóвен, но éсли говорúт, то говорúт дéло. *Vasily doesn't talk much, but when he does say something, he talks sense.*

делá идýт, контóра пúшет—*everything is fine, business as usual*

«Как делá?»—спросúл Олéг. «Делá идýт, контóра пúшет»—ответúла Лéна. *"How are things?" asked Oleg. "Everything is fine, business as usual," Lena answered.*

делá—как сáжа белá—(in answers) *don't even ask!*

«Как делá?»—«Как сáжа, белá.»—*"How are things going?"—"Don't even ask!"*

дéло бы́ло к вéчеру—*get to be evening*

Дéло бы́ло к вéчеру, когдá я решúл вернýться домóй. *It was getting to be evening when I decided to head for home.*

дéло в том—*the fact of the matter is*

Дéло в том, что её обвинúли, хотя́ онá невиновáта. *The fact of the matter is that although she was accused, she is really innocent.*

дéло деся́тое (or **двадцáтое**)—*be of little significance*

Вопрóс о покýпке хрустáльных бокáлов мы отложúли, так как э́то дéло деся́тое. *The question of purchasing the crystal glasses was put off, since it's a matter of little significance.*

дéло за деньгáми—*it's a question of money*

Решéние пострóить дáчу прúняли; тепéрь дéло за деньгáми. *They decided to build the summer cottage—now it's just a question of money.*

дéло пáхнет керосúном—*be in big trouble; things are in a bad way*

Счетá бухгáлтера бы́ли не в поря́дке, и мы почýвствовали, что дéло пáхнет керосúном. *The accountant's books weren't in order, and we felt we were in big trouble.*

де́ло—таба́к (or труба́)!—*have had it; it's tough luck; things are bad*

Когда́ меня́ уво́лили, я ду́мал, что де́ло—таба́к! *"Tough luck," I thought when they fired me.*

как дела́?—*How are you? What's the news?*

При встре́че он всегда́ спра́шивал: «Как дела́?» *"What's the news?" he always asked when we met.*

моё де́ло сторона́; э́то не мое де́ло—*it's none of my business*

Вы де́лайте что хоти́те, а моё де́ло—сторона́. *You can do whatever you want, it's none of my business.*

не ле́зь(те) в чужи́е дела́—*mind your own business*

Я вам сове́тую не ле́зть в чужи́е дела́. *I suggest you mind your own business.*

не у дел—*be out of work* (or *a job*)

По́сле реорганиза́ции в на́шем отде́ле я оста́лся не у дел. *After the reorganization in our department, I was out of work.*

по де́лу—*on business*

О́льга прие́хала по ва́жному де́лу. *Olga has arrived on important business.*

серде́чные дела́—*love affairs*

В фи́рме все зна́ли о его́ серде́чных дела́х. *At work everybody knew about his love affairs.*

день—*day*

в бы́лые дни́—*in olden days*

В бы́лые дни́ лю́ди телеви́зора не зна́ли. *People didn't know television in the olden days.*

днём с огнём—*be hard to find*

Тако́го че́стного челове́ка, как Оле́г, днём с огнём не найдёшь. *It's hard to find such an honest person as Oleg.*

за́втрашний день—*the future*

Име́я доста́точный дохо́д, не́чего боя́ться за́втрашнего дня. *No need to worry about the future if one has enough income.*

изо дня́ в день—*day by day; day afer day*

Изо дня́ в день нáше положéние фи́рмы улучшáется. *Day after day our situation is getting better.*

кáждый бóжий день—*every blessed day*

Бори́с ходи́л ко мне кáждый бóжий день. *Every blessed day Boris would visit me.*

на чёрный день—*for a rainy day*

Мы сберегли́ небольшу́ю су́мму на чёрный день. *We saved up a small sum of money for a rainy day.*

среди́ бéлого дня́—*in broad daylight*

Среди́ бéлого дня́ ограбили бáнк. *The bank was robbed in broad daylight.*

я́сно как бóжий день—*clear as the light of day*

Почему́ ты не понимáешь, ведь э́то я́сно как бóжий день. *How come you don't get it when it's clear as the light of day?*

дéньги—*money*

бéшеные дéньги—*a fortune; a bundle; heaps* (or *tons) of money*

Егó коллéкция рéдких почтóвых мáрок стóила бéшеные дéньги. *His rare stamp collection cost him a bundle.*

бросáть дéньги на вéтер—*squander one's money*

Получи́в наслéдство, он стал бросáть дéньги на вéтер. *As soon as he received his inheritance, he began to squander it.*

дéнег в обрéз—*not to have a penny to spare; every penny is spoken for*

Я не могу́ откры́ть нóвый магази́н, потому́ что у меня́ дéнег в обрéз. *I can't open a new shop, because every penny I've got is already spoken for.*

дéньги на мéлкие расхóды—*pocket money*

Дéньги на мéлкие расхóды мáльчик трáтит на жвáчку. *The boy spends his pocket money on chewing gum.*

класть (or **выклáдывать**) **дéньги на бóчку**—*pay on the spot*

Пóсле заключéния контрáкта нам сказáли положи́ть дéньги на бóчку. *After the signing of the contract they said that we should pay on the spot.*

крóвные дéньги—*hard-earned money*

Они́ купи́ли мáленький дом за свои́ крóвные дéньги. *They bought a small house with their hard-earned money.*

не в дéньгах счáстье—*money isn't everything*

«Не в дéньгах счáстье»—поду́мала Ли́за и вы́шла зáмуж за бéдного поэ́та. *"Money isn't everything," Lisa thought, and married a poor poet.*

ни за каки́е дéньги—*not for the (whole) world; not for all the tea in China*

Ни за каки́е дéньги я не продáм карти́ну, подáренную мáтерью. *I wouldn't sell the picture my mother gave me for the whole world.*

десятóк—*ten*

не из рóбкого десятка—*not to be the timid type* (or *sort*)

Михаи́л не из рóбкого деся́тка: во врéмя пожáра он вы́нес сестру́ из горя́щего дóма. *Mikhail is not the timid sort—he brought his sister out of the burning house.*

детáль—*detail*

вдавáться в детáли—*go into (all kinds of) detail*

В своём репортáже он всё врéмя вдавáлся в детáли. *In his report he kept going into all kinds of detail.*

дéтский—*children's*

по-дéтски—*childish*

Иногдá Алексéй рассуждáл по-дéтски. *Aleksey's opinions sometimes sounded childish.*

дéтство—*childhood*

впадáть в дéтство—*be in one's second childhood; become senile*

В стáрости онá совсéм впáла в дéтство. *She became quite senile in her old age.*

дешёвый—*cheap*

дёшево и сердúто—*good bargain* (or *deal*)

В э́том магазúне всё дёшево и сердúто. *You get a good deal on everything in this store.*

отдéлаться дёшево—*get off lucky* (or *cheap*)

Мы попáли в авáрию, но дёшево отдéлались. *We were in an accident, but we got off lucky.*

дно—*bottom*

вверх дном—*go topsy-turvy*

Йз-за приéзда президéнта в нáшем городкé всё пошлó вверх дном. *Because of the President's arrival everything was topsy-turvy in our little town.*

до дна!—*bottoms up!*

«Пей до дна!»—кричáли мужчúны в кабакé. *"Bottoms up!" the men in the tavern cried.*

опустúться на дно—*sink to the bottom of society*

Пётр стал наркомáном и опустúлся на дно. *Peter sank to the bottom of society, when he became a dope addict.*

добро́—*good*

добро́ пожа́ловать!—*Welcome!*

Добро́ пожа́ловать!—сказа́ла хозя́йка. *"Welcome!" the hostess said.*

не к добру́—*it's a bad omen*

По мне́нию суеве́рных, но́мер трина́дцать не к добру́. *The number "13" is considered a bad omen by the superstitious.*

не приведёт к добру́—*no good will come of it*

Обма́н не приведёт к добру́. *No good ever comes of fraud.*

помина́ть добро́м—*remember kindly*

Мои́х зарубе́жных друзе́й я всегда́ вспомина́ю добро́м. *I always remember kindly my friends abroad.*

до́брый—*good; kind*

бу́дь(те) добр(ы́)—*be so kind*

Будь добр, сде́лай мне э́то! *Would you be so kind as to do this for me?*

всего́ до́брого—*all the best*

Жела́ю вам всего́ до́брого! *I wish you all the best!*

дове́рие—*confidence*

втира́ться в дове́рие—*worm oneself into someone's confidence*

И́горь с лицеме́рием втира́лся в дове́рие дире́ктору. *Igor wormed himself into the manager's confidence under false pretenses.*

злоупотребля́ть дове́рием—*abuse one's confidence*

Ива́н злоупотребля́л дове́рием свои́х друзе́й. *Ivan abused the confidence of his friends.*

дождь—*rain*

дождь льёт как из ведра́—*it's raining cats and dogs*

Весь день дождь льёт как из ведра́. *It's been raining cats and dogs all day.*

идёт проливно́й дождь—*it's coming down in sheets*

Óсенью чáсто идýт проливны́е дожди́. *In the fall the rain often comes down in sheets.*

под сáмым дождём—*right in the rain*

Мы стоя́ли и разговáривали под сáмым дождём. *We just stood there and kept talking right in the rain.*

долг—*debt; duty*

быть в долгý, как в шелкý—*be in debt up to one's neck* (or *ears*)

Рáньше он бросáл дéньги на вéтер, а тепéрь он в долгý, как в шелкý. *He spent his money so recklessly that now he is in debt up to his neck.*

вы́йти из долгóв—*get out of the red*

Егó извéчная проблéма, как вы́йти из долгóв. *His eternal problem is how to get out of the red.*

отдáть послéдний долг—*pay final respects*

На похоронáх мы отдáли емý послéдний долг. *We paid him our final respects at the funeral.*

пéрвым дóлгом—*first of all*

Пéрвым дóлгом ты дóлжен зарабáтывать дéньги. *First of all you need to make some money.*

по дóлгу слýжбы—*in an official capacity; on business*

Меня́ послáли по дóлгу слýжбы за грани́цу. *I was sent abroad in an official capacity.*

дóлго—*long time*

не дóлго дýмая—*wasting no time; without thinking twice*

Не дóлго дýмая, он реши́л жени́ться. *Without thinking twice he decided to get married.*

дóля—*part; portion*

вы́пасть на дóлю—*get as one's share; fate bestows something upon one*

На егó дóлю вы́пали войнá и гóлод. *He got the war and hunger as his share.*

дом—*house*

отбиться от дóма—*hardly ever to be at home* (with one's family)

Посещáя ночнóй клуб, он отбился от дóма. *He was hardly ever at home, because of all the night-clubbing he did.*

скучáть (or **тосковáть**) **по дóму**—*be* (or *feel* or *get*) *homesick*

Прожив мéсяц за границей, студéнтка скучáла по дóму. *After a month abroad the student felt homesick.*

дóма—*at home*

не все дóма—SEE: **винтика не хватáет в головé**

дорóга—*road*

выбиться на дорóгу—*make one's way in life; find one's niche in society* (or *life*)

Своéй прилéжностью он обязáтельно выбьется на дорóгу. *Given his diligence, he's bound to find his niche in society.*

идти (or **слéдовать**) **своéй дорóгой**—*follow one's own path*

Никтó не мóжет влиять на негó, он идёт своéй дорóгой. *No one can persuade him to do anything; he follows his own path.*

на дорóге не валяется—*is hard to come by; is difficult to get*

Такóй хорóший друг, как Пётр, на дорóге не валяется. *A really good friend, such as Peter, is hard to come by.*

стать (or **стоять**) **на дорóге** (or **поперёк дорóги**)—*be an obstacle; be in one's way*

Мой начáльник стоит на дорóге к моемý профессионáльному успéху. *My boss at work is an obstacle to my professional advancement.*

тудá комý **и дорóга!**—*it serves one right!*

За растрáту егó заключили в тюрьмý. Тудá емý и дорóга! *He got arrested for embezzlement—serves him right!*

дорогóй—*dear; expensive*

себé дорóже стóит—*something is more trouble than it's worth*

Отремонти́ровать ста́рый, изно́шенный автомоби́ль себе́ доро́же сто́ит. *To repair an old used car is more trouble than it's worth.*

доро́жка—*path*

идти́ по проторённой доро́жке—*keep to the beaten track*

Что́бы не сде́лать оши́бки, иди́ по проторённой доро́жке. *If you don't want to make a mistake, keep to the beaten track.*

доска́—*board*

до гробово́й доски́—*to one's dying day*

Лю́ди ре́дко рабо́тают в той же фи́рме до гробово́й доски́. *People seldom work at the same place to their dying day.*

от доски́ до доски́—SEE: **от А до Я**

ста́вить на одну́ до́ску—*put one on the same level; consider as an equal*

Пётр пренебрега́л все́ми и никого́ не ста́вил на одну́ до́ску с собо́й. *Peter looked down on everyone never considering anyone as an equal.*

(худо́й) как доска́—*be excessively thin; be thin as a toothpick*

Заболе́в, она́ ста́ла худа́я как доска́. *Because of her illness, she became thin as a toothpick.*

дочь; до́чка—*daughter*

дочь Е́вы—*female; woman*

Ве́чером в кафе́ собира́лись одни́ до́чери Е́вы. *It was all women in the cafe in the evening.*

ма́менькина до́чка—*spoiled little girl; (little) princess*

Э́та ма́менькина до́чка капри́зничала весь день. *This spoiled little girl was acting up all day.*

дрова́—*firewood*

налома́ть дров—*do silly things; make one mistake after another; screw things up*

Ско́лько они́ налома́ли дров и́з-за незна́ния де́ла. *They made one mistake after another, due to their lack of expertise.*

дрожь—*trembling*

дрожа́ть кру́пной дро́жью—*be all shook (shaken) up*

Когда́ он идёт к зубно́му врачу́, он дрожи́т кру́пной дро́жью. *When he goes to the dentist, he gets all shook up.*

дру́жба—*friendship*

войти́ в дру́жбу—*strike up a friendship with someone*

Бори́с стара́лся всéми путя́ми войти́ в дру́жбу со мно́й. *Boris spared no effort to strike up a friendship with me.*

дуда́—*pipe*

дуде́ть в ста́рую дуду́—*sound like a broken record*

Де́душка постоя́нно расска́зывал о войне́, дудя́ в ста́рую дуду́. *Grandpa talks so much about the war that he sounds like a broken record.*

ду́мать—*think*

на́до ду́мать—*probably; chances are that...*

На́до ду́мать, наш сын бу́дет музыка́нтом. *Chances are that our son will become a musician.*

дура́к—*fool*

нашёл (нашли́) дурака́!—*I'm not such a fool as you think*

За такúе дéньги рабóтать? Нашлú дуракá! *To work for so little? I'm not such a fool as you think!*

набúтый дурáк—*damn fool*

Что от негó ожидáть, ведь он набúтый дурáк. *What can you expect of him? He is such a damn fool.*

остáвить (or **остáться**) **в дуракáх**—*make a fool of someone; be left holding the bag*

Мой партнёр отказáлся поделúть прúбыль, и такúм óбразом я остáлся в дуракáх. *My partner refused to share in the profits, and I was left holding the bag.*

дух—*mind; spirit*

бежáть во весь дух—*run at full speed; as fast as one can; all steam ahead*

Увúдев медвéдя, мы бежáли во весь дух. *We ran as fast as we could when we caught sight of the bear.*

быть в дýхе—*be in a good frame of mind; be in high spirits*

Сегóдня я в дýхе. *I'm in high spirits today.*

быть не в дýхе—*be in an ill humor; be in a bad mood*

Вчерá я был не в дýхе. *I was in a bad mood yesterday.*

пáдать дýхом—*lose heart; give up; be* (or *get*) *discouraged*

Когдá егó увóлили с рабóты, он упáл дýхом. *He got all discouraged when they fired him.*

придавáть дýху (or **дýха**)—*give someone a pep-talk; encourage someone*

Врач придáл дýху больнóму. *The doctor gave the patient some pep-talk.*

душá—*soul*

душá в дýшу—*in perfect harmony*

Мы с мýжем живём душá в дýшу. *My husband and I live in perfect harmony.*

душá не лежи́т—*not one's cup of tea*

К изучéнию матемáтики у меня́ дýша не лежи́т. *Studying math isn't my cup of tea.*

душá не на мéсте—*be awfully worried; be worried sick*

У негó стóлько хлопóт, что душá не на мéсте. *He has so much trouble that he is worried sick.*

душá уйдёт в пя́тки—*one's heart sinks*

Пéред оперáцией у меня́ душá ушлá в пя́тки. *My heart sank before the operation.*

есть (or **имéется) за душóй**—*have (*or *own) things*

Бори́с óчень богáт, у негó мнóго áкций за душóй. *Boris is rich—he's got lots of bonds.*

зáячья душá—*timid person; chicken*

Ивáн всегó бои́тся—у негó зáячья душá. *Ivan is such a chicken—everything scares him.*

по душé—*be pleased with something; rather to like something*

Э́то плáтье мне по душé. *I rather like this dress.*

скóлько душé угóдно—*as much as one's heart desires*

Пожáлуйста, кýшайте скóлько душé угóдно! *Please eat as much as your heart desires!*

хватáть зá душу—*touch one to the quick*

Расскáзы о концентрациóнном лáгере меня́ всегдá хватáют зá душу. *The stories about the concentration camp always touch me to the quick.*

дыхáние—*breath*

не переводя́ дыхáния—*1. in one fell swoop; in a jiffy 2. nonstop; incessantly*

1. Бори́с вы́пил стакáн вóдки не переводя́ дыхáния. *Boris drank down his vodka in one fell swoop.*
2. Никúта рабóтал не переводя́ дыхáния. *Nikita kept on working nonstop.*

Е

едвá—*barely*

едвá-едвá—*scarcely, hardly*

Мы провели́ сто́лько вре́мени на тамо́жне, что едвá-едвá успе́ли к самолёту. *We spent so much time at customs that we barely reached our plane in time.*

едвá ли—*hardly*

«Хвáтит у нас вре́мени на обе́д?»—«Едвá ли.» *"Do we have time for a sit-down dinner?"—"Hardly."*

едвá ли не—*just about*

В нáшем клáссе он едвá ли не лу́чший учени́к. *He's just about the best student in our class.*

едвá не; чуть не—*almost; nearly; all but*

Натáша чуть не рассказáла нáшу тáйну. *Natasha almost gave away our secret.*

еди́ный—*single*

все до еди́ного (челове́ка)—*all without exception; to a man; every last*

Пассажи́ры все до еди́ного остáвили то́нущий парохо́д. *The sinking boat was abandoned by every last person.*

е́здить—*to go (*by conveyance*); ride*

е́здить (верхо́м) на кого́-либо—*order one around*

Мой начáльник на мне всегдá верхо́м е́здит. *My boss keeps ordering me around.*

е́здить на свои́х двои́х—*walk*

У меня́ автомоби́ля нет, я е́зжу на свои́х двои́х. *I've no car, I always walk.*

ерундá—*nonsense*

ерундá (or **чепухá**) **на по́стном мáсле**—*a lot of rubbish* (or *nonsense); horsefeathers*

Всё, что он говори́л в тот ве́чер, бы́ло чепухо́й на по́стном ма́сле. *Everything he said that evening was a lot of nonsense.*

есть—*be*

то́ есть—*that is; in other words*

Ава́рия случи́лась в понеде́льник, то́ есть ро́вно неде́лю тому́ наза́д. *The accident happened on Monday, that is, exactly a week ago.*

есть—*eat*

есть про́сит—*be in need of repair*

Моя́ о́бувь уже́ есть про́сит. *My shoes are in need of repair.*

ещё—*some more*

ещё бы!—*1. of course, and how! 2. just what I wanted! (*negatively*)*

1.«Хо́чешь вы́играть в лотере́ю?»—«Ещё бы!» *"Would you like to win the lottery?"—"But of course, and how!"*

2.«Хо́чешь пла́вать в оледене́лом о́зере?»—«Ещё бы!» *"Do you want to swim in an icy lake?"—"Just what I wanted."*

ёлка—*fir (-tree)*

быть на ёлке—*be at a Christmas (*or *New Year's) party*

Мы бы́ли на ёлке у на́ших друзе́й. *We were at the Christmas party at our friends'.*

Ж

жар—*heat*

дава́ть (or **задава́ть**) **жа́ру**—*make it hot for someone; give one hell*

И́горь не сде́ржен и всегда́ задаёт всем жа́ру. *Igor is unable to restrain himself—he makes it hot for everybody.*

поддава́ть (or **поддавля́ть**) **жа́ру**—*1. add fuel to the fire 2. get moving*

1. Мои́ замеча́ния подда́ли Бори́су жа́ру, и он совсе́м потеря́л контро́ль над собо́й. *My remarks added fuel to the fire and Boris lost all self control.*
2. Мои́ слова́ подда́ли ему́ жа́ру, и он взя́лся за рабо́ту. *I gave him a pep talk, and so he started to work.*

жва́чка—*chewing*

жева́ть (or **пережёвывать**) **жва́чку**—SEE: **дуде́ть в ста́рую дуду́**

ждать—*wait*

ждать не дожда́ться—*wait impatiently; be on tenterhooks*

Мать сы́на ждёт не дождётся. *The mother is on tenterhooks expecting her son.*

того́ и жди—*any minute now; just you wait*

То́рмоз на́до отремонти́ровать, а то, того́ и жди́, попадёшь в ава́рию. *You need to fix the brakes now, or you'll be in an accident!*

желе́зка—*piece of iron*

жать (or **нажима́ть**) **на всю́ желе́зку**—*throw into high gear*

Полице́йские, догоня́я престу́пников, жа́ли на всю́ желе́зку. *The police threw the car into high gear as they were chasing after the criminals.*

желе́зо—*iron*

вы́жечь калёным желе́зом—*root out (mercilessly); eliminate*

Ка́жется, что наркома́нию из совреме́нного о́бщества и калёным желе́зом нельзя́ вы́жечь. *There seems to be no way of rooting out drug abuse in modern society.*

куй желе́зо пока́ горячо́—*make hay while the sun shines*

Сего́дня ло́вится ры́ба хорошо́. «Куй желе́зо пока́ горячо́»—ду́мал рыба́к и оста́лся рыба́чить до ве́чера. *The fish are running well today. "Make hay while the sun shines," thought the fisherman and kept fishing till nightfall.*

жени́ть—*marry*

без меня́ меня́ жени́ли—*without my knowledge; get one into something*

Колле́ги реши́ли судьбу́ моеё фи́рмы—без меня́ меня́ жени́ли. *The colleagues decided the fate of my company without my knowledge.*

жени́х—*fiance*

смотре́ться женихо́м—*be as happy as a lark; walk on air*

Вы́играв в лотере́ю, Ива́н смотре́лся женихо́м. *When Ivan won the lottery, he was as happy as a lark.*

живо́й—*alive*

в живы́х—*remain alive; survive*

По́сле паде́ния самолёта то́лько тро́е оста́лись в живы́х. *There were only three survivors after the plane crashed.*

жив-здоро́в; жив и здоро́в—*safe and sound; alive and kicking*

Бори́с вы́шел из ава́рии жив и здоро́в. *Boris emerged from the accident alive and kicking.*

ни жив(о́й), ни мёртв(ый)—*be half dead with fright*

Заме́тив надвига́ющуюся лави́ну, мы ста́ли ни живы́ ни мертвы́. *We were half dead with fright when we noticed the avalanche coming toward us.*

ре́зать по живо́му—*touch* (or *hit) a sensitive nerve; hit a sore spot*

Пётр не сказа́л Ма́ше, что она́ о́чень пополне́ла; он не хоте́л ре́зать по живо́му. *Peter didn't tell Masha that she's gotten too fat—he didn't want to hit a sore spot.*

живо́т—*stomach*

надрыва́ть живо́т со́ смеху (or **от хо́хота**)—*split one's sides with laughter*

Когда́ Бори́с расска́зывает анекдо́ты, мы всегда́ надрыва́ем животы́ со́ смеху. *Whenever Boris tells jokes, our sides are splitting with laughter.*

подтя́гивать живо́т—*tighten one's belt*

Поско́льку я потра́тил все де́ньги на но́вый автомоби́ль, мне пришло́сь подтяну́ть живо́т на мно́гие ме́сяцы. *Since I spent all my money on a new car, I had to tighten my belt for months.*

жизнь—*life*

брать всё от жи́зни—*enjoy life to the full*

Бу́дучи молоды́м и бога́тым, Ива́н берёт всё от жи́зни. *Ivan is both rich and young—he enjoys life to the full.*

воплоща́ть (or **претворя́ть**) **в жизнь**—*turn into reality*

Па́влу удало́сь претвори́ть свои́ мечты́ в жизнь. *Pavel succeeded in turning his dreams into reality.*

входи́ть в жизнь—*become usual; a matter of routine*

Фина́нсовые пробле́мы входи́ли в на́шу жизнь. *Financial worries became a matter of routine for us.*

жи́зни свое́й не жале́ть—*not to spare oneself; give one's all*

Солда́ты, защища́я свою́ ро́дину, жи́зни свое́й не жале́ли. *The soldiers gave their all in the defense of their country.*

жизнь бьёт ключо́м—*life is in full swing; there's lots of activity; be buzzing with activity*

Во время́ футбо́льных соревнова́ний жизнь бьёт ключо́м в на́шем го́роде. *During the football season our town is buzzing with activity.*

жизнь на широ́кую но́гу—*high living; live high on the hog*

Па́вел лю́бит жизнь на широ́кую но́гу. *Pavel likes to live high on the hog.*

зарабáтывать на жизнь—*make one's living*

Йгорь своим пóтом зарабáтывал на жизнь. *Igor made his own living with the sweat of his brow.*

клянýсь жи́знью!—*upon* (or *on) my life (*or *my word of honor)*

Я прáвду говорю́, клянýсь жи́знью! *On my word of honor, I'm telling you the truth!*

не жизнь, а мáсленица—*live high on the hog; one has it made*

Пóсле удáчных биржевы́х махинáций у Михайла стáла не жизнь, а мáсленица. *Mikhail started to live high on the hog after some successful manipulations at the stock exchange.*

прожигáть жизнь—*lead a fast life*

Все вечерá Бори́с провóдит в ресторáнах и́ли в кинó; он прожигáет жизнь. *Boris spends each evening either in a restaurant or at the movies—he leads a fast life.*

таковá жизнь!—*that's life for you; c'est la vie*

Ники́та окóнчил свой расскáз словáми: «Таковá жизнь». *Nikita ended his story with the words: "Well, c'est la vie!"*

жилéтка—*vest*

плáкаться в жилéтку—*cry on someone's shoulder*

Пóсле развóда онá недéлями плáкалась мне в жилéтку. *After her divorce she was crying on my shoulder for weeks.*

жилéц—*tenant*

не жилéц на бéлом свéте (or **на э́том свéте**)—*be on the verge of death; be not long for this world*

Сýдя по егó ви́ду, я́сно, что он не жилéц на бéлом свéте. *Judging by his appearance, it was plain that he was on the verge of death.*

жир—*fat*

беси́ться от жи́ра (or **с жи́ру**)—*go nuts (*on one's riches or wealth*)*

Получи́в наслéдство, он бéсится от жи́ра. *His inheritance drove him nuts.*

лóпаться от жи́ра—*fall apart with obesity; get as fat as a pig*
Бори́с так мнóго и чáсто ест, что лóпается от жи́ра. *Boris eats so much and so often that he's falling apart with obesity.*

жить—*live*

жил-был—*once upon a time*
«Жи́ли-бы́ли корóль и королéва»—так начинáется моя́ люби́мая скáзка. *"Once upon a time there was a king and a queen"—so starts my favorite fairy tale.*

жить припевáючи—*live on Easy Street; live high on the hog*
Вы́йдя на хорóшую пéнсию, Пётр жил припевáючи. *Peter lived on Easy Street after his advantageous retirement.*

как живёте-мóжете?—*How are you doing?*
При встрéче Мáша спрáшивала: «Как живёте-мóжете?» *"How are you doing?" Masha asked when we met.*

жуть—*terror; awe*

до жу́ти—*terribly; incredibly; awfully*
Дéвочка до жу́ти боится темноты́. *The little girl is awfully afraid of the darkness.*

З

забóта—*care*

нé было забóты!—*that's the last thing* (or *all*) *one needed; there was trouble enough to spare without it*
Очки́ разби́лись—нé было забóты! *My glasses broke—that's the last thing I needed!*

не моя́ забóта—*I don't care; it's not my headache* (or *concern*)

Как он спра́вится со свои́ми пробле́мами, не моя́ забо́та. *It's not my headache how he solves his problems.*

забы́ть—*forget*

что я там (or тут) забы́л?—*what business do I have being there?*

Заче́м мне туда́ идти́? Что я там забы́л? *Why should I go there? What business have I got being there?*

заве́са—*curtain; screen*

заве́са упа́ла с глаз—*the scales fell from one's eyes; suddenly to see clearly*

По́сле его́ объясне́ния с на́ших глаз упа́ла заве́са. *After his explanations, the scales fell from our eyes.*

завести́—*lead*

как (or **сло́вно** or **то́чно**) **заведённый**—*incessantly; like a machine; nonstop*

Са́ша рабо́тал как заведённый. *Sasha was working like a machine.*

за́висть—*envy*

ло́пнуть от за́висти—*burst with envy; be green with envy*

Когда́ он уви́дел но́вый автомоби́ль сосе́да, он чуть не ло́пнул от за́висти. *He was green with envy when he saw his neighbor's new car.*

за́втра—*tomorrow*

до за́втра!—*see you tomorrow!*

Михаи́л попроща́лся со слова́ми: «До за́втра!» *Mikhail said good-bye with the words "see you tomorrow!"*

за́втрак—*breakfast*

корми́ть за́втраками—*feed someone with (empty) promises*

Ско́ро нам ста́ло я́сно, что он ко́рмит нас за́втраками. *It became soon evident to us that he was feeding us with empty promises.*

загвóздка—*difficulty*

вот в чём загвóздка—*there's the rub*

Мы хотим уéхать в óтпуск, но дéнег нет—вот в чём загвóздка. *We want to go on a vacation, but we have no money—there's the rub.*

зад—*back*

зáдом наперёд—*wrong way around*

По рассéянности он надéл пуловéр зáдом наперёд. *Being absent-minded, he put his sweater on the wrong way.*

задвóрки—*backyard*

быть (or **держáть) на задвóрках**—*take the back seat; be put on the backburner*

При жизни писáтель был на задвóрках, извéстность пришлá пóсле смéрти. *During his lifetime the writer took the back seat—his fame came only after his death.*

задýматься—*muse*

о чём ты задýмался?—*a penny for your thoughts!*

Ты весь вéчер смóтришь мечтáтельными глазáми. О чём ты задýмался? *All evening long you've been daydreaming. A penny for your thoughts!*

зажить—*begin to live*

зажить по-нóвому; зажить нóвой жизнью—*begin a new life; turn over a new leaf*

Борис решил зажить по-нóвому и женился. *Boris decided to turn over a new leaf and got married.*

зазрéние

без зазрéния сóвести—*without a twinge of conscience; remorselessly*

Вор забрáл мои дéньги без зазрéния сóвести. *The thief took my money without a twinge of conscience.*

закáт—*decline*

на закáте дней—*in one's declining years*

Пётр чáсто болéл на закáте свои́х дней. *Peter was often sick in his declining years.*

заклёпка—*rivet*

заклёпок не хватáет—SEE: **ви́нтика не хватáет**

заключéние—*conclusion*

дéлать поспéшные заключéния—*jump to conclusions*

Сáша был нетерпели́в и чáсто дéлал поспéшные заключéния. *Sasha was impatient and would frequently jump to conclusions.*

закóн—*law*

закóн не пи́сан—*not to go by the book; not to live by the rules*

Ники́та ведёт себя́ настóлько беззастéнчиво, что емý закóн, очеви́дно, не пи́сан. *Nikita is so uninhibited that he obviously doesn't live by the rules.*

закýска—*hors d'oeuvre; snack*

на закýску—*as a special treat* (or *favor*)

В концé вéчера на закýску арти́ст спел нáшу люби́мую пéсню. *At the end of the evening the artist sang our favorite song as a special favor.*

замечáние—*remark*

бéглое замечáние—*passing remark*

При разговóре он сдéлал бéглое замечáние, что сегóдня я плóхо вы́гляжу. *During our conversation he made the passing remark that I wasn't looking good today.*

замирáние—*dying down; going out*

с замирáнием сéрдца—*with a sinking* (or *palpitating*) *heart*

Бори́с шёл на экзáмен с замирáнием сéрдца. *Boris went to his examination with a sinking heart.*

замóк—*lock*

за семью́ (or **десятью́**) **замкáми**—*under seven seals; under lock and key*

Секрéтные докумéнты находи́лись за семью́ замкáми. *The secret documents were kept under seven seals.*

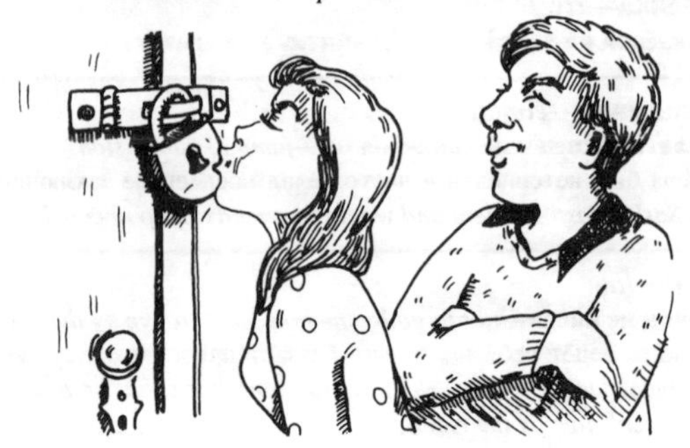

поцеловáть замóк—*go somewhere in vain; not to be received; no one is in*

Он пригласи́л нас в гóсти, а сам ушёл, и мы поцеловáли замóк. *He invited us to his place but he himself was gone, so we had gone there in vain.*

секрéтный замóк—*combination lock*

С цéлью безопáсности у нас смонти́ровали секрéтный замóк. *For safety reasons, we had a combination lock established.*

зáмуж—*married*

вы́скочить зáмуж—*to get married in a (real) hurry*

Окóнчив шкóлу, Лéна вы́скочила зáмуж. *Having finished school, Lena got married in a real hurry.*

запáл—*fuse, primer*

в запáле; под запáл—*in the heat of the moment*

Во врéмя задушéвной бесéды Пáвел в запáле вы́сказал свои тáйные мы́сли. *In the midst of the heart-to-heart talk, Pavel spilled his secret thoughts in the heat of the moment.*

запятáя—*comma*

до послéдней запятóй—*down to the smallest detail*

Аркáдий изучи́л библиотековéдение до послéдней запятóй. *Arkady learned librarianship down to the smallest detail.*

зарéз—*disaster*

до зарéзу; хоть зарéжь(те)—*desperately*

Мне до зарéзу нужны́ дéньги. *I need money desperately.*

заря́—*dawn*

вечéрняя заря́—*sunset*

С верши́ны горы́ мы любовáлись вечéрней зарёй. *We delighted in the sunset from the mountaintop.*

от зари́ до зари́—*all the live-long day; from dawn to dusk*

Бори́с рабóтал от зари́ до зари́. *Boris kept working from dawn to dusk.*

ýтренняя заря́—*sunrise*

Мы встáли с ýтренней зарёй. *We got up with the sunrise.*

заставля́ть—*make*

не заставля́й(те) себя́ проси́ть!—*help yourself!*

Пожáлуйста, кýшайте и не заставля́йте себя́ проси́ть! *Please, help yourselves, eat as much as you will!*

не заставля́ть себя́ дóлго ждáть—*not to keep someone waiting; waste no time*

Врач позвони́л, что он сейчáс приéдет, не заставля́ет себя́ дóлго ждáть. *The doctor phoned that he'll be there right away—he won't waste any time.*

зáяц—*hare*

пройти́ зáйцем—*sneak in free; crash the gate*

В кинó он прошёл зáйцем. *He snuck into the movie free.*

убúть двух зáйцев—*kill two birds with one stone*

С решéнием э́того вопрóса мы убúли двух зáйцев. *By resolving this question we killed two birds with one stone.*

звездá—*star*

звёзд с нéба не хватáть—*not to be known for one's excellence; be no genius*

Он хорóший специалúст, но звёзд с нéба не хватáет. *He is a good specialist but is not a genius.*

считáть звёзды—*twiddle one's thumbs*

От скýки Никúта считáет звёзды. *Nikita is twiddling his thumbs with boredom.*

зверь—*beast*

как затрáвленный зверь—*like a beast at bay*

Он убежáл и спря́тался как затрáвленный зверь. *He ran off and hid like a beast at bay.*

смотрéть звéрем—*have a ferocious look*

Он не любúл людéй и смотрéл на них звéрем. *He disliked people and looked at them with a ferocious look.*

зги

(ни) згú не видáть (or **не вúдно)**—*it's pitch dark*

В безлýнной нóчи ни зги не вúдно. *It's pitch dark on moonless nights.*

здорóвый—*healthy*

бýдь(те) здорóв(ы)—*1. good bye! 2. bless you! 3. cheers!*

1. Прощáясь, Пáвел сказáл: «Бýдьте здорóвы!» *Pavel said "good-bye" when he left.*
2. Когдá я чихнýла, он сказáл: «Бýдьте здорóвы!» *He said "bless you" when I sneezed.*

3. Когда́ мы чо́кались, Никола́й говори́л: «Бу́дьте здоро́вы!» *Nikolay said "cheers" when we clinked glasses.*

земля́—*earth*

бу́дто (or **сло́вно** or **то́чно**) **из-под земли́ появи́ться**—*appear out of the (clear) blue (sky); out of nowhere* (or *thin air)*

Он неожи́данно появи́лся, сло́вно из-под земли́ вы́рос. *He appeared suddenly, as if out of the clear blue sky.*

земли́ под собо́й не слы́шать (or **чу́ять**)—*be on the top of the world; be in seventh heaven*

Узна́в о вы́игрыше, Пётр земли́ под собо́й не слы́шал. *Having heard that he won, Peter was in seventh heaven.*

земля́ и не́бо—*all the difference in the world; like Mutt and Jeff*

Э́ти два бра́та как земля́ и не́бо. *These two brothers are like Mutt and Jeff.*

зени́ца—*pupil (*of the eye*)*

бере́чь (or **храни́ть**) **как зени́цу о́ка**—*cherish as the apple of one's eye*

Э́ти рели́квии она́ бережёт как зени́цу о́ка. *She guarded these old things like the apple of her eye.*

зло—*evil*

вымеща́ть (or **срыва́ть**) **зло**—*vent one's anger* (or *spleen) on someone*

Когда́ Ива́н возвраща́лся домо́й, то зло вымеща́л на жене́. *When Ivan went home, he vented his anger on his wife.*

пря́мо зло берёт!—*really maddening*

Опя́ть очки́ потеря́л, пря́мо зло берёт! *I lost my glasses again—really maddening!*

зло́ба—*spite; malice*

зло́ба дня—*topic of the day; burning issue*

Тайфу́н стал зло́бой дня́. *The topic of the day was the typhoon.*

пита́ть зло́бу—*have ill-feeling towards one*

Я ни к комý злóбы не питáю. *I entertain no ill-feeling towards anyone.*

змея́—*snake*

отогрéть (or **пригрéть**) **змею́ на груди́**—*nurture a snake in one's bosom*

За мою́ добротý он оплати́л мне злóм, и я пóнял, что отогрéл змею́ на груди́. *He repaid my kindness with evil and then I understood that I had been nurturing a snake in my bosom.*

знакóмство—*acquaintance*

шáпочное (or **шля́почное**) **знакóмство**—*nodding acquaintance*

О нём не могý ничегó сказáть, у нас тóлько шáпочное знакóмство. *I can't say anything about him—ours is but a nodding acquaintance.*

знать—*know*

знай нáших—*find out who you're dealing with! Look at what we (I) can do!*

Мы тебé отомсти́м—знай нáших! *We'll get even with you—find out who you're dealing with!*

знать не знáю—*not to have the faintest idea*

Как слóжится в бýдущем моя́ жизнь, я знать не знáю. *I haven't the faintest idea how my life will turn out later.*

как знать—*goodness knows*

Как знать, полýчится э́то хорошó и́ли плóхо. *Goodness knows if this will come out all right or not.*

наскóлько я знáю—*as far as I know*

Наскóлько я знáю, он не женáт. *He's not married, as far as I know.*

то и знáй—*incessantly; all the time; constantly*

Мои́ дéти, то и знáй, кричáт весь день. *My kids are screaming all day long incessantly.*

зре́ние—*sight*

оскорбля́ть зре́ние—*be an eyesore*

Му́сор на у́лице оскорбля́ет зре́ние. *The garbage in the street is an eyesore.*

зуб—*tooth*

дать по зуба́м—*pay someone back*

Ива́н дал Петру́ по зуба́м за оскорбле́ние. *Ivan paid Peter back for the insult.*

держа́ться (or **ухвати́ться**) **зуба́ми**—*hang on to something for dear life; stick to something tooth and nail*

Он держа́лся за свою́ рабо́ту зуба́ми. *He stuck to his work tooth and nail.*

зуб на́ зуб не попада́ет—*someone's teeth are chattering*

От моро́за у Ива́на зуб на́ зуб не попада́ет. *Ivan's teeth are chattering from the cold.*

зу́бы облома́ть—*come a cropper; be ruined*

Он взя́лся за тако́е, что мог себе́ зу́бы облома́ть. *He started a business that he could be ruined in.*

име́ть зуб—*hold a grudge*

За оби́ду Па́вел име́л зуб на А́нну. *Ivan held a grudge at Anna for the insult.*

кла́сть зу́бы на по́лку—*tighten one's belt*

У нас де́нег ма́ло, придётся кла́сть зу́бы на по́лку. *We've got little money—we need to tighten our belt.*

не по зуба́м—*too difficult for one; not to be able to manage*

Бы́ло я́сно, что киберне́тика ему́ не по зуба́м. *It was clear that computer science was beyond his intellectual capacity.*

чеса́ть зу́бы—*gossip; flail* (or *wag) one's tongue*

Стару́шки чеса́ли зу́бы о свои́х сосе́дях. *The old women were gossiping about their neighbors.*

И

Ива́н—*Ivan*

Ива́н кива́ет на Петра́—*blame one another for something*

Ива́н кива́ет на Петра́, а де́ло стои́т. *Ivan and Peter blame one another—the work stands still.*

ива́новский

(крича́ть) во всю́ ива́новскую—*(shout* or *yell) at the top of one's voice* (or *lungs)*

Бори́с рассерди́лся и крича́л во всю́ ива́новскую. *Boris got mad and was shouting at the top of his voice.*

иго́лка—*needle*

иго́лку (or **иго́лки**) **не́где** (or **не́куда**) **воткну́ть**—*be jam-packed*

На пля́же бы́ло сто́лько люде́й, что иго́лку не́где бы́ло воткну́ть. *There were so many people on the beach that it was jam-packed.*

не иго́лка—*not to be easily missed; not to be a needle that can get lost in a haystack*

«Ку́да Никола́й исчёз?»—спроси́ла взволно́ванная Ма́ша. «Не бо́йся, он не иго́лка—не потеря́ется»—споко́йно отве́тила

Натáша. *"Where did Nikolay disappear to?" Masha asked excitedly. "Don't worry, he is no needle that can get lost in a haystack."*

с игóлки (or **игóлочки)**—*brand new*

На Петрé одéжда с игóлочки. *Peter has a brand new suit on.*

сидéть как на игóлках—*be on pins and needles*

Собрáние затя́гивалось, и он сидéл как на игóлках. *The meeting got dragged out and he was sitting on pins and needles.*

игрá—*play*

игрá не стóит свеч—*it's not worth the trouble; the game isn't worth the gamble*

Зачéм поддéлывать копéйки? Игрá не стóит свеч. *Why forge false pennies (kopecks)? The game isn't worth the gamble.*

(твоя́) игрá сы́гранна—*you have had it; you've shot your wad* (or *ammunition)*

Ты мне бóльше ничегó не говори́—твоя́ игрá сы́гранна. *Don't you tell me anything anymore—you've shot your wad.*

игру́шка—*plaything*

как (or **слóвно) игру́шка**—*be pretty as a picture*

Невéста моегó сы́на краси́ва как игру́шка. *My son's fiancée is as pretty as a picture.*

и́дол—*idol*

сидéть (or **стоя́ть) и́долом**—*sit* (or *stand) like a statue*

В дóме стóлько рабóты, а ты стои́шь и́долом. *There's a lot of work to be done at home, and you're just standing there like a statue.*

идéя—*idea*

блестя́щая идéя—*brainchild; smarts*

За егó блестя́щие идéи егó вы́брали дирéктором. *He was chosen director because of his smarts.*

навя́зчивая идéя—*obsession*

Месть за бра́та ста́ла у Ники́ты навя́зчивой иде́ей. *It became Nikita's obsession to avenge his brother.*

по иде́е—*in principle; theoretically*

По иде́е они́ давно́ должны́ бы́ли быть до́ма. *Theoretically, they ought to have been home a long time ago.*

изве́стно—*it is known*

как изве́стно—*as is (generally) known*

Перелётные пти́цы, как изве́стно, о́сенью улета́ют на юг. *Migratory birds fly south in the autumn, as it is (generally) known.*

издалека́—*from far off*

начина́ть издалека́—*begin in a roundabout way*

Расска́з о свое́й жени́тьбе он на́чал издалека́. *He started telling the story of his marriage in a roundabout sort of way.*

изжива́ть—*eliminate*

изжива́ть себя́—*become outdated*

Зако́ны социа́лизма в Росси́и изжи́ли себя́. *The laws of socialism in Russia have become outdated.*

изли́шек—*surplus*

э́того хва́тит с изли́шком—*that will be enough, and to spare*

Заче́м ещё гото́вить? Э́того хва́тит с изли́шком. *Why cook more? This'll be enough and to spare.*

измени́ть—*be unfaithful*

изменя́ть себе́—*be untruthful to oneself; contradict oneself*

Ста́рый холостя́к, жени́вшись, измени́л себе́. *The old bachelor contradicted himself when he got married.*

имени́нник—*one whose name-day it is*

вы́глядеть (or **смотре́ть**) **имени́нником**—SEE: **смотре́ться женихо́м**

име́ть—*have*

ничего́ не име́ть про́тив—*not to mind*

Е́сли вы ничего́ не име́ете про́тив, то я закурю́. *If you don't mind, I'll light up.*

и́мя—*name*

открыва́ть своё и́мя—*reveal one's identity*

Мы не зна́ли, кто он, пока́ он не откры́л своё и́мя. *We didn't know who he was, until he revealed his identity.*

па́чкать до́брое и́мя—*disgrace someone's name*

«Не сме́й па́чкать моё до́брое и́мя!»—сказа́л оте́ц сы́ну. *"Don't you disgrace my good name!" the father said to his son.*

сде́лать себе́ и́мя—*become known* (or *famous); make oneself a name*

Свои́ми рома́нами Толсто́й сде́лал себе́ и́мя. *Tolstoy became famous for his novels.*

с и́менем—*known; established; a (big) name*

Он поэ́т с и́менем. *He's an established poet.*

ино́й—*someone else*

никто́ ино́й, как—*none other than*

Таку́ю карти́ну мо́жет написа́ть никто́ ино́й, как тала́нтливый худо́жник. *None other than a gifted artist can paint a picture like this.*

интере́с—*interest*

из спорти́вного интере́са—*just for the fun* (or *hell) of it*

Из спорти́вного интере́са инжене́р стал писа́ть стихи́. *The engineer started to write poems just for the hell of it.*

ока́зываться (or **остава́ться) при пи́ковом интере́се**—*be out in the cold; be left holding the bag* (or *the socks)*

Моя́ неве́ста вы́шла за́муж за друго́го, а я оста́лся при пи́ковом интере́се. *My fiancée married another guy, and I was left holding my socks.*

иска́ть—*look for*

ищи́ свищи́—*you can kiss it good-bye*

Вор убежа́л, твой кошелёк—ищи́ свищи́! *The thief has run off—you can kiss your wallet good-bye!*

и́скра—*spark*

и́скры из глаз посы́пались—*one saw stars*

От уда́ра у меня́ посы́пались и́скры из глаз. *I saw stars from the blow.*

искусствове́д—*art historian*

искусствове́д в шта́тском—*plain-clothes agent*

По́сле паде́ния коммуни́зма вы́яснилось, что Никола́й был искусствове́дом в шта́тском. *After the fall of Communism it became known that Nikolay was a plain-clothes agent.*

испечённый—*baked*

вновь испечённый—*brand new; newly fledged; new*

Наш вновь испечённый дире́ктор произвёл на нас отли́чное впечатле́ние. *Our new director made a good impression on us.*

испу́г—*fright*

брать на испу́г—*frighten someone*

Он чáсто брал на испýг своих одноклáссников. *He frequently frightened his classmates.*

истéрика—*hysterics*

впадáть в истéрику; закáтывать истéрику; устрáивать истéрики—*make a hysterical scene; throw a tantrum*

Когдá ребёнку чтó-то захотéлось, он впадáл в истéрику. *Whenever the child wanted something, he threw a tantrum.*

йстина—*truth*

прописнáя йстина—*cliché; hackneyed truth*

Ничегó оригинáльного в словáх Олéга нет, он тóлько повторя́ет прописны́е йстины. *There's nothing original to Oleg's words—all he does is repeat clichés.*

истóрия—*history*

вéчная (or **обы́чная**) **истóрия**—*the same old story; here we go again!*

Он снóва потеря́л ключи́—э́то вéчная истóрия. *He lost his keys again—it's the same old story.*

войти́ в истóрию—*become famous; go down in history; become a part of history*

Пастéр вошёл в истóрию свои́ми медици́нскими изобретéниями. *Pasteur became a part of history because of his medical discoveries.*

истóрия умáлчивает—*history doesn't say; be a deep dark secret*

С кем Бори́с провёл врéмя в Пари́же, об э́том истóрия умáлчивает. *With whom Boris spent his time in Paris is a deep dark secret.*

истукáн—*idol, statue*

сидéть (or **стоя́ть**) **истукáном**—SEE: **сидéть** (or **стоя́ть**) **и́долом**

итóг—*total*

в конéчном итóге—*in the end*

В конéчном итóге мы поженúлись. *In the end we got married.*

йóта—*jot (iota)*

ни на йóту—*not one iota*

Ни на йóту он не отошёл от своúх прúнципов. *He didn't budge from his principles—not one iota.*

К

каблýк—*heel*

быть под каблукóм—SEE: **быть под башмакóм**

кáждый—*every; each*

кáждому своё—*to each his (or their) own; it's a matter of taste*

Никúта лю́бит классúческую мýзыку, Óльга лю́бит поп-мýзыку—кáждому своё. *Nikita likes classical music, Olga likes pop—to each their own.*

казáк—*Cossack*

вóльный казáк—*be free as a bird; be foot-loose and fancy-free*

Женá уéхала, а он вóльный казáк. *His wife's gone; he is foot-loose and fancy-free.*

как—*how*

вот как—*really*

Вот как! А я об э́том не знал. *Really? I didn't know that.*

как бýдто—*as if*

Э́то бы́ло как бýдто во снé. *This was as if in a dream.*

как бы то ни́ было—*anyway; in any event; no matter what*

Как бы то ни́ было, а я в Аме́рику уе́ду. *I'm going to America anyway.*

как же—*why, yes!; what a (silly) question*

«Вы зна́ете Ле́рмонтова?»—«А как же!» *"Do you know Lermontov?"—"Of course, what a silly question."*

как мо́жно бо́льше—*as much as you can; as much as possible*

Принеси́ как мо́жно бо́льше де́нег. *Bring with you as much money as you possibly can.*

как-ника́к—*after all*

К ве́черу он почу́вствовал го́лод—как-ника́к он с утра́ не ку́шал. *He got hungry by evening time; after all he hadn't eaten since the morning.*

как раз—*just*

Как раз я о тебе́ ду́мал, и ты пришёл. *I was just thinking of you when you arrived.*

как сле́дует—*as is expected; comme il faut; as one should*

Он поблагодари́л хозя́йку за обе́д как сле́дует. *He thanked the hostess for dinnner as is expected.*

как то́лько—*as soon as; just as*

Как то́лько я освобожу́сь, я к тебе́ приду́. *I'll visit you just as soon as I get some free time.*

как э́то так не—*have every reason to do something; why should one not do something?*

Как э́то так не волнова́ться, е́сли я опа́здываю на по́езд. *Why shouldn't I worry, when I am about to miss my train?*

како́в—*what, how*

како́в собо́й? како́в из себя́?—*what does one look like?*

«А како́в он собо́й?»—«Он хоро́ш собо́й.» *"And what does he look like?"—"Quite handsome."*

како́вский—*what*

по-како́вски?—*what language?*

По-какóвски эту пéсню поют? *What language are they singing in?*

какóй—*what*

какóй бы (ни)—*no matter what someone is like; regardless how...*

Какóй бы ни был мой сын, я люблю егó. *I love my son, no matter what he's like.*

смотря какóй—*it depends*

«Ты пойдёшь в кинó с нáми?»—«Смотря какóе бýдет у меня настроéние.» *"Will you come to the movies with us?"—"Depends on how I feel."*

каланчá—*watch tower*

каланчá пожáрная—*beanpole*

Пéредо мной в кинó сидéл человéк, слóвно каланчá пожáрная. *There sat a man in front of me in the movie theater who was as tall as a beanpole.*

калáч—*kalach (*kind of fancy bread*)*

калачóм не замáнишь—*you can't get one (*out of a certain place*) for love or money*

Он не лю́бит гóрод—егó калачóм в Москвý не замáнишь. *He doesn't like the city—you can't make him come to Moscow for love or money.*

на калачи́ достáться—*get what is coming to one; get one's comeuppance*

За прокáзы емý на калачи́ достáлось. *He got what was coming to him for his pranks.*

тёртый калáч—*old hand; old pro*

Егó не обмáнешь, он тёртый калáч. *You can't fool him—he's an old pro.*

калéние—*incandescence*

доводи́ть до бéлого калéния—*rouse one to fury*

Он своей истерикой доводил меня до белого каления. *He roused me to a fury with his hysterics.*

калиф—*caliph*

калиф на час—*be king for a day; have but temporary influence*

Я бы охотно для вас всё сделал, но дело в том, что я калиф на час. *I would gladly do everything for you, but I've only got temporary influence.*

калоша—*galosh*

посадить в калошу—*put someone into a mess; embarrass someone*

Он посадил меня в калошу тем, что всем рассказал о моих странных привычках. *He embarrassed me by telling everyone about my odd habits.*

сесть в калошу—*get into a mess* (or *fix* or *pickle* or *stink*)

Не зная обычаи чужой страны, он сел в калошу. *He got himself into a pickle by being ignorant about the habits of the foreign country.*

ка́мень—*stone*

броса́ть ка́мень (or **ка́мешек**) **в огоро́д**—*make a snide remark; take a dig at someone*

Де́лая неприя́тное замеча́ние об иностра́нцах, сосе́д броса́л ка́мень в мой огоро́д. *My neighbor took a dig at me by making an unpleasant remark about foreigners.*

держа́ть (or **име́ть**) **ка́мень за па́зухой**—*have evil intentions against someone*

Меня́ предупреди́ли, что мой партнёр де́ржит ка́мень за́ па́зухой. *They told me that my partner had evil intentions against me.*

ка́мень на душе́ (or **се́рдце**)—*have a heavy heart*

С тех пор, как я узна́л по телеви́зору о траги́ческой ги́бели люде́й во вре́мя гражда́нской войны́, у меня́ ка́мень на душе́. *I've had a heavy heart ever since I heard on TV about the tragic death of the people in the civil war.*

ка́мень с души́ (or **се́рдца**) **сва́лится**—*a load off one's mind*

Услы́шав о повыше́нии зарпла́ты, у меня́ ка́мень с души́ свали́лся. *Having heard that I got a raise in salary was a big load off my mind.*

ка́мня на ка́мне не оста́вить—*raze to the ground; level completely*

Бомбёжки в Берли́не ка́мня на ка́мне не оста́вили. *The bombardments leveled Berlin completely.*

ка́пать—*drip*

не ка́плет—*take one's time; there is no hurry*

Зачем так торопи́ться? Не ка́плет над на́ми. *Why such rush? We can take our time.*

ка́пелька—*small drop; droplet*

ни ка́пельки—*not a bit; not a grain*

У него́ ни ка́пельки терпе́ния нет. *He hasn't got a bit of patience.*

В егó словáх ни кáпельки и́стины нет. *There's not a grain of truth in his words.*

кáпля—*drop*

как кáпля в мóре—*a drop in the ocean; a drop in the bucket*

Сто дóлларов заплати́ть за мои́ долги́—э́то как кáпля в мóре. *To pay a hundred dollars on my debts is only a drop in the bucket.*

кáпля за кáплей; кáпля по кáпле—*gradually; bit by bit*

Они́ собрáли на дом кáпля по кáпле. *They saved for their house bit by bit.*

кáпля моегó (твоегó ...) мёду есть—*have a finger in the pie; make a contribution to something*

В успéхе Аркáдия и кáпля моегó мёду есть, ведь я финанси́ровал егó учёбу. *I made a contribution to Arkady's success as I was the one who financed his education.*

похóжи как две кáпли воды́—*(as similar as) two peas in a pod*

Двойня́шки Éва и Агнéса, похóжи как две кáпли воды́. *The twins, Eva and Agnes, are like two peas in a pod.*

капýста—*cabbage*

руби́ть (or **изруби́ть**) **в капýсту**—*make mincemeat out of someone*

Васи́лий причини́л мне стóлько неприя́тностей, что я изруби́л бы егó в капýсту, éсли бы встрéтил. *Vasily caused me so much trouble that I'd make mincemeat out of him if we met.*

карандáш—*pencil*

взя́ть на карандáш—*put down; take notes*

Он взял на карандáш мои́ совéты. *He put down my suggestions.*

караýл—*guard*

караýл!—*help!*

Во вре́мя землетрясе́ния бы́ло слы́шно изо всех сторо́н: «Карау́л!» *At the time of the earthquake one could hear "help!" from everywhere.*

хоть карау́л кричи́—*one could just climb the walls*
Ситуа́ция така́я, что хоть карау́л кричи́. *In such a situation one could just climb the walls.*

карма́н—*pocket*

бить (or **уда́рить) по карма́ну**—*hit someone in the wallet* (or *pocket)*
Внеза́пная сва́дьба до́чери уда́рила отцу́ по карма́ну. *His daughter's unexpected wedding hit the father in the pocket.*

держи́ карма́н (ши́ре)—*not a chance!*
«Наде́юсь быть дире́ктором фирмы»—«Держи́ карма́н ши́ре!» *"I hope I'll be the manager of the firm!"—"Not a chance!"*

залеза́ть в карма́н—*put one's hands in someone else's pocket; have greasy fingers*
Мы на́шему бухга́лтеру доверя́ли, зна́я, что он в чужо́й карма́н не зале́зет. *We trusted our bookkeeper since we knew that he didn't have greasy fingers.*

не по карма́ну—*not to be able to afford it; be beyond one's means*
Да́ча мне не по карма́ну. *I can't afford a summer house.*

в карма́не свисти́т—SEE: **ве́тер свисти́т в карма́не**

ка́рта—*map; card*

(и) ка́рты (or **кни́ги) в ру́ки**—*be just the person; be (right) up one's alley*
В на́шем бракоразво́дном де́ле вам, как адвока́ту, и ка́рты в ру́ки. *Since you are an attorney, our divorce case is right up your alley.*

ка́рта би́та—*game is up*
Когда́ раскры́ли его́ манипуля́ции, его́ ка́рта была́ би́та. *When his manipulations became known, the game was up.*

откры́ть (or **раскры́ть**) **свои́ ка́рты**—*show one's hand; come clean*

Под давле́нием ему́ пришло́сь откры́ть свои́ ка́рты. *He had to show his hand under pressure.*

поста́вить всё на одну́ ка́рту—*put all one's eggs in one basket*

Неу́мное де́ло поста́вить всё на одну́ ка́рту. *It's silly to put all one's eggs in one basket.*

после́дняя ка́рта—*last chance; last resort*

Пётр пропусти́л после́днюю ка́рту и оста́лся холостяко́м. *Peter lost his last chance and remained a bachelor.*

карти́нка—*picture*

оде́т как карти́нка—*dressed fit to kill*

Во вре́мя пе́рвого свида́ния А́нна была́ оде́та как карти́нка. *Anna was dressed fit to kill on her first rendezvous.*

карто́фель or **карто́шка**—*potatoes*

карто́фель (or **карто́шка**) **в мунди́ре**—*potatoes baked (*or *boiled) in their jackets*

К столу́ пода́ли карто́шку в мунди́ре. *They served potatoes baked in their jackets.*

не карто́шка—*no joking matter*

Любо́вь не карто́шка. *Love is no joking matter.*

каса́ться—*to touch*

что каса́ется—*as regards; as to*; *as far as one is concerned*

Что каса́ется меня́, я согла́сен с тобо́й. *As far as I'm concerned, I agree with you.*

ка́сса—*cash box; cash register*

не отходя́ от ка́ссы—*right away; right there; on the spot*

По́сле разво́да Валенти́на бы́стро вы́шла за́муж, как говори́тся, не отходя́ от ка́ссы. *After the divorce Valentina got married on the spot, as they say.*

ка́чество—*quality*

в ка́честве—*as; in the capacity of; by way of*

Мой брат рабо́тал в на́шей фи́рме в ка́честве секретаря́. *My brother was working at our company in the capacity of secretary.*

кафта́н—*caftan*

Три́шкин кафта́н—*rob Peter to pay Paul*

Из отло́женных на пальто́ де́нег я взял для опла́ты за све́т—сло́вно Три́шкин кафта́н. *I took away money set aside for a coat in order to pay the electric bill—I robbed Peter to pay Paul.*

ка́ша—(cooked) *cereal*

завари́ть ка́шу—*make a muddle of things; stir up trouble.*

Куда́ он не пойдёт, он везде́ зава́рит ка́шу. *Wherever he goes, he stirs up trouble.*

ка́ша в голове́—*be a muddled head; have one's head muddled*

От пробле́м у неё ка́ша в голове́. *She's got her head muddled with all of her problems.*

ка́ша во рту—*mumble*

Когда́ Алексе́й пьян, у него́ ка́ша во рту. *Aleksey always mumbles when he's drunk.*

ка́ши не свари́ть—*be impossible to get along with someone; get nowhere with someone*

Он тако́й упря́мый, с ним ка́шу не сва́ришь. *He is so stubborn that there's no getting along with him.*

ка́ши про́сят—*they are in need of repair (*said about shoes, boots)

Мой сапоги́ уже́ давно́ ка́ши про́сят. *My boots have been in need of repair for a long time.*

ка́шу ма́слом не испо́ртишь—*it's never* (or *one can't have) too much of a good thing*

Я двáжды поднял бокáл за егó здорóвье, считáя, что кáшу мáслом не испóртишь. *I raised my glass to his health twice, thinking that you can't have too much of a good thing.*

мáло кáши ел—*be inexperienced; be a greenhorn*

По егó рассуждéниям вúдно, что он мáло кáши съел. *It's evident from his remarks that he is inexperienced.*

расхлёбывать кáшу—*face the music; be called on the carpet for something*

Йз-за их ошúбок всю кáшу расхлёбывать пришлóсь нам. *We had to face the music for their mistakes.*

сам кáшу заварúл, сам и расхлёбывай—*you've made your (own) bed, now lie in it*

Сáша женúлся прóтив вóли своúх родúтелей, и когдá появúлись проблéмы, отéц сказáл: «Сам кáшу заварúл, сам и расхлёбывай.» *Sasha got married against his parents' wishes, and when problems cropped up his father said, "You've made your own bed, now lie in it."*

с кáшей съем—*fix one's little red wagon (*said to children or in jest*)*

Éсли ты не бýдешь слýшаться, я тебя́ с кáшей съем. *I'll fix your little red wagon if you won't obey me!*

каштáн—*chestnut*

таскáть каштáны из огня́—*pull the burning chestnuts out of the fire*

Когдá Ивáн стал дирéктором, я пóнял, что таскáл каштáны из огня́ для другóго. *When Ivan became the director, I understood that I had pulled the burning chestnuts out of the fire for someone else.*

квадрáт—*square*

в квадрáте—*a complete; a total*

Мой сосéд—лгун в квадрáте. *My neighbor is a total liar.*

квартира—*apartment*

квартира и стол—*board and lodging*

В мой студенческие годы я снял квартиру и стол у родственников. *During my student years I had board and lodging with my relatives.*

кишка—*intestine*

вымотать все кишки—*bother life* (or *hell*) *out of someone*

Мой начальник мне вымотал все кишки. *My boss kept bothering the hell out of me.*

кишка тонка—*not to have the guts*

Он своё мнение начальнику не скажет, у него кишка тонка. *He doesn't have the guts to tell his boss his opinion.*

клапан—*valve*

закрой клапан!—*shut your mouth; keep your mouth shut*

Перестань кричать! Закрой клапан! *Stop yelling! Shut your mouth!*

клёпка—*rivet*

не хватает (or **достаёт**) **(одной) клёпки в голове**—SEE: **винтика не хватает в голове**

клещи—*pincers*

клещами вытягивать (or **тащить**) **слово**—*be like pulling teeth; one has to tease every word out of someone*

Каждое слово из него приходится клещами вытягивать. *To get a word out of him is like pulling teeth.*

клин—*wedge*

клином не вышибешь (or **выколотишь**)—*you can't knock something out of someone's head; can't change someone's mind*

Е́сли Васи́лий что́-то заду́мал сде́лать, то э́то из него́ и кли́ном не вы́шибешь. *Whenever Vasily decides to do something, you can't knock it out of his head.*

клони́ть—*incline; bend*

куда́ вы кло́ните?—*what are you driving at?*

Вы́слушав меня́, Никола́й спроси́л: «Куда́ вы кло́ните?» *Nikolay listened to me and then asked, "What are you driving at?"*

кни́га—*book*

кни́га за семью́ печа́тями—*sealed book; beyond one's comprehension; way over one's head*

Астроно́мия—э́то для меня́ кни́га за семью́ печа́тями. *Astronomy is way over my head.*

кно́пка—*button*

нажима́ть на все кно́пки (or **педа́ли**)—*pull strings; move heaven and earth*

Что́бы жени́ться на А́нне, Бори́с нажима́л на все кно́пки. *Boris moved heaven and earth to be able to marry Anna.*

коври́жка—*honey-cake*

ни за каки́е коври́жки—*not for the (whole wide) world; not (even) for a farm down east; not for all the tea in China*

Унасле́дованный от роди́телей дом я ни за каки́е коври́жки не прода́м. *I wouldn't sell the house I inherited from my parents for the whole (wide) world!*

когда́—*when*

есть когда́—*no time for it*

«Пойдёшь со мной в кино́?»—«Есть когда́ мне!» *"Will you come to the movies with me?"—"I've got no time for that!"*

когда́ бы ни—*whenever*

Когда́ бы Бори́с ни пришёл, Ири́ны не́ было до́ма. *Whenever Boris came, Irina wasn't home.*

когда́ как—*sometimes this way, sometimes that way; comme ci, comme ça*

Когда́ как: то со́лнце све́тит, то дождь идёт. *Sometimes the sun is shining, sometimes it is raining.*

когда́ како́й—*once it's like this, then it's like that*

Жизнь когда́ кака́я: то хоро́шая, то плоха́я. *Life is sometimes good, and sometimes bad.*

когда́-когда́—*every now and then; every once in a while* (or *blue moon)*

Когда́-когда́ я его́ уви́жу. *I see him every once in a while.*

ко́готь—*claw*

держа́ть в когтя́х—*keep someone under one's thumb*

Финанси́руя мои́ расхо́ды, он держа́л меня́ в когтя́х. *By financing my expenses, he kept me under his thumb.*

облома́ть ко́гти—*render* (or *make) one harmless*

Ю́рий причини́л сто́лько хлопо́т, что пора́ ему́ облома́ть ко́гти. *Yury has caused so much trouble already that it is time to make him harmless.*

пока́зывать свои́ ко́гти—*show one's teeth*

Мы счита́ли Ива́на поря́дочным, пока́ он свои́ ко́гти не показа́л. *We considered Ivan a nice person until he showed his teeth.*

попа́сть в ко́гти—*fall into the clutches of someone*

Лу́чше жить че́стно, чем попа́сть в ко́гти престу́пников. *It's better to live honestly than fall into the clutches of criminals.*

ко́жа—*skin*

быть в че́й-либо ко́же—*be in someone's shoes*

Что́бы понима́ть его́ страда́ния, ну́жно быть в его́ ко́же. *In order to understand his suffering, we'd have to be in his shoes.*

вы́лезть (or **ле́зть**) **из ко́жи вон**—*bend over backwards; do one's utmost*

Пётр из ко́жи вон ле́зет, что́бы понра́виться нача́льнику. *Peter bends over backwards in order to please his boss.*

ко́жа да ко́сти—*a bag of bones; skin and bones*

Стра́шно смотре́ть на Бори́са, лишь ко́жа да ко́сти. *It's terrible to look at Boris, he's just skin and bones.*

ни ко́жи ни ро́жи—*look awful*; *be very unattractive*; *ugly (as sin)*

Как Ири́на мо́жет люби́ть Ива́на? Ведь у него́ ни ко́жи ни ро́жи. *How can Irina love Ivan? He's so very unattractive.*

коза́—*goat*

драть (or **лупи́ть** or **поро́ть** or **сечь) как си́дорову козу́**—*beat the crap out of one; give a sound thrashing*

Сосе́д драл сы́на как си́дорову козу́. *Our neighbor gave his son a sound thrashing.*

на козе́ не подъе́дешь—*hard to approach one*

Мой ста́рый друг стал президе́нтом на́шей фи́рмы, и к нему́ с тех пор на козе́ не подъе́дешь. *My old friend became president of our company, and since then it's hard to approach him.*

козёл—*goat*

козло́м петь—*sing in a false voice; caterwaul*

Он пел козлóм, и э́то всех раздражáло. *He sang in a false voice and set everyone's nerves on edge.*

пусти́ть козлá в огорóд—*send the wolf to keep the sheep; send a fox to keep one's geese; put the cat near the goldfish bowl*

Растрáтчику поручи́ть бухгалтéрию—э́то пусти́ть козлá в огорóд. *To entrust an embezzler with the bookkeeping is like sending a fox to keep one's geese.*

козырёк—*visor*

брать под козырёк—*salute*

Привéтствуя генерáла, солдáты брáли под козырёк. *The soldiers saluted in greeting the general.*

кол—*stake; picket*

кóлом (or **кóмом**) **стоя́ть в гóрле**—*1. be unable to get the words out 2. become disgusted with*

1. Когдá Лéна уви́дела гнев в глазáх Петрá, у неё словá стáли кóлом в гóрле. *Seeing the rage in Peter's eyes, Lena couldn't get the words out.*
2. Постоя́нные упрёки Николáя у меня́ стоя́ли кóлом в гóрле. *I was disgusted with Nikolay's constant reproaches.*

ни колá ни двора́—*not a thing to one's name*

Пóсле наводнéния у старýшки не остáлось ни колá ни дворá. *After the flood the old woman didn't have a thing left to her name.*

хоть кол на головé теши́—*be an extremely stubborn person; be impossible to beat anything into one's thick head*

Ивáну хоть кол на головé теши́, он своё мнéние не измéнит. *Ivan is an extremely stubborn person, he refuses to change his mind.*

колбасá—*sausage*

кати́сь колбасóй!—*off with you!; get lost; beat it!*

Когдá егó поведéние мне надоéло, я закричáл: кати́сь колбасóй! *"Get lost!" I shouted at him, when I got fed up with his behavior.*

колéно—*knee*

до седьмóго колéна—*back to the seventh generation*

В семьé Николáя все худóжники до седьмóго колéна. *In Nikolay's family everybody is an artist, seven generations back.*

постáвить на колéни—*bring to one's knees*

Свои́ми аргумéнтами Ивáн постáвил всех на колéни. *Ivan brought everyone to their knees with his arguments.*

кóлер—*color*

подогнáть (or **подвести́**) **всех под оди́н кóлер**—*treat everyone alike*

Начáльник подгоня́л всех под оди́н кóлер незави́симо от их ли́чности. *The boss treated everyone alike regardless of their personality.*

колесни́ца—*chariot*

привязáть себя́ к колесни́це—*hitch one's wagon to another's star*

Пётр привязáл себя́ к колесни́це победи́телей. *Peter hitched his wagon to the star of the victors.*

колесо́—*wheel*

быть на колёсах—*constantly to be on the road*

До́ма Бори́са не заста́нешь, он всегда́ на колёсах. *You won't find Boris at home—he's on the road all the time.*

верте́ться колесо́м—SEE: **верте́ться** (or **кружи́ться**) **как бе́лка в колесе́**

подма́зывать колёса—*grease someone's palm*

Что́бы получи́ть но́вый контра́кт, Пётр подма́зал колёса у дире́ктора. *In order to get a new contract, Peter greased the director's palm.*

пя́тое колесо́ в колесни́це (or **теле́ге**)—*fifth wheel*

С молодожёнами я чу́вствовал себя́, как пя́тое колесо́ в теле́ге. *I felt like a fifth wheel beside the newlyweds.*

колея́—*rut*

войти́ в колею́ (or **ру́сло**)—*settle down; get back into the old routine*

По́сле о́тпуска тру́дно войти́ в колею́. *It's hard to get back into the old routine after a vacation.*

вы́бить из колеи́—*disrupt one's regular routine*

Э́ти собы́тия нас вы́били из колей. *These events disrupted our regular routine.*

ко́локол—*bell*

звони́ть во все колокола́—*spread the news far and wide; divulge*

А́нна звони́ла во все колокола́ о своём заму́жестве. *Anna spread the news of her marriage far and wide.*

колоко́льня—*church* (or *bell) tower*

смотре́ть со свое́й колоко́льни—*see only one's own point of view; not to see beyond one's nose*

Ива́н уме́л смотре́ть на собы́тия то́лько со свое́й колоко́льни. *Ivan could only see the events from his own point of view.*

колпа́к—*cap*

держа́ть под стекля́нным колпако́м—*keep someone in cotton wool; overprotect someone*

Роди́тели свою́ дочь держа́ли под стекля́нным колпако́м. *The parents overprotected their daughter.*

помести́ть (or **поста́вить) себя́ под стекля́нный колпа́к**—*live in seclusion; avoid publicity; turn into a hothouse flower*

Бу́дучи нелюди́мым, он помести́л себя́ под стекля́нный колпа́к. *Being a loner, he kept avoiding publicity.*

колыбе́ль—*cradle*

с (or **от) колыбе́ли**—*from the cradle; from* (or *since) early childhood on*

С колыбе́ли Ми́ша уже́ люби́л му́зыку. *Misha loved music from early childhood on.*

кома́нда—*command*

как по кома́нде—*in unison; as if at a command*

Когда́ Ива́н входи́л, все как по кома́нде встава́ли. *When Ivan entered, everybody stood up in unison.*

комáр—*mosquito*

комарá не зашибёт—*one wouldn't hurt even a fly*

Он такóй дóбрый, комарá не зашибёт. *He is such a good man that he wouldn't hurt a fly.*

комéдия—*comedy*

игрáть (or **разы́грывать) комéдию**—*put on an act; try to fool someone*

Мы вéрили емý, но вы́яснилось, что он тóлько игрáл комéдию пéред нáми. *We believed him until we found out that he was putting on an act for us.*

комментáрий—*commentary*

комментáрии изли́шни—*it speaks for itself*

Егó поведéние такóе, что комментáрии изли́шни. *His behavior is such that it speaks for itself.*

компáния—*company*

води́ть компáнию—*associate with someone*

Мы с сосéдями не вóдим компáнию, потомý что мы не понимáем их язы́к. *We don't keep company with our neighbors, because we don't speak their language.*

за компáнию—*just to be sociable*

Спирт я не люблю́, но за компáнию я реши́л вы́пить глотóк. *I don't drink alcohol, but I took a sip just to be sociable.*

не компáния—*not to be suitable company*

Криводу́шный человéк мне не компáния. *A hypocrite is not suitable company for me.*

при всей честнóй компáнии—SEE: **при (всём) (честнóм) нарóде**

комплимéнт—*compliment*

напрáшиваться на комплимéнты—*fish for compliments*

Жáлуясь на своúю фигýру, Áнна напрáшивалась на комплимéнты. *By complaining about her own figure, Anna was fishing for compliments.*

конёк—*small horse*

садúться на своегó (любúмого) конькá; оседлáть своегó (любúмого) конькá—*launch into one's pet subject; mount* (or *ride) one's (favorite) hobby horse*

Дéдушка, расскáзывая о войнé, садúлся на своегó любúмого конькá. *Talking about the war grandpa launched into his pet subject.*

конéц—*end*

в óба концá—*round trip*

Билéт на самолёт дешéвле, éсли брать в óба концá. *Air fare is cheaper if you purchase it as a round-trip.*

в концé концóв—*after all*

Мне, в концé концóв, всё равнó, что Ивáн дéлает. *It's all the same to me what Ivan's doing, after all.*

во все концы́—*in all directions; all over*

Мы разослáли пúсьма своúм друзья́м во все концы́ страны́. *We sent letters to our friends all over the country.*

дéлать (or **начинáть) не с тогó концá**—*put the cart before the horse*

Пóсле убóрки крáсить стéны—э́то начинáть не с тогó концá. *To paint the walls after cleaning the house is like putting the cart before the horse.*

едвá (or **éле** or **кóе-как) сводúть концы́ с концáми**—*make ends meet*

Едвá сводúли концы́ с концáми, так как дéнег бы́ло мáло. *We had so little money that we could hardly make ends meet.*

концá-крáю нет; концá-крáя нет; ни концá ни крáю нет; ни концá ни крáя нет—*there is no end to it*

Нáшим страдáниям ни концá ни крáя нет. *There's no end to our trials and tribulations.*

концóв не найтú—*be unable to get to the bottom of the matter*

Дéло так запýтано, что концóв не найтú. *The matter is so involved that it's impossible to get to the bottom of it.*

положúть конéц—*make an end; put an end to something*

Борúс решúл положúть конéц холостя́цкой жúзни. *Boris decided to put an end to his bachelorhood.*

пря́тать концы́—*cover one's tracks*

Борúс умéл пря́тать концы́ своúх преступлéний. *Boris knew how to cover the tracks of his crimes.*

на худóй конéц—*if worst comes to worst*

На худóй конéц, мы мóжем купúть билéты в кредúт. *If worst comes to worst, we can buy the tickets on credit.*

контóра—*office; bureau*

шарáшкина контóра—*shady business*

Лýчше не свя́зываться с Пáвлом, у негó шарáшкина контóра. *It's better not to be associated with Pavel—he is involved in shady businesses.*

концéрт—*concert*

кошáчий концéрт—*caterwaul; cacophony; singing falsely, in the wrong key*

Что э́то за кошáчий концéрт? Рáзве мóжно так петь? *What is all this cacophony? How can anybody sing like that?*

кóнчик—*tip*

до кóнчиков ногтéй—*through and through; all the way; entirely*

Он чéстный до кóнчиков ногтéй. *He's an entirely honest person.*

кóнчить—*finish*

всё кóнчено—*everything's lost; all gone with the wind*

Наш дом конфискова́ли. Всё ко́нчено. *They foreclosed our house on us—it's all gone with the wind.*

конь—*horse*

не в коня́ корм—*wasted effort; waste something on someone*

Иностра́нные языки́ для Алексе́я не в коня́ корм. *Foreign languages are wasted on Aleksey.*

коньки́—*skates*

отбро́сить коньки́—*kick the bucket; cash in one's chips*

Ста́рый плут отбро́сил коньки́. *The old swindler kicked the bucket.*

копе́йка; копе́ечка—*kopeck*

дрожа́ть над ка́ждой копе́йкой—*pinch pennies*

Ста́рый и скупо́й Васи́лий дрожи́т над ка́ждой копе́йкой. *The old and stingy Vasily pinched every penny.*

копе́йка в копе́йку—*exactly to a penny*

Расчёт сошёлся копе́йка в копе́йку. *The bill was exact to the penny.*

обойти́сь (or **стать**) **в копе́йку** (or **копе́ечку**)—*cost a pretty penny*

Постро́йка ви́ллы обойдётся нам в копе́ечку. *The building of the villa will cost us a pretty penny.*

копы́то—*hoof*

отки́нуть (or **отбро́сить) копы́та**—SEE: **отбро́сить коньки́**

ко́рень—*root*

в ко́рне пресе́чь—*nip in the bud*

Прави́тельство реши́ло в ко́рне пресе́чь восста́ние. *The government decided to nip the rebellion in the bud.*

врасти́ (or **прирасти́) корня́ми**—*take* (or *grow) roots*

Я к э́тому го́роду прирóс корня́ми. *I grew roots in this city.*

гляде́ть (or **смотре́ть) в ко́рень**—*get to the root of the matter*

Ива́н всегда́ стара́ется смотре́ть в ко́рень. *Ivan always tries to get to the root of the matter.*

ко́роб—*box*

наобеща́ть с три ко́роба—*promise the moon (and the stars)*

Пе́ред сва́дьбой Ива́н наобеща́л Ма́ше с три ко́роба. *Before the wedding Ivan promised Masha the moon.*

це́лый ко́роб новосте́й—*whole bunch of news*

Са́ша расска́зал нам це́лый ко́роб новосте́й. *Sasha gave us a whole bunch of news.*

ко́ротко—*briefly*

ко́ротко (or **коро́че) говоря́**—*in short; in brief; to make a long story short*

Коро́че говоря́, мы пожени́лись. *We got married, to make a long story short.*

коса́—*scythe*

нашла́ коса́ на ка́мень—*one has met one's match; diamond cuts diamond*

При игре́ в ша́хматы Ма́ша не уступа́ла Ива́ну—нашла́ коса́ на ка́мень. *Masha is just as good in chess as Ivan—he has met his match.*

ко́сточка—*small bone*

вое́нная (or **солда́тская**) **ко́сточка**—*a soldier to the core*

По вы́правке Михаи́ла мо́жно бы́ло ви́деть, что он вое́нная ко́сточка. *It is apparent in Mikhail's bearing that he's a soldier to the core.*

разбира́ть по ко́сточкам—*1. go over something very thoroughly 2. pick someone to pieces*

1. Занима́ясь хи́мией, он разбира́л её по ко́сточкам. *He went over his chemistry very thoroughly.*
2. Стару́шки на ла́вочке разбира́ли по ко́сточкам проходя́щих. *The old women sitting on the bench picked every passer-by to pieces.*

кость—*bone*

бе́лая кость—*blue blood*

Он аристокра́т, у него́ бе́лая кость. *He's an aristocrat—he's got blue blood.*

кость от ко́сти и плоть от пло́ти—*one's flesh and blood*

Когда́ сы́на арестова́ли, Бори́с вскри́кнул: «Как он мо́жет быть престу́пником, когда́ он кость от ко́сти и плоть от пло́ти!» *"How can he be a criminal," Boris exclaimed when his son got arrested. "After all he is my flesh and blood!"*

одни́ ко́сти—*bag of bones*

Она́ так похуде́ла, что одни́ ко́сти оста́лись. *She lost so much weight that she looked like a bag of bones.*

промёрзнуть до косте́й—*be frozen to the marrow*

Мы попа́ли в пургу́ и промёрзли до косте́й. *We got into a snow storm and were frozen to the marrow.*

промо́кнуть до косте́й—*get drenched to the bone; get wet to the skin*

Мы попа́ли под проливно́й дождь и промо́кли до косте́й. *We got into such a downpour that we became soaked to the bone.*

широ́кая кость; широ́к ко́стью; широ́к в кости́—*stocky man*
Ви́дно, что он штанги́ст: у него́ широ́кая кость. *It's obvious that he's a weight lifter—he's such a stocky man.*

костю́м—*suit*

в костю́ме Ада́ма (or **Е́вы**)—*in one's birthday suit*
Когда́ Са́ша появи́лся на собра́нии в костю́ме Ада́ма, его́ увезли́ в сумасше́дший дом. *Sasha was taken to the nutfarm when he showed up at the meeting in his birthday suit.*

кот—*tomcat*

кот напла́кал—*nothing to speak of; next to nothing*
У нас де́нег как кот напла́кал. *We've got next to no money.*

купи́ть кота́ в мешке́—*buy a pig in a poke*
Вы́йти за́муж—всё равно́ что купи́ть кота́ в мешке́. *Getting married is like buying a pig in a poke.*

смотре́ть как кот на смета́ну—*like a cat looks at a canary*
Па́вел смотре́л на сосе́дку как кот на смета́ну. *Pavel looked at the lady next door like a cat looks at a canary.*

тяну́ть кота́ за хво́ст—*hem and haw*

Арка́дий отвеча́л на мой вопро́с кра́йне ме́дленно, сло́вно тяну́л кота́ за хво́ст. *Arkady answered my question very slowly, hemming and hawing.*

котёл—*caldron; kettle*

(как) в котле́ кипе́ть (or **вари́ться**)—*be all keyed-up; be in a pressure cooker*

У них сто́лько рабо́ты—они ва́рятся, как в котле́. *They've got so many projects going that they are constantly in the pressure cooker.*

котело́к—*pot*

котело́к ва́рит—*one's brain is working; one's sure got brains*

«Ничего́, ва́рит котело́к!» сказа́л дово́льный оте́ц, просма́тривая аттеста́т сы́на. *"He's sure got brains!" the father said upon looking at his son's grade report.*

кошелёк—*purse*

кошелёк или жи́знь!—*your money or your life!*

Банди́т крича́л: «Кошелёк или жизнь!» *The hold-up man cried, "Your money or your life!"*

ко́шка—*cat*

бе́гать как угоре́лая ко́шка—*run like mad (*in frenzy*); run like a chicken with its head cut off*

Когда́ муж оста́вил её, бе́дная Ири́на бе́гала как угоре́лая ко́шка. *When her husband left her, poor Irina was running around like a chicken with its head cut off.*

ко́шки скребу́т на душе́ (or **се́рдце**)—*something is gnawing at one's heart; be sick at heart*

У меня́ ко́шки скребу́т на душе́, когда́ я ви́жу состоя́ние мое́й страны́. *I'm sick at heart when I see the condition of my country.*

(чёрная) ко́шка пробежа́ла (or **проскочи́ла**)—*be at loggerheads; there is bad blood between two people*

Из-за де́вушки ме́жду Петро́м и Ива́ном пробежа́ла чёрная ко́шка. *Peter and Ivan are at loggerheads because of a girl.*

кра́ешек—*edge*

ви́деть кра́ешком or **кра́ем гла́за**—*catch a glimpse of; see out of the corner of one's eye*

Ка́жется, милиционе́р не смо́трит, но он всё ви́дит кра́ешком гла́за. *It seems that the cop isn't looking, but he sees everything out of the corner of his eye.*

край—*edge*

в на́ших края́х—*in our neck of the wood(s)*

Когда́ бу́дете в на́ших края́х, заезжа́йте! *Come and visit us when you get to our neck of the woods!*

из кра́я в край or **от кра́я (и) до кра́я**—*all over; from end to end*

Мы объе́здили страну́ из кра́я в край. *We've traveled all over the country.*

на край све́та (or **земли́**)—*at the back of beyond, at the world's ends*

Я за тобо́й пойду́ на край све́та. *For you I'd go even to the end of the world.*

непоча́тый край рабо́ты—*no end to work; overwhelming amount of chores*

У нас рабо́ты непоча́тый край. *We've got an overwhelming amount of work to do.*

услы́шать кра́ем у́ха—*overhear something by accident*

Э́ту но́вость я услы́шал кра́ем у́ха. *This news I overheard by accident.*

хлебну́ть го́ря че́рез край—*have one's share of hardship; drink the bitter cup to the bottom*

Мы во вре́мя войны́ хлебну́ли го́ря че́рез край. *During the war we drank the bitter cup to the bottom.*

кра́йность—*extreme*

вдава́ться (or **впада́ть) в кра́йности**—*run to extremes*

У Ива́на не́ было золото́й середи́ны, он всегда́ вдава́лся в кра́йности. *Ivan knew no golden mean—he always ran to extremes.*

кра́ска—*paint*

кра́ска броса́ется в лицо́—*blush; blood rushes into one's face*

От стыда́ у Ири́ны кра́ска бро́силась в лицо́. *Irina blushed with shame.*

не жале́я кра́сок—*spare no words; lay it on thick*

Об охо́те Миха́ил расска́зывал не жале́я кра́сок. *Mikhail spared no words to describe the hunt.*

сгуща́ть кра́ски—*lay it on thick; exaggerate*

Пётр сгуща́л кра́ски, когда́ расска́зывал о прие́зде в Аме́рику. *Peter laid it on thick when he told the story of his arrival to the States.*

креди́т—*credit*

отпуска́ть в креди́т—*sell on credit*

В э́том магази́не все това́ры отпуска́ют в креди́т. *This store sells everything on credit.*

кре́ндель—*pretzel*

выде́лывать кренделя́ (or **кре́ндели)**—*stagger; walk crookedly*

Пья́ный идёт по у́лице, выде́лывая кренделя́. *He's staggering in the street—he's drunk.*

кре́ст—*cross*

поста́вить крест—*cross off the list; give up for lost; kiss something good-bye*

Муж давно́ уе́хал в Аме́рику, и Мари́я, оста́вшись в Ки́еве, поста́вила на нём крест. *With her husband having left for the States a long time ago, Maria, who remained back in Kiev, gave him up for lost.*

креста́ нет—*have no conscience; be heartless*

Лев никогда́ никому́ не помога́л, и всем бы́ло я́сно, что на нём креста́ нет. *Everybody knew that Lev was heartless, because he never helped anyone.*

пойти́ крест-на́-крест—*go bust*

С прие́здом дру́га наш брак пошёл крест-на́-крест. *With the arrival of our friend, our marriage went bust.*

кри́во—*crookedly*

улыба́ться (or **усмехну́ться**) **кри́во**—*smirk* (or *grin*) *with embarrassment*

Слу́шая неприли́чные расска́зы, А́нна кри́во улыба́лась. *Upon hearing the off-color stories, Anna grinned with embarrassment.*

крик—*shout*

кри́ком крича́ть; крича́ть во всю́ ива́новскую—*shout at the top of one's voice*

Когда́ на неё набро́сился банди́т, Ири́на кри́ком крича́ла. *Irina shouted at the top of her voice when the bandit attacked her.*

после́дний крик мо́ды—*the latest vogue* (or *fashion*)

Ната́ша одева́лась по после́днему кри́ку мо́ды. *Natasha dressed according to the latest vogue.*

кри́тика—*criticism*

быть ни́же вся́кой кри́тики; не выде́рживать (никако́й) кри́тики—*not to hold water; be beneath criticism; be no good at all*

Но́вая пье́са сезо́на ни́же вся́кой кри́тики. *The new play of the season is below all criticism.*

кров—*roof; shelter*

лиши́ться кро́ва—*be homeless*

Лиши́вшись кро́ва, Па́вел спа́л на у́лице. *Being homeless, Pavel slept in the street.*

кровь—*blood*

кровь за кровь—*an eye for an eye; tooth for a tooth*

Дре́вний зако́н гласи́т: кровь за кровь. *The old law demands an eye for an eye and a tooth for a tooth.*

кровь с молоко́м—*the very picture of health, bursting with health*

Акули́на—настоя́щая дереве́нская краса́вица; как говори́тся, кровь с молоко́м. *Akulina is a real village beauty—as they say, she is the very picture of health.*

испо́ртить (or **перепо́ртить) мно́го кро́ви**—*cause much trouble* (or *headache)*

Свои́ми постоя́нными замеча́ниями Пётр перепо́ртил мне мно́го кро́ви. *Peter caused me much trouble with his constant negative remarks.*

(хоть) кровь из но́су (or **но́са)**—*no matter what; come hell or high water*

Ты до́лжен вы́полнить э́ту рабо́ту, хоть кровь из но́су. *You've got to complete this work come hell or high water.*

круг—*circle*

враща́ться в кругу́—*frequent someone's society; move in someone's circle*

В Москве́ Пётр постоя́нно враща́лся в кругу́ акаде́миков. *Peter moved constantly in the circle of academics in Moscow.*

на круг—*on the average*

Моя́ зарпла́та на круг ты́сяча до́лларов. *My income is $1,000 on the average.*

сде́лать круг—*go a roundabout way; make a detour*

Йз-за ава́рии на доро́ге нам пришло́сь сде́лать круг. *We had to make a detour because of the road accident.*

кругозо́р—*horizon; mental outlook*

кури́ный кругозо́р—*have a worm's viewpoint; be low-minded*

Бори́с, бу́дучи необразо́ванным, име́ет кури́ный кругозо́р. *Boris has a worm's viewpoint on everything because of his lack of education.*

круго́м—*around*

ходи́ть круго́м да о́коло—*beat around the bush*

Па́вел не дал прямо́го отве́та на мой вопро́с, а ходи́л круго́м да о́коло. *Pavel gave no straight answer to my question—he kept beating around the bush.*

кру́то—*steeply*

кру́то прихо́дится—*be in a tight spot; be in dire circumstances; have rough times*

Йз-за увольне́ния с рабо́ты ему́ кру́то прихо́дится. *He is having rough times after losing his job.*

крыло́—*wing*

опуска́ть кры́лья—*become discouraged*

Так как его́ кни́гу не изда́ли, Пётр опусти́л кры́лья. *Peter became discouraged when the publisher rejected his book.*

придава́ть кры́лья—*give someone wings; make someone happy*

Любо́вь придава́ла кры́лья поэ́ту. *Love gave the poet wings.*

крыть—*cover*

крыть не́чем—*there's nothing one can say*

Па́влу крыть бы́ло не́чем, когда́ его́ растра́та обнару́жилась. *There was nothing Pavel could say when his embezzling was discovered.*

кры́шка—*lid*

тут и кры́шка!—*one's number's up! one's goose is cooked!*
Наконе́ц Андре́я посади́ли в тюрьму́—тут ему́ и кры́шка! *At last Andrey was arrested—his goose is cooked!*

кста́ти—*to the point*

как нельзя́ кста́ти—*just at the right moment*
Нам по́мощь нужна́, ты пришла́ как нельзя́ кста́ти. *We need some help and you've come just at the right moment!*

кто—*who*

кто бы ни—*whoever; no matter who*
Кто бы ни позвони́л, скажи́те, что я за́нят. *Whoever calls, (please) tell them that I am busy.*

куда́—*where*

куда́ лу́чше—*far better*
Икра́ куда́ лу́чше ветчины́. *Caviar is far better than ham.*

не зна́ть куда́ дева́ться—*not to know where to hide (*for shame *or* from embarrassment*)*
Когда́ раскры́лась его́ ложь, он не зна́л, куда́ дева́ться от стыда́. *When his lie became known, he didn't know where to hide for shame.*

не зна́ть куда́ дева́ть себя́—*not to know what to do with oneself*
У моего́ сосе́да сто́лько вре́мени, что от безде́лья он не зна́ет куда́ деть себя́. *My neighbor has so much time that he doesn't know what to do with himself.*

хоть куда́—*excellent; couldn't be better*
Его́ отме́тки ра́ньше бы́ли посре́дственные, а тепе́рь хоть куда́. *His grades used to be average, but now they're excellent.*

кула́к—*fist*

держа́ть в кулаке́—*keep someone under one's thumb*

Он свою́ семью́ держа́л в кулаке́. *He held his family under his thumb.*

сжима́ть (or **собира́ть**) **себя́ в кула́к**—*get hold of oneself; pull oneself together*

В тру́дную мину́ту Ива́н всегда́ сжима́л себя́ в кула́к. *In difficult moments Ivan always pulled himself together.*

смея́ться в кула́к—*laugh up one's sleeve*

Па́вел обма́нывал клие́нтов и смея́лся в кула́к. *Pavel cheated his clients and laughed up his sleeve.*

кулёк—*bag*

из кулька́ в рого́жку—SEE: **из огня́ да в по́лымя**

купи́ть—*buy*

за что купи́л, за то и продаю́—*I am saying it the way I heard it; not to be responsible for the validty (*of hearsay *or* gossip*)*

Расска́зывая исто́рию, Ива́н предупреди́л: за что купи́л, за то и продаю́. *When Ivan told the story he warned that he was not responsible for its truthfulness.*

купи́ть втри́дорога—*pay through one's nose*

Наш дом мы купи́ли втри́дорога. *We paid through our nose when we bought our house.*

кур—*rooster;* **ку́ра**—*hen*

де́нег ку́ры не клюю́т—*roll in money; have money to burn*

Бори́с вы́играл в лотере́ю, и сейча́с у него́ де́нег ку́ры не клюю́т. *Boris won the lottery and now he's got money to burn.*

ку́рам на́ смех—*enough to make a horse laugh*

Расска́зы о про́махах иностра́нцев—про́сто ку́рам на́ смех. *The tales about the foreigner's goof-ups are enough to make a horse laugh.*

попа́сть как кур во щи (or **в о́щип**)—*get into a fix; be* (or *get into*) *a pickle*

Бори́с верну́лся из командиро́вки и заста́л меня́ с его́ жено́й. Я попа́л как кур во щи. *Boris returned from his business trip and found me with his wife. Now I'm really in a pickle!*

ку́рица—*chicken*

мо́края ку́рица—*weakling; chicken; chicken-heart; milksop*

Са́ша производи́л впечатле́ние мо́крой ку́рицы. *Sasha gave the impression of a chicken.*

писа́ть как ку́рица ла́пой—*have a handwriting like chicken scratch*

Его́ по́черк нельзя́ разобра́ть, он пи́шет как ку́рица ла́пой. *His handwriting is illegible—it is all chicken-scratch.*

слепа́я ку́рица—*as blind as a bat*

Не ищи́ ключи́, они́ здесь, ты слепа́я ку́рица. *Stop looking for the keys—here they are—you're as blind as a bat!*

курс—*course*

быть в ку́рсе—*be well posted* (or *informed)*

Президе́нт был в ку́рсе фронтовы́х собы́тий. *The president was well informed of the events on the front.*

держа́ть курс (or **ли́нию)**—*be working toward*

Мы держáли курс на аттестáт зрéлости. *We were workin toward a high-school diploma.*

читáть курс по чемý-либо—*lecture on something*

Бýдучи профéссором лингвúстики, мой муж читáет кýрсы п языкознáнию. *Since he is a professor of linguistics, m husband lectures on the language sciences.*

курьéрский—*express*

как на курьéрских—*at breakneck speed; posthaste*

Мы éхали домóй как на курьéрских. *We were heading home a breakneck speed.*

кусóк (or **кусóчек**)—*lump*

кусóк в гóрло не идёт—*hardly be able to swallow a bite; it won go down one's throat*

От волнéния Ивáну кусóк в гóрло не идёт. *Ivan can hardl swallow a bite in his excitement.*

проносúть кусóк мúмо рта—*miss out on an opportunity; let g of a good deal*

Ѝз-за рассéянности Олéг проносúл кусóк мúмо рта. *Because o his absent-mindedness Oleg let go of a good deal.*

собирáть кускú—*go begging; live on handouts*

Не получáя пéнсию, Ирúна вы́нуждена былá собирáть кускı *Since she didn't get a pension, Irina was reduced to living o handouts.*

куст—*bush*

смотрéть (or **глядéть**) **в кусты́**—*try to duck* (or *back*) *out*

Хотя́ я обещáл Сáше хорóшую зарплáту за рабóту н строúтельстве, он смотрéл в кусты́. *Although I offered Sash a good salary to work on the construction, he tried to duck ou*

уходúть в кусты́—*chicken out*

Мы не боя́лись купа́ться в ледяно́й воде́ о́зера, но Никола́й, как всегда́, ушёл в кусты́. *We weren't afraid to take a swim in the icy lake, but Nikolay as always, chickened out.*

ку́ча—*heap*

вали́ть всё в одну́ ку́чу—*make a muddle of things; lump everything together*

Плохо́й реда́ктор вали́л всё в одну́ ку́чу—и настоя́щие расска́зы и спле́тни. *The bad editor lumped together the real stories and the gossip.*

Л

ла́вочка—*store*

э́то одна́ ла́вочка; настоя́щая ла́вочка; ну и ла́вочка—*sing the same tune; totally to agree with someone*

По их поведе́нию я по́нял, что э́то одна́ ла́вочка. *It became evident from their behavior that they're singing the same tune.*

закрыва́ть ла́вочку—*1. stop an activity; put the shutters up; call it quits 2. shut one's mouth; clam up*

1. Уста́в от рабо́ты, мы сказа́ли: дава́йте закро́ем ла́вочку. *When we got tired of work, we said, "Let's call it quits."*
2. Когда́ Оле́г на́чал говори́ть гру́бости, мы окли́кнули его́, чтобы он закры́л ла́вочку. *When Oleg started to talk rudely, we told him to shut up.*

лавр—*laurel*

ла́вры не даю́т спать—*be green with envy*

Ла́вры моего́ конкуре́нта не даю́т мне спать. *I'm green with envy because of the success of my competitor.*

ла́герь—*camp*

де́йствовать на два ла́геря—*have a foot in each camp*

Васи́лий не явля́ется чле́ном ни одно́й из па́ртий, но де́йствует на два ла́геря. *Vasily is no member of any party, but he has a foot in each camp.*

ла́д—*harmony; concord*

быть (or **жи́ть) в ладу́** (or **в лада́х)**—*live in harmony with someone; get on well*

Мы с му́жем живём в ладу́. *My husband and I get on well with one another.*

идёт на лад—*things, life, etc. are taking a turn for the better*

В э́том году́ у нас бо́льше де́нег, и поэ́тому жизнь идёт на лад. *This year we have more money, and therefore our life has taken a turn for the better.*

на все лады́—*in every possible way* (or *manner)*

Арка́дий тверди́л свою́ правоту́ на все лады́. *Arkady affirms his own right in every possible way.*

на свой лад—*in one's own way (*or *fashion)*

О́льга ме́бель в кварти́ре расста́вила на свой лад. *Olga arranged the furniture in the apartment in her own way.*

ладо́нь—*palm*

ви́ден как (бу́дто) на ладо́ни—*be spread before the eyes*

С ба́шни го́род ви́ден как на ладо́ни. *You can see the town spread out before your eyes from the tower.*

ла́па—*paw*

накла́дывать ла́пу—*get one's grubby paws on someone else's things; to steal*

Фёдор люби́л накла́дывать ла́пу на чужо́е иму́щество. *Fedor liked to get his grubby paws on other people's property.*

попа́сть в ла́пы—*fall into someone's clutches*

Он попа́л в ла́пы банди́тов. *He fell into the bandits' clutches.*

ла́пка—*small paw*

ходи́ть (or **стоя́ть) на за́дних ла́пках**—*flatter someone; kowtow to someone*

Ива́н стоя́л пе́ред нача́льником на за́дних ла́пках. *Ivan kept kowtowing to the boss.*

ла́поть—*bast shoe*

не ла́птем щи хлеба́ть—*know a thing or two; not to be naive*

Не объясня́й нам как себя́ вести́, мы то́же не ла́птем щи хлеба́ем. *Don't explain to us how to behave—we, too, know a thing or two.*

ла́рчик—*small box*

ла́рчик про́сто открыва́лся—*the explanation was quite simple; it wasn't hard to figure out*

По́сле дли́тельного молча́ния А́нна сообщи́ла, что до́лго боле́ла; ла́рчик про́сто открыва́лся. *After a lengthy silence Anna told us that she was ill for a long time—the explanation was quite simple.*

ла́сточка—*swallow*

одна́ ла́сточка весны́ не де́лает—*one swallow doesn't make a summer.*

Америкáнский банк откры́лся в Москвé пéред 1990 гóдом. Пессими́сты говори́ли: «Одна́ лáсточка весны́ не дéлает.» *An American bank was opened in Moscow before 1990. The pessimists said: "One swallow doesn't make a summer."*

пéрвая лáсточка—*early bird*

При откры́тии нóвого магази́на Ивáн оказáлся пéрвой лáсточкой. *Ivan was the first early bird when they opened the new store.*

легкó—*easy*

легкó отдéлаться—*lucky to emerge from a dangerous situation; get off light*

Во врéмя автокатастрóфы он легкó отдéлался. *He got off light from the car accident.*

лёд—*ice*

лёд трóнулся—*things are moving; the ice is broken*

С получéнием креди́та лёд трóнулся, и мы нáчали стрóить дом. *When we got the credit, things got moving and we were able to begin building the house.*

лежáть—*lie*

плóхо лежи́т—*be left lying around; be within reach*

Сосéдский мáльчик уходя́ от нас, уноси́л с собóй всё, что плóхо лежáло. *When the neighbor's little boy left, he took with him everything within his reach.*

лéкция—*lecture*

читáть лéкции—*read lectures; give lectures*

Бýдучи извéстным поэ́том, он читáет лéкции в рáзных университéтах. *Being a famous poet, he keeps giving lectures at various universities.*

читáть лéкцию—*tell someone what to do; preach to someone*

Мать чáсто читáла лéкцию нам о прáвильном поведéнии. *Mother often lectured us on proper behavior.*

ле́нь—*laziness*

все, кому́ не лень—*everybody who feels like it*

Бори́са критику́ют все, кому́ не лень. *Everybody who feels like it, is criticizing Boris.*

лес—*woods*

кто в лес, кто по дрова́—*one pulls one way, and the other pulls the other way; everyone does his own thing*

Нача́льник говори́т одно́, а замести́тель друго́е—кто в лес, кто по дрова́. *The boss says one thing, his substitute another—one pulls one way, the other pulls the other way.*

смотре́ть (or **гляде́ть**) **в лес**—*look for greener pastures*

«Что я то́лько для него́ не де́лаю, а он всё в лес гляди́т»—жа́ловалась ба́бушка на вну́ка. *"There's nothing I wouldn't do for him, and yet he's looking for greener pastures" the grandmother complained about her grandson.*

тёмный лес—*terra incognita; not to have a clue about; be Greek to someone*

Киберне́тика для меня́—тёмный лес. *I don't have a clue about computer science.*

ле́стница—*stairs*

спуска́ть с ле́стницы—*show someone the door; get rid of someone*

Па́вел нам нагруби́л, и мы его́ спусти́ли с ле́стницы. *Pavel was rude to us, so we showed him the door.*

лёт—*flight*

лови́ть (or **хвата́ть**) **на лету́** (or **с лёту**)—*be quick in the uptake; be a quick study*

Ска́занные на́ми слова́ Ива́н лови́л на лету́. *Ivan was a quick study—he got our meaning right away.*

лета́—*years*

войти́ в лета́—*be advanced in years; get old*

Войдя́ в лета́, Са́ша ушёл на пéнсию. *Sasha got his retirement, since he became advanced in years.*

с ма́лых лет—*since (early) childhood*

С ма́лых лет я люби́л петь. *I've loved to sing ever since my early childhood.*

сóрок лет с хвóстиком—*past forty; forty-something*

Мне ужé сóрок лет с хвóстиком. *I am forty-something.*

лéто—*summer*

ба́бье лéто—*Indian summer*

У нас сейча́с тёплые дни ба́бьего лéта. *We are living the warm days of an Indian summer.*

скóлько лет, скóлько зим (не вида́лись or **не встреча́лись)**—*it's ages since we met! I haven't seen you for ages!*

При встрéче Пётр сказа́л: «Скóлько лет, скóлько зим!» *When we met Peter said, "I haven't seen you for ages!"*

лéший—*wood-goblin*

иди́ (or **пошёл** or **ну тебя́) к лéшему!**—*to hell with you! go to hell!*

Рассерди́вшись, он сказа́л: ну тебя́ к лéшему! *"Go to hell!" he said when he got mad at me.*

на кой лéший?—*what on earth* (or *what the hell) for?*

На кой лéший мне такóй друг? *What on earth do I need such a friend for?*

хоть к лéшему на рога́—*even to the end of the world*

От свои́х врагóв он готóв бежа́ть хоть к лéшему на рога́. *He is ready to run even to the end of the world from his enemies.*

лимóн—*lemon*

как вы́жатый лимóн—*worn out; spent*

К концу́ недéли я совсéм как вы́жатый лимóн. *I'm all worn out at the end of the week.*

отда́ть лимóн—*pay* (or *fork over) a million*

«Ско́лько лимо́нов ты отда́л за свой Мерседе́с?»—спросил Петров у своего коллеги нувори́ша. *"How many millions did you fork over for your Mercedes?" Petrov asked his nouveau riche colleague.*

ли́ния—*line*

вести́ (or **держа́ть) свою́ ли́нию**—*follow one's own course of action*

Како́й бы ни да́ли Бори́су сове́т, он держа́л свою́ ли́нию. *No matter what advice one gave Boris, he kept following his own course of action.*

же́нская ли́ния—*mother's side*

По же́нской ли́нии она́ аристокра́тка. *On her mother's side she's an aristocrat.*

по ли́нии—*in the field of something*

Мой оте́ц—специали́ст по ли́нии пожа́рного де́ла. *My father is a specialist in the field of fire prevention.*

по прямо́й (ли́нии)—*1. as the crow flies 2. direct lineage (of descent)*

Сосе́дний го́род в сорока́ киломе́трах от нас по прямо́й. *The neighboring town is forty kilometers from us, as the crow flies.* 2. Всё иму́щество доста́лось насле́дникам по прямо́й ли́нии. *All of the inheritance went to the relatives of direct lineage.*

отцо́вская ли́ния—*father's side*

По отцо́вской ли́нии у него́ неме́цкое происхожде́ние. *On his father's side he is of German extraction.*

ли́пка—*young linden tree*

обдира́ть (or **обира́ть** or **облу́пливать) как ли́пку**—*take someone to the cleaners; fleece someone*

По́сле разво́да меня́ ободра́ли как ли́пку. *I was taken to the cleaners after my divorce.*

лиса́—*fox*

Лиса́ Патрике́евна—*sly fox*

Мне казáлось, что Ли́за чéстная, но вы́яснилось, что онá Лисá Патрикéевна. *I thought that Lisa was honest, but it turned out that she's a sly fox.*

лист—*leaf*

привязáться (or **пристáть) как бáнный лист**—*stick like a burr*

От Бори́са никáк не избáвишься, он пристаёт как бáнный лист. *You'll never get rid of Boris—he sticks like a burr.*

ли́хо—*evil*

не поминáть ли́хом—*think kindly of someone; remember someone kindly*

При прощáнии он сказáл: «Не поминáйте меня́ ли́хом.» *"Remember me kindly," he said as we parted.*

лицó—*face; person*

в лицé; от лицá—*on behalf of someone*

Председáтель говори́т от лицá организáции. *The chairman spoke on behalf of the organization.*

знать в лицó—*know someone by sight*

Мы никогдá не разговáривали, но я знал егó в лицó. *We have never talked to each other, but I knew him by sight.*

кидáть в лицó—*reproach someone; tell someone off*

Áнна ки́нула мýжу в лицó, что он сли́шком мнóго пьёт. *Anna reproached her husband for drinking too much.*

к лицý—*look good on someone; suit one*

Ей бéлое плáтье к лицý. *White dresses suit her well.*

лицá (живóго) нет—*be as pale as a ghost*

Пóсле тяжёлой оперáции на нём лицá нет. *He was pale as a ghost after major surgery.*

лицóм к лицý—*face to face*

Поворáчивая за ýгол, я встрéтился с подрýгой лицóм к лицý. *I met my girlfriend face to face after turning the corner.*

лицóм не вы́шел—*be ugly; homely; unattractive*

Актри́са была́ тала́нтлива, но лицо́м не вы́шла. *The actress was gifted but homely.*

на одно́ лицо́—*nearly identical*

Не́которые совреме́нные дома́ на одно́ лицо́. *Some modern houses are nearly identical.*

не уда́рить лицо́м в грязь—*not to fall on one's face; not to disgrace oneself*

В но́вой шко́ле наш сын не уда́рил лицо́м в грязь. *Our son didn't fall on his face at the new school.*

смести́ (or **стере́ть) с лица́ земли́**—*raze to the ground*

Бомбардиро́вки стёрли го́род с лица́ земли́. *The bombardments razed the city to the ground.*

ли́шний—*unnecessary*

не ли́шне (бы́ло бы)—*it would be good if; it wouldn't hurt a bit if*

Не ли́шне бы́ло бы име́ть бо́льше де́нег. *It wouldn't hurt a bit for us to have more money.*

позво́лить себе́ ли́шнее—*1. live beyond one's means 2. allow oneself more than is called for; take liberties*

1. Он позво́лил себе́ ли́шнее и влез в больши́е долги́. *He ran up a huge debt by living beyond his means.*
2. Свои́ми выска́зываниями И́горь позво́лил себе́ ли́шнее. *Igor took liberties with his pronouncements.*

с ли́шним—*odd; (a bit) over*

Э́то сто́ит сто рубле́й с ли́шним. *This costs a bit over a hundred rubles.*

лоб—*forehead*

заруби́ть на лбу́—*commit to memory; remember well*

Сове́ты ма́тери Пётр заруби́л себе́ на лбу́. *Peter committed to memory his mother's advice.*

лоб в лоб—*right into each other; face to face*

У переу́лка мы вдруг сошли́сь с Миха́йлом лоб в лоб. *Mikhail and I suddenly came face to face with one another at the crossroads.*

ме́дный лоб—*blockhead; dumb; slow-witted*

Бори́са не переубеди́шь, у него́ ме́дный лоб. *You can't convince Boris—he is a blockhead.*

на лбу́ (or **на лице́) напи́сано**—*be written all over one's face*

Как Ната́ша не стара́лась скрыть, но на лбу́ бы́ло напи́сано, что говори́т непра́вду. *No matter how hard Natasha tried, it was written all over her face that she wasn't telling the truth.*

лове́ц—*fisherman; hunter*

на ловца́ и зверь бежи́т—*speak of the devil and he appears; just the person one needs*

«На ловца́ и зверь бежи́т»—вскри́кнула Ли́за, когда́ Арка́дий вошёл. «Ведь я тебя́ ищу́ весь день.» *"Speak of the devil and he appears!" Lisa cried, when Arkady stepped into the room. "I have been looking for you all day."*

ло́жка—*spoon*

утопи́ть в ло́жке воды́—*one would like to see another person hanged*

От не́нависти Пётр гото́в утопи́ть меня́ в ло́жке воды́. *Peter hates me so much he would love to see me hanged.*

ло́пнуть—*break*

хоть ло́пни—*even if you burst*

Хоть ло́пни, но на́шу та́йну никому́ не расска́зывай! *Don't you tell our secret to anyone, even if you burst!*

ло́шадь—*horse*

я не я, и ло́шадь не моя́—*it's none of my business* (or *affair*)

Ты мне об э́том не расска́зывай, я не я, и ло́шадь не моя́. *Don't tell me about this—it's none of my business.*

лука́вый—*sly; cunning*

не му́дрствуя лука́во—*without subterfuge; directly*

Са́ша выска́зывался не му́дрствуя лука́во. *Sasha cleared his chest of everything without subterfuge.*

луна́—*moon*

под луно́ю (луно́й)—*under the sun; in this world*

Для долгожи́теля ничто́ не но́во под луно́ю. *There's nothing new under the sun if you live long enough.*

с луны́ свали́ться—*come from another planet*

Он всё так стра́нно понима́ет, сло́вно с луны́ свали́лся. *He interprets everything so strangely as if he came from another planet.*

лунь—*chicken hawk*

бе́лый (or **седо́й**) **как лунь**—*white-haired; snow-white*

Он верну́лся с фро́нта бе́лый как лунь. *His hair had turned snow-white by the time he returned from the front.*

лу́чше—*better*

как мо́жно лу́чше; как нельзя́ лу́чше—*in the best possible way; excellently*

Я хочу́ как мо́жно лу́чше свой о́тпуск провести́. *I want to spend my vacation in the best possible way.*

тем лу́чше—*(all) the better*

Е́сли ты мно́го де́нег зараба́тываешь, тем лу́чше для тебя́. *All the better for you if you make lots of money.*

лу́чший—*best*

оставля́ть жела́ть лу́чшего—*leave lots* (or *a great deal) to be desired*

Его́ рабо́та оставля́ет жела́ть лу́чшего. *His work leaves a lot to be desired.*

лы́жи—*skis*

навостри́ть лы́жи—*skip out; take to one's heels*

Ле́на уже́ навостри́ла лы́жи. *Lena has skipped out already.*

лы́ко—*tree bark*

не лы́ком шит—*be nobody's fool*

Он в любо́й ситуа́ции вы́йдет из положе́ния—не лы́ком шит. *He emerges unscathed from any situation—he's nobody's fool.*

лы́ка не вя́жет—*stammer; not to be able to talk straight*

От пья́нства он лы́ка не вя́жет. *He's stammering with drunkenness.*

любе́зность—*courtesy; kindness*

не откажи́те в любе́зности—*please; be so kind as; be kind enough to do something*

Помоги́те мне, не откажи́те в любе́зности. *Please be kind enough to give me a hand!*

сде́лать любе́зность—*do a favor*

Бу́дьте добры́, сде́лайте мне любе́зность! *Be so kind, do me a favor!*

любо́вь—*love*

горя́чая любо́вь—*passionate love*

Ма́ша относи́лась к Бори́су с горя́чей любо́вью. *Masha felt passionate love for Boris.*

из любви́ к иску́сству—*just for the fun of it; for the love of something*

Он э́то де́лает не из-за де́нег, а из любви́ к иску́сству. *He's not doing this for money but for the love of it.*

крути́ть любо́вь—*flirt*

Ната́ша меня́ не лю́бит, а то́лько кру́тит любо́вь со мной. *Natasha isn't in love with me—she's just flirting.*

любо́вь зла—полю́бишь и козла́—*love is blind*

Во вре́мя разво́да Васи́лий не мог поня́ть, как он мог жени́ться на Ната́ше. Но ведь любо́вь зла—полю́бишь и козла́. *At the time of their divorce Vasily couldn't understand how he could have married Natasha, but then love is blind.*

объясня́ться (or **призна́ться) в любви́**—*make someone a declaration of love*

Гуля́я в па́рке, Ива́н объясни́лся Ма́ше в любви́. *Ivan declared his love to Masha while they were walking in the park.*

любопы́тство—*curiosity*

дви́жимый любопы́тством—*be dying of curiosity*

Са́ша был дви́жим любопы́тством, что́бы узна́ть но́вости. *Sasha was dying of curiosity to find out what the news was.*

лю́ди—*people*

быть на лю́дях—*be without* (or *have no) privacy all the time; be in company*

Изве́стная актри́са была́ всегда́ на лю́дях. *The famous actress had no privacy at any time.*

вы́биться (or **вы́йти) в лю́ди**—*make a career; have "arrived"*

Ива́н все свои́ си́лы напря́г, что́бы вы́биться в лю́ди. *Ivan spared no effort to make a career.*

люде́й посмотре́ть да себя́ показа́ть—*see and be seen*

Пётр пошёл на конце́рт изве́стного дирижёра люде́й посмотре́ть и себя́ показа́ть. *Peter went to the concert of the famous conductor in order to see and be seen.*

ни лю́дям, ни соба́кам; ни лю́дям, ни себе́—*be unwanted; not to be needed by anyone*

Как он не стара́лся, он был ни лю́дям, ни соба́кам. *No matter how hard he tried, nobody wanted him.*

ля́мка—*strap*

тере́ть (or **тяну́ть) ля́мку**—*drudge; toil*

Они́ всю жизнь тяну́ли ля́мку. *They were toiling all their lives long.*

ля́сы

точи́ть ля́сы—*chew the fat; shoot the breeze*

Никола́й весь ве́чер точи́л ля́сы. *Nikolay was shooting the breeze all evening long.*

M

мазь—*ointment; grease*

на мази́—*something is going smoothly; something is almost all set*

В до́ме сде́лан ремо́нт, расста́влена ме́бель—всё на мази́, что́бы пересели́ться. *They did all the repair work in the house, the furniture is all in place, everything is almost all set for the move.*

Мака́р—*Makar*

куда́ Мака́р теля́т не гоня́л—SEE: **куда́ во́рон косте́й не занесёт**

ма́ленький—*small*

ма́ленький, да уда́ленький—*be strong for one's size; small can be strong*

Ма́льчик стал чемпио́ном—вот вам ма́ленький, да уда́ленький. *The boy became a champion—behold how small can be strong!*

ма́ло—*few*

ма́ло-ма́льски—*halfway; half-*

Да́же вся́кий ма́ло-ма́льски образо́ванный челове́к зна́ет Пу́шкина. *Even a half-educated person has heard about Pushkin.*

ма́ло-пома́лу—*little by little*

Ма́ло-пома́лу собрала́сь толпа́. *The crowd gathered little by little.*

ма́ло того́, что—*not only*

Ма́ло того́, что опозда́л, он ещё нас обвини́л. *Not only was he late—he blamed us for it!*

ма́ло ли что—*it doesn't matter*

Ма́ло ли что оте́ц ду́мает, я живу́ свое́й жи́знью. *It doesn't matter what my father thinks—I'm living my own life.*

ма́лый—*small*

без ма́лого (or **ма́ла**)—*almost; just under; nearly*

Ей без ма́лого сто лет. *She's almost a hundred years old.*

до́брый (or **сла́вный**) **ма́лый**—*decent fellow; regular guy*

Мой сосе́д—сла́вный ма́лый. *My neighbor is a decent fellow.*

мал мала́ ме́ньше—*one is smaller than the other; line up like organ pipes*

У нас детей мал, мала́, ме́ньше. *Our kids line up like organ pipes.*

от ма́ла до вели́ка—*big and small; young and old*

На пра́зднике уча́ствовали все, от ма́ла до вели́ка. *Everybody, big and small participated in the festivities.*

Мамáй—*Mamay* (name of the Tartar khan)

как (or **бýдто** or **слóвно** or **тóчно**) **Мамáй прошёл**—*it looks as if an army had marched through; complete disorder*

Пóсле бýри в гóроде—как Мамáй прошёл. *After the storm the city looks as if an army had marched through it.*

манéра—*manner*

вся́кими манéрами; на вся́кие манéры—*in every possible way*

Никúта вся́кими манéрами старáлся добúться успéха. *Nikita tried to achieve success in every possible way.*

живы́м манéром—*in a jiffy; in no time*

Он тóлько что пришёл и живы́м манéром исчéз. *He had hardly arrived, when he disappeared in no time.*

мáнна—*manna*

ждать (or **жáждать**) **как мáнны небéсной**—*thirst for; look forward to; yearn for something*

Устáлый, я ждал óтпуска, как мáнны небéсной. *I was yearning for a vacation, I was so exhausted.*

мановéние—*beck; nod*

бýдто (or **как** or **слóвно** or **тóчно**) **по мановéнию волшéбного жéзла** (or **волшéбной пáлочки**)—*as if by magic*

Бýдто по мановéнию волшéбной пáлочки вертолёт спустúлся на мóре и спас нас. *The helicopter descended to the sea and rescued us, as if by magic.*

мáрка—*stamp*

вы́сшей (or **пéрвой**) **мáрки**—*1. of the top quality; first-class 2. be notorious for something*

1. Мы купúли машúну вы́сшей мáрки. *We bought a top quality car.*
2. Мой сосéд лгун вы́сшей мáрки. *My neighbor is a notorious liar.*

под мáркой—*under the guise of*

Под мáркой благотворúтельности он скопúл себé дéньги. *Under the guise of charitableness, he grabbed the money for himself.*

пóртить мáрку—*spoil one's good reputation*

Своúм поведéнием Никúта пóртил мáрку нáшей семьú. *Nikita spoiled the good reputation of our family with his behavior.*

мáсло—*oil; butter*

идёт (or **течёт** or **кáтится**) **как по мáслу**—*go smoothly; proceed well*

С егó пóмощью рабóта пошлá как по мáслу. *With his help the work went smoothly.*

как бýдто мáслом по сéрдцу—*be like music to one's ears*

Бýрные аплодисмéнты для актёра, как бýдто мáслом по сéрдцу. *The thunderous applause was like music to the actor's ears.*

лить (or **подливáть**) **мáсла в огóнь**—*add fuel to the flame*

Стрóгим запрещéнием курúть, отéц подливáл мáсла в огóнь. *With his strong injunction against smoking, the father added fuel to the flame.*

мáсса—*mass*

в (óбщей) мáссе—*as a whole; on the whole; in the mass; in the bulk*

Продýкты нáшего магазúна в óбщей мáссе кáчественные. *The wares in our store are of high quality, on the whole.*

мáстер—*foreman*

мáстер на все рýки—*Jack-of-all-trades*

Хорошó имéть в семьé мáстера на все рýки. *It's a good thing if there's a Jack-of-all-trades in one's family.*

мáстер своегó дéла—*expert*

Он хорóший инженéр, настоя́щий мáстѐр своегó дéла. *He is a good engineer—a real expert of his trade.*

масть—*color*

всех (or **любы́х** or **рáзных) мастéй**—*of every stripe and color*

В нáшем клýбе лю́ди всех мастéй. *There are people of every stripe and color in our club.*

однóй (or **такóй) же мáсти; под однý масть**—*birds of a feather; equals*

Óльга и Йгорь однóй мáсти. *Olga and Igor are birds of a feather.*

мат—*obscene language*

кричáть благúм мáтом—*shout at the top of one's voice; shout one's head off*

От бóли Пáвел кричáл благúм мáтом. *Pavel was shouting at the top of his voice with pain.*

мать—*mother*

мать честнáя!—*Holy Mother!; Heavens!; oh my God!*—SEE: **бóже мой!**

показа́ть ку́зькину мать—*make it hot for someone; put the fear of God into someone*

Ники́та грози́л: «Покажу́ тебе́ ку́зькину мать.» *Nikita threatened, "I'll put the fear of God into you!"*

мах—*motion*

дать ма́ху—*make a blunder; mess up something; shoot wide of the mark*

Свои́м заму́жеством О́льга дала́ ма́ху. *Olga made a blunder of her marriage.*

одни́м (or **еди́ным**) **ма́хом**—*at one stroke; at one go; at one blow*

Одни́м ма́хом он сбил почти́ все ке́гли. *He knocked down almost all the pins at one stroke.*

с ма́ху—*rashly*

С ма́ху не реша́ют больши́е пробле́мы. *Don't make a rash decision on important matters.*

маши́на—*machine*

а́дская маши́на—*time bomb*

Нерешённые пробле́мы легко́ мо́гут преврати́ться в а́дскую маши́ну. *Unsolved problems can easily become a time bomb.*

мгнове́ние—*instant; moment*

в мгнове́ние о́ка; в одно́ мгнове́ние—*in the twinkling of an eye; between two shakes of a lamb's tail; instantly*

Компью́тер реша́ет зада́чи в одно́ мгнове́ние. *Computers can solve tasks in the twinkling of an eye.*

ме́бель—*furniture*

для ме́бели—*sitting around doing nothing*

У нас ма́сса рабо́ты, а Ли́за сиди́т для ме́бели. *We have an awful lot of work while Lisa just sits around doing nothing.*

мёд—*honey*

не мёд—*no great joy; not one's cup of tea*

Моя́ рабо́та не мёд. *My work is no great joy.*

медвéдь—*bear*

делúть шкýру неубúтого медвéдя—*count one's chicken before they are hatched*

Подождú немнóжко, не делú шкýру неубúтого медвéдя. *Hang on a bit longer—don't count your chickens before they're hatched.*

медвéдь (or **слон**) **нá ухо наступúл**—*have no ear for music; be tone-deaf*

Емý медвéдь нá ухо наступúл—он музыкáнтом не бýдет. *He'll be no musician—he's got no ear for music.*

мéжду—*between*

а мéжду тем—*although; albeit*

Алексéй мнóго говорúл, а мéжду тем суть не рассказáл. *Although Aleksey talked a lot, he failed to relate the essence of the matter.*

мéжду нáми (говорá)—*between you and me; between ourselves*

Мéжду нáми говорá, Ивáн чáсто врёт. *Between ourselves, Ivan often lies.*

мéжду прóчим—*incidentally; by the way*

Ме́жду про́чим, Са́ша вчера́ сде́лал ава́рию. *By the way, Sasha was in an accident yesterday.*

ме́жду тем как—*while*

Ме́жду тем как они́ разгова́ривали, мы накры́ли стол. *While they were conversing, we set the table.*

ме́лко—*shallow*

ме́лко пла́вать—*be of poor* (or *mediocre) caliber*

Бори́с как архите́ктор ме́лко пла́вает. *Boris is mediocre as an architect.*

ме́лочь—*detail*

разме́ниваться на ме́лочи—*fritter away one's energy*

Ива́н ничего́ не дости́г, так как разме́нивался на ме́лочи. *Ivan never achieved anything—he frittered away his energy.*

мель—*shoals*

сади́ться на мель—*get stranded; get into a fix*

Й́з-за безде́нежья мы со свое́й констру́кцией се́ли на мель. *We got stranded with the construction due to a lack of money.*

ме́нее—*less*

ме́нее всего́—*least of all*

Ме́нее всего́ я рассчи́тывал на помо́щь Са́ши. *It was Sasha's help I counted on the least.*

тем не ме́нее—*nevertheless; in spite of something*

Хотя́ он меня́ обману́л, тем не ме́нее я не оби́делся. *In spite of the fact that he cheated me, I did not get offended.*

ме́ра; ме́рка—*measure*

в значи́тельной ме́ре—*to a large extent*

Э́то в значи́тельной ме́ре зави́сит от вас. *This depends to a large extent on you.*

в ме́ру—*within limits; in moderation*

Хотя́ мы пи́ли во́дку, но в ме́ру. *We drank some vodka all right, but in moderation.*

всему́ есть ме́ра—*everything has a limit*
Так себя́ вести́ нельзя́, всему́ есть ме́ра. *One mustn't act like that—everything has a limit.*

ме́ра терпе́ния перепо́лнилась—*be* (or *get*) *fed up with someone* (or *something*)
Ме́ра моего́ терпе́ния перепо́лнилась, и я его́ вы́гнал. *I got fed up with him and told him to get out.*

ме́рить то́ю же ме́рою; ме́рить в ту же ме́ру—*repay in kind; pay someone in his own coin*
Я стара́лся ме́рить Ива́на той же ме́рою. *I was trying to repay Ivan in kind.*

ме́рить свое́й ме́рой—SEE: **ме́рить на свой арши́н**

не знать ме́ры—*go to extremes*
Он ни в чём не зна́ет ме́ры. *He goes to extremes in everything.*

по кра́йней ме́ре—*at least*
Строи́тельство до́ма потре́бует по кра́йней ме́ре два го́да. *The construction will take at least two years.*

приня́ть все ме́ры—*take all necessary measures*
Мы при́няли все ме́ры для охра́ны го́рода. *We took all necessary measures for the defense of the city.*

мертве́цки

мертве́цки пьян—*drunk as a marine*
Ники́та лежа́л в лу́же мертве́цки пьян. *Nikita lay in the puddle, drunk as a marine.*

спать мертве́цки; спать мертве́цким сно́м—*sleep like a log*
От уста́лости он спал мертве́цки. *He was so tired he slept like a log.*

местéчко—*borough; small town*

тёплое (or **тёпленькое**) **местéчко**—*snug* (or *cushy*) *job*

Ивáн нашёл себе тёплое местéчко. *Ivan found himself a cushy job.*

мéсто—*place*

имéть мéсто—*happen; take place*

Собы́тие, о котóром он рассказáл, имéло мéсто во врéмя войны́. *The events he related took place during the war.*

не к мéсту—*out of place; off the topic*

Бори́с говори́т всегдá не к мéсту. *Boris keeps talking off the topic.*

не находи́ть (себé) мéста—*fret; be beside oneself with worry*

Ду́мая о возмóжности развóда, Ири́на не находи́ла себé мéста. *Irina was beside herself with worry because of the possibility of a divorce.*

нет мéста; не должнó быть мéста—*must not happen; is out of place*

Неприли́чному поведéнию нет мéста. *Indecent behavior is out of place.*

ни с мéста—*1. entirely still 2. don't move!; stay put!*

1. Как мы не старáемся, а дéло нáше ни с мéста. *No matter how hard we try, our business stands entirely still.*
2. «Ни с мéста!»—сказáл полицéйский. *"Don't move!" the policeman said.*

отказáть от мéста—*fire someone*

Начáльник отказáл Бори́су от мéста. *The boss fired Boris.*

пустóе мéсто—*nobody*

Мой начáльник—э́то пустóе мéсто. *My boss is a nobody.*

с мéста в карьéр—*straight away; right off the bat*

Окóнчив университéт, Пáвел стал дирéктором, с мéста в карьéр. *After Pavel finished the university, he became a director right off the bat.*

ста́вить себя́ на ме́сто—*put oneself in someone else's shoes* (or *place* or *position)*

Пре́жде чем ты сде́лаешь мне замеча́ние, поста́вь себя́ на моё ме́сто. *Before you make remarks about me, try to put yourself in my place.*

я бы на твоём ме́сте—*if I were you*

Я бы на твоём ме́сте не кури́л. *I wouldn't smoke if I were you.*

мета́лл—*metal*

презре́нный мета́лл—*money; filthy lucre*

Оле́г всё вре́мя говори́л о презре́нном мета́лле. *Oleg kept talking about the money all the time.*

метёлка—*whisk*

под метёлку—*clean sweep*

Взло́мщики очи́стили весь дом под метёлку. *The burglars made a clean sweep of the entire house.*

мех—*fur*

на ры́бьем меху́—*ragged* (or *shabby) coat giving no protection from the cold*

Э́то пальто́ на ры́бьем меху́. *This is a shabby coat that gives no protection from the cold.*

меч—*sword*

вложи́ть меч в но́жны—*bury the hatchet*

По́сле спо́ра мы вложи́ли мечи́ в но́жны. *After our dispute we buried the hatchet.*

мечта́ть—*dream*

мечта́ть о себе́ (мно́го or **высоко́)**—*think highly of oneself*

Актри́са мечта́ла о себе́ высоко́. *The actress thought very highly of herself.*

мешо́к—*sack*

мешо́к с соло́мой—*be dull-witted* (or *slow-witted)*

С Па́влом посове́товаться нельзя́, у него́ голова́—мешо́к с соло́мой. *It's not worth asking for Pavel's advice—he is so dull-witted.*

сиде́ть мешко́м—*hang loosely; be baggy; slouch around*

Но́вое пла́тье сиди́т мешко́м на А́нне. *The new dress hangs loosely on Anna.*

мешо́чек—*small bag*

яйцо́ в мешо́чек—*semi-hardboiled egg; three-minute egg*

На за́втрак я ем яйцо́ в мешо́чек. *I eat a three-minute egg for breakfast.*

миг—*moment*

ми́гом—*in no time*

Я ми́гом верну́сь. *I'll be back in no time.*

мизи́нец—*little finger*

не сто́ит мизи́нца—*cannot hold a candle to someone*

Брат не сто́ит мизи́нца сестры́. *The brother can't hold a candle to his sister.*

с мизи́нец; на мизи́нец—*hardly anything; next to nothing; almost nothing*

Его́ успе́хи с мизи́нец. *His successes amount to next to nothing.*

ми́лость—*favor; grace*

ми́лости про́сим—1.—SEE: **добро́ пожа́ловать**

сде́лай(те) ми́лость—*1. do me a favor 2. you are welcome*

1. Сде́лайте ми́лость, помоги́те мне. *Do me a favor—help me!*
2. «Мо́жно воспо́льзоваться ва́шей ру́чкой на мину́точку?»—" «Сде́лайте ми́лость, ско́лько хоти́те.» *"May I use your pen for a moment?"—"You're welcome to use it any time."*

скажи́(те) на ми́лость—*1. tell me, please 2. for Goodness' sake!*

1. Скажи́те на ми́лость, ско́лько вре́мени? *Tell me, please, what time is it?*
2. Скажи́те на ми́лость, ско́лько мо́жно издева́ться! *For Goodness' sake, how much mocking can one indulge in?*

ми́на—*mien; expression*

де́лать хоро́шую ми́ну при плохо́й игре́—*put up a bold front; put a good face on the matter*

Ната́ша зна́ла, что речь идёт о недоста́тках её му́жа, но она́ де́лала хоро́шую ми́ну при плохо́й игре́. *Natasha knew that they were talking about her husband's shortcomings, but she put up a bold front.*

мину́та—*minute*

без пяти́ мину́т—*be a step away from becoming something; one will become something very soon*

Ната́шин сын без пяти́ мину́т инжене́р. *Natasha's son is a step away from becoming an engineer.*

жить мину́той—*live for the present*

Не ду́мая о бу́дущем, И́горь жил мину́той. *Igor didn't think of the future—he was living for the moment.*

мину́та в мину́ту—*to the minute*

Он пришёл мину́та в мину́ту. *He arrived to the minute.*

одну́ мину́ту!—*just a minute! wait a minute!*

Одну́ мину́ту! Я сейча́с обслужу́ вас. *Just a minute! I'll serve you right away!*

сию́ мину́ту—*this very minute; at once*

Ты до́лжен заня́ться рабо́той сию́ мину́ту. *You've got to start working this very minute.*

с мину́ты на мину́ту (or **мину́тку** or **секу́нду**)—*any minute (now)*

С минýты на минýту он дóлжен прийтú. *He's got to arrive any minute.*

мир—*world; community*

идтú (or **ходúть) пó миру**—*live as a beggar; go begging*

Совсéм обеднéв, Сáша ходúл пó миру. *Entirely impoverished, Sasha went begging.*

не от мúра сегó—*live in a fool's paradise; live in one's own world*

Извéстный поэ́т Алексéй Петрóв был не от мúра сегó. *Alexey Petrov, the famous poet, lived in his own world.*

переверну́ть весь мир—SEE: **переверну́ть весь свет**

пустúть пó миру—*ruin someone completely*

Своúм пья́нством он пустúл пó миру свою́ семью́. *He ruined his family completely with his alcoholism.*

с мúру по нúтке—*a little bit from here and there*

Для оперáции мáльчику жúтели гóрода собрáли дéньги с мúру по нúтке. *The inhabitants of the town collected money for the boy's operation—a little bit from here and there.*

старó как мир—*as old as the hills*

Э́та истóрия старá как мир. *This story is old as the hills.*

мировáя—*peaceful settlement; amicable agreement*

пойтú на мировýю—*settle something among themselves; come to an amicable agreement*

Пóсле длúтельных разговóров стóроны пошлú на мировýю. *After long negotiations, the partners came to an amicable agreement.*

мнéние—*opinion*

расходúться во мнéниях—*disagree*

К сожалéнию, мы расхóдимся во мнéниях. *Unfortunately, we disagree.*

мно́го—*much*

ни мно́го ни ма́ло—*not less than*

За дом он уплати́л ни мно́го ни ма́ло: че́тверть миллио́на. *He paid no less than a quarter million for his house.*

моги́ла—*grave*

бра́тская моги́ла—*common grave*

Бе́дного Мо́царта похорони́ли в бра́тской моги́ле. *Poor Mozart was buried in a common grave.*

горба́того одна́ моги́ла испра́вит—*the leopard does not change its spots; boys will be boys*

Он то́лько что освободи́лся из тюрьмы́ и уже́ вору́ет. Да, горба́того одна́ моги́ла испра́вит. *Hardly had he gotten out of jail, he started to steal again. Well, the leopard doesn't change its spots.*

мо́жно—*can*

мо́жно сказа́ть—*so to say* (or *speak)*

Бори́с говори́л ма́ло, мо́жно сказа́ть, ничего́. *Boris said but little; almost nothing, so to speak.*

мозг—*brain*

быть с мозга́ми—*clever fellow*

Он с мозга́ми, по́этому он быстре́е устро́ится, чем други́е. *He is a clever fellow, so he can find jobs faster than others.*

дави́ть на мозги́—*put pressure on someone; try to brainwash someone*

Не дави́ на мозги́, я сам зна́ю, что мне ну́жно де́лать. *Don't put pressure on me, I know what to do by myself.*

мозги́ ва́рят—*have brains; have the smarts; be a smart cookie*

У Ма́ши мозги́ ва́рят, по́этому у неё прогре́сс в ли́чной жи́зни. *Masha is a smart cookie, that's why she's getting ahead in life.*

вправля́ть мозги́—*straighten someone out*

Оте́ц детя́м вправля́л мозги́. *Father straightened the kids out.*

раскúдывать (or **шевелúть) мозгáми**—*rack one's brain*

Над э́той проблéмой пришлóсь шевелúть мозгáми. *We had to rack our brains over this problem.*

мозóль—*corn*

наступúть на (любúмую) мозóль—*touch someone to the quick; touch a nerve*

Своúми выскáзываниями Пётр наступúл на мою́ любúмую мозóль. *With his outspokenness, Peter touched me to the quick.*

молодéц—*good boy; fine fellow*

молодéц к молодцу́—*all good to a man; be equally good* (or *outstanding)*

Моú брáтья молодéц к молодцу́. *My brothers are all equally outstanding.*

молодóй—*young*

мóлодо-зéлено—*unripe; green; wet behind the ears*

Моú дéти ещё мóлоды-зéлены, но со врéменем онú измéнятся. *My kids are still wet behind the ears, but with time they'll change.*

мóлодость—*youth*

не пéрвой мóлодости—*past one's prime; no spring chicken*

Мáша ужé не пéрвой мóлодости. *Masha is no spring chicken.*

молокó—*milk*

молокó на губáх не обсóхло—*be wet behind the ears; be a milksop; be a greenhorn*

Молокó на губáх не обсóхло, а он меня́ у́чит. *He's a mere greenhorn, yet he teaches me already!*

на молокé обжёгся, и на вóду ду́ет—*once bitten, twice shy*

Пóсле развóда он боя́лся встречáться с жéнщинами—обжёгшись на молокé, бу́дешь дуть и на вóду. *He was afraid to date women after his divorce—once bitten, twice shy.*

тóлько пти́чьего молокá нет—*there's everything under the sun; you name it*

Дéлать покýпки в Амéрике—прóсто прéлесть: тóлько пти́чьего молокá нет. *Shopping in the States is a real pleasure—there is everything under the sun.*

мóлот; молотóк—*hammer*

быть (or **находи́ться** or **попáсть) мéжду мóлотом и наковáльней**—*between the devil and the deep blue sea; between a rock and a hard place*

Мéжду мýжем и любóвником Áнна находи́лась как мéжду мóлотом и наковáльней. *Between her husband and her lover Anna felt caught between the devil and the deep blue sea.*

продавáть с молоткá—*sell by auction*

Стáрую карти́ну прóдали с молоткá. *The old picture was sold at an auction.*

молчáние—*silence*

обходи́ть молчáнием—*pass by* (or *over) in silence*

Он обошёл э́тот вопрóс молчáнием. *He passed by this question in silence.*

моме́нт—*moment*

в любо́й моме́нт—*any time; in any moment* (or *minute)*

Вулка́н мо́жет взорва́ться в любо́й моме́нт. *The volcano may erupt any minute.*

в моме́нт—*immediately*

«Я ва́шу о́бувь в моме́нт отремонти́рую»—сказа́л сапо́жник. *"I'll fix your shoes in a minute," said the shoe repair man.*

лови́ть (or **улучи́ть) моме́нт**—*seize the opportunity*

Разгова́ривая о бу́дущем, Бори́с улучи́л моме́нт и сде́лал А́нне предложе́ние. *Talking about the future, Boris seized the opportunity, and popped the question to Anna.*

упусти́ть моме́нт—*miss* (or *neglect) an opportunity*

Ива́н упусти́л моме́нт, что́бы жени́ться на америка́нской миллионе́рше. *Ivan missed the opportunity to marry the American millionairess.*

монасты́рь—*monastery*

в чужо́й монасты́рь со свои́м уста́вом не хо́дят—SEE: **с волка́ми жить, по-во́лчьи выть**

моне́та—*coin*

гони́ моне́ту!—*pay up!*

Ты мне до́лжен. Гони́ моне́ту! *You owe me! Pay up!*

оплати́ть той же моне́той—SEE: **ме́рить той же ме́рою; ме́рить в ту же ме́ру**

принима́ть за чи́стую моне́ту—*take at face value*

Ива́на легко́ обману́ть, он принима́ет всё за чи́стую моне́ту. *It's easy to cheat Ivan, he takes everything at face value.*

мо́ре—*sea*

мо́ре по коле́но (or **по коле́на)**—*be a dare-devil; nothing fazes one*

Он высо́вывается из окна́ на 80-ом этаже́—ему́ и мо́ре г коле́но. *He's leaning out the window on the 80th floor—he's dare-devil.*

ждать у мо́ря пого́ды; сиде́ть у мо́ря и ждать пого́ды—*b waiting for the plums to fall into one's mouth*

Лу́чше труди́ться, чем ждать у мо́ря пого́ды. *It's better to b working than to wait for the plums to fall into one's mouth.*

моро́з—*frost*

моро́з по ко́же (or **по спине́) дерёт** (or **пробега́ет)**—*it gives on the creeps; send shivers up and down ones's spine*

От стра́ха у Ири́ны моро́з по ко́же пробега́л. *Fear gave Irina th creeps.*

моро́з пробира́ет до косте́й—*be chilled to the bone*

В пургу́ нас моро́з пробра́л до косте́й. *We were chilled to th bone in the snowstorm.*

стои́т моро́з—*there's frost*

В январе́ моро́з стои́т на дере́вьях. *There's frost on the trees i January.*

Москва́—*Moscow*

не вдруг Москва́ стро́илась—*Rome was not built in a day*

Набери́сь терпе́ния, ведь Москва́ не сра́зу стро́илась. *B patient—(after all) Rome wasn't built in one day!*

моча́лка—*loofah*

жева́ть моча́лку (or **моча́ло)**—*keep repeating the same thing*

Разгово́р с Алексе́ем был неинтере́сен: он опя́ть жева́ моча́лку. *The discussion with Aleksey wasn't interesting—h keeps repeating the same thing.*

мочь—*power; might*

во всю мочь; из(о) всей мо́чи; что есть мо́чи—*with all one' might* (or *power); 1. as hard as one can 2. as fast as one can*

Боксёр уда́рил своего́ проти́вника изо всей мо́чи. *The boxer hit his opponent as hard as he could.*

Во всю мочь Алексе́й бежа́л от банди́тов. *Aleksey was running away from the bandits as fast as he could.*

мо́чи нет; мо́чи не ста́ло—*one can't endure* (or *stand) something*

Ле́том иногда́ так жа́рко, что мо́чи нет. *It can be so hot in the summer that one can't stand it.*

мошна́—*pouch; purse*

больша́я (or **то́лстая** or **туга́я**) **мошна́**—*be a fat purse*

О́льга променя́ла любо́вь на туѓую мошну́. *Olga traded in her love for a fat purse.*

наби́ть мошну́—*feather one's nest; line one's pocket; fill one's purse*

Обману́в свои́х партнёров, Ива́н наби́л мошну́. *Ivan feathered his nest by cheating his partners.*

тряхну́ть мошно́й—*spend one's money recklessly; throw money around*

На сва́дьбе Ма́ши оте́ц тряхну́л мошно́й. *Father spent money recklessly for Masha's wedding.*

мрак—*darkness*

кроме́шный мрак—*pitch-dark*

В пеще́ре стоя́л кроме́шный мрак. *It was pitch-dark inside the cave.*

покры́т(о) мра́ком неизве́стности—*shrouded in mystery*

Про́шлое Па́вла покры́то мра́ком неизве́стности. *Pavel's past is shrouded in mystery.*

мудрёный—*strange; odd*

(не) мудрено́; (не) мудрено́, что—*no wonder, that; small wonder that...*

Не мудрено́, что он тала́нтливый музыка́нт, в его́ семье́ все музыка́нты. *No wonder he is such a talented musician—everybody in his family is a musician.*

му́зыка—*music*

му́зыка не та; му́зыка друга́я—*it's a different story* (or *a horse of another color)*

Бори́с ра́ньше был транжи́рой, но с тех пор, как он жени́лся, му́зыка не та. *Boris used to spend money recklessly, but since his marriage it's been a different story.*

му́ка—*suffering*

му́ка му́ченическая—*torture; torment of hell; unbearable suffering*

Потеря́в сы́на на войне́, бе́дная А́нна переноси́ла му́ку му́ченическую. *When she lost her son in the war, poor Anna endured the torment of hell.*

мука́—*flour*

переме́лется—мука́ бу́дет—*things will be OK in the end; every cloud has a silver lining*

И́горь и О́льга поссо́рились. Чепуха́! Переме́лется—мука́ бу́дет. *Igor and Olga fell out with one another—Nothing to it! Things will be OK in the end.*

мура́шки—*ants; creeps; shivers*

мура́шки бе́гают (or **по́лзают) по спине́; мура́шки бе́гают** (or **по́лзают) по те́лу; покрыва́ться мура́шками**—SEE: **моро́з по ко́же дерёт** (or **пробега́ет)**

му́ха—*fly*

быть под му́хой—*have one drink too many; be three sheets to the wind*

На вечери́нке го́сти бы́ли под му́хой. *At the evening party the guests were three sheets to the wind.*

де́лать из му́хи слона́—*make a mountain out of a molehill*
На но́вом ме́сте рабо́ты Ива́н де́лал из му́хи слона́. *Ivan made a mountain out of a molehill at his new job.*

до бе́лых мух—*till the snow falls*
«С ката́нием на са́нках придётся ждать до бе́лых мух»—мать объясня́ла де́тям. *"You have to wait with the sleigh riding till the snow falls," the mother said to the children.*

(кака́я) му́ха укуси́ла?—*what's the matter with him?; what got into him?; what's eating him?*
Он так кричи́т... Кака́я му́ха его́ укуси́ла? *He's shouting so... What's the matter with him?*

слы́шно как му́ха пролети́т—*one might hear a pin drop*
В ко́мнате така́я тишина́, что слы́шно, как му́ха пролета́ет. *It's so quiet in the room that one might hear a pin drop.*

(то́чно) му́ху проглоти́л—*make* (or *pull) a sour* (or *wry) face*
Не получи́в чаевы́х, официа́нт то́чно му́ху проглоти́л. *Since he didn't get a tip, the waiter pulled a sour face.*

мысль—*idea*

без за́дней мы́сли—*without mental reservation; without an ulterior motive; without a secret purpose*

Он всегда́ говори́т, что ду́мает, без за́дней мы́сли. *He always says what he thinks without mental reservation.*

носи́ться с мы́слью—*cherish a thought; nurture a plan*

Са́ша всю жизнь носи́лся с мы́слью уе́хать в А́фрику, но так и не уе́хал. *Sasha nurtured the plan all his life to go to Africa, yet he never went.*

мытьё—*washing*

не мытьём, так ка́таньем—*by hook or by crook; no matter what; come hell or high water*

Мы на́шей це́ли дости́гнем не мытьём, так ка́таньем. *We'll reach our goal by hook or by crook.*

мышь—*mouse*

наду́лась как мышь на крупу́—*turn up one's nose at something; make a long face*

Я то́лько шути́л, а она́ наду́лась как мышь на крупу́. *I was merely joking, yet she turned up her nose at me.*

мя́гко—*softly*

мя́гко выража́ться—*to put it mildly; putting it mildly*

Его́ поведе́ние вчера́ бы́ло, мя́гко выража́ясь, неприли́чное. *His behavior yesterday was unbecoming, to put it mildly.*

Н

на—*on*

вот тебе́ и на!—*there goes nothing*

Вот тебе́ и на! У нас уже́ ни копе́йки не оста́лось. *There goes nothing! We haven't got a penny left!*

на все сто—*magnificently; excellently*

Ты сего́дня вы́глядишь на все сто. *You really look magnificent today!*

набóр—*recruitment; set*

набóр слов—*empty words; mere verbiage*

Его́ доклáд оказáлся не интерéсным выступлéнием, а набóром слов. *His report was not an interesting presentation—it was mere verbiage.*

наверняќа—*definitely*

бить наверняќа—*bet on a sure thing*

Ужé со стáрта Никńта бил наверняќа. *Nikita bet on a sure thing from the start.*

навсегдá—*for good*

раз (и) навсегдá—*once and for all; forever; for good*

Раз и навсегдá он покóнчил с курéнием. *He quit smoking for good.*

навстрéчу—*toward*

идтń навстрéчу—*be polite; be considerate toward someone*

Сáша всем шёл навстрéчу. *Sasha was considerate toward everyone.*

пойтń навстрéчу—*to meet halfway*

Пóсле длńтельных переговóров стóроны пошлń навстрéчу друг дрýгу. *After long discussions the parties met halfway.*

наготá—*nudity*

во всей (своéй) наготé—*showing one's true colors; revealing one's true nature*

Когдá Борńс стал начáльником, егó харáктер проявńлся во всей наготé. *When Boris became the boss, he showed his true colors.*

надéжда—*hope*

в надéжде—*hoping; expecting; expect; with the hope that*

В надéжде на сóлнечную погóду мы не взя́ли зóнтик. *Hoping the weather would be sunny we took no umbrella with us.*

возлага́ть наде́жды—*pin one's hopes on someone; place hope in someone*

Роди́тели возлага́ли наде́жды на свои́х дете́й. *The parents pinned their hopes on their children.*

льстить себя́ наде́ждой; пита́ть наде́жду (or **наде́жды**)—*entertain* (or *cherish) (a) hope(s)*

Я пита́л наде́жду на повыше́ние зарпла́ты. *I was entertaining hopes for a salary raise.*

подаёт наде́жду (or **наде́жды**)—*show great promise; have a promising future*

Ма́ленький сын моего́ сосе́да, тала́нтливо игра́ющий на скри́пке, подаёт наде́жды. *My neighbor's little boy who plays the violin so well, has a promising future.*

пусты́е наде́жды—*pie in the sky; pipe dream*

Мои́ пла́ны на бу́дущее оказа́лись пусты́ми наде́ждами. *My plans for the future turned out to be pie in the sky.*

на́до—*to have to*

о́чень мне на́до!—*what do I care?*

Жа́луется, что у него́ долги́. О́чень мне на́до! *He complains about his debts... What do I care?*

так вам и на́до!—*it serves someone right*

Из-за ле́ности его́ уво́лили. Так ему́ и на́до! *It serves him right that he was fired for his laziness.*

надыша́ться—*inhale; breath in*

не навы́шится; не мо́жет надыша́ться—*dote on* (or *upon)*

Ната́ша не мо́жет надыша́ться на своего́ ребёнка. *Natasha is doting on her baby.*

нажи́ть—*gain*

как на́жито, так и про́жито—*easy come, easy go*

Наслéдство Ивáн скóро растрáтил. Как нáжито, так и прóжито. *Ivan soon squandered his inheritance—easy come, easy go!*

наказáние—*punishment*

наказáние мне—*a pain in the neck*

Перестáнь кричáть! Наказáние мне с тобóй! *Stop yelling! You're a pain in the neck!*

сýщее наказáние!—*what a nuisance!*

Я опоздáл на пóезд. Сýщее наказáние! *I missed my train! What a nuisance!*

налёт—*raid*

с налёта; с налёту—*in one fell swoop*

Пётр отвечáл на все вопрóсы с налёту. *Peter answered all the questions in one fell swoop.*

намёк—*hint*

тóнкий намёк—*delicate hint*

При разговóре он сдéлал тóнкий намёк на мой долг. *During the course of the conversation he made a delicate hint at my indebtedness.*

тóнкий намёк на тóлстое обстоя́тельство—*hint at the obvious*

В пóзднее врéмя гость не уходи́л. Хозя́ин нáчал зевáть, и э́то был тóнкий намёк на тóлстое обстоя́тельство. *Late at night the guest hadn't left yet, and so the host started to yawn, hinting at the obvious.*

наобýм—*at random*

наобýм (Лáзаря)—*without using one brains; without thinking*

Прошý тебя́ серьёзно отнести́сь и не отвечáть наобýм. *Please take the question seriously and don't answer without thinking.*

напáсть—*attack*

не на тогó напáл—*underestimate one*

Он дýмал, что я емý повéрил. Не на тогó напáл. *He thought I believed him—he underestimated me.*

наплевáть—*spit*

мне наплевáть!—*I don't give a damn!*

Мне наплевáть, что онú обо мнé дýмают! *I don't give a damn what they think of me!*

напрáво—*to the right*

напрáво-налéво; напрáво и налéво—*to tell everybody and his dog; to the whole world; to every Tom, Dick and Harry*

Áнна расскáзывала о своéй любвú напрáво и налéво. *Anna told everybody and his dog about her love.*

напропалýю—*desperately*

идтú напропалýю—*decide to take desperate measures; act desperately*

Боя́сь банкрóтства, Пáвел шёл напропалýю. *Being afraid of bankruptcy, Pavel decided to take desperate measures.*

нарасхвáт—*be sold*

продавáться нарасхвáт—*sell like hot cakes*

Биле́ты на конце́рты Сти́нга продава́лись нарасхва́т. *The tickets for the Sting concert sold like hot cakes.*

покупа́ть нарасхва́т—*there is a great demand for something*

Кни́ги о жи́зни ца́рской семьи́ покупа́ют нарасхва́т. *There is a great demand for books about the life of the Czar's family.*

наро́д—*people*

вы́йти из наро́да—*be of humble origin*

Миллионе́р Арка́дий вы́шел из наро́да. *Arkady, the millionaire, was of humble origin.*

при (всём) (честно́м) наро́де; при всей честно́й компа́нии—*in public; in front of everyone*

Молодожёны держа́лись за ру́ки при всей честно́й компа́нии. *The newlyweds were holding hands in front of everyone.*

нару́жу—*outside*

всё нару́жу—*be very outspoken; be honest; wear one's heart on one's sleeve*

Он сли́шком и́скренен, у него́ всё нару́жу. *He's too sincere—he wears his heart on his sleeve.*

вы́йти нару́жу—*come to light; be revealed*

Тепе́рь вы́шло нару́жу, что у Бори́са была́ связь с ма́фией. *It came to light recently that Boris was mixed up with the Mafia.*

наряду́—*side by side*

наряду́ с э́тим—*at the same time*

Он был до́брым, но наряду́ с э́тим иногда́ груби́л. *He was a good man, but at the same time he was sometimes rude.*

наско́лько—*as far as*

насто́лько, наско́лько—*as much as*

Я ему́ помога́л насто́лько, наско́лько мо́жно бы́ло. *I helped him as much as I could.*

настáивать—*insist on*

настáивать на своём—*insist on having it one's own way*

Что бы я емý не предлагáл, он настáивал на своём. *No matter what I proposed to him, he insisted on having his own way.*

настроéние—*mood*

быть не в настроéнии—*be in low spirits; be out of sorts*

Пéред экзáменом Ивáн всегдá не в настроéнии. *Before an exam Ivan is always in low spirits.*

чемодáнное настроéние—*wanderlust; have itchy feet*

Ещё недéля до отъéзда, но у меня́ ужé чемодáнное настроéние. *There's still a week before my trip, but I've got itchy feet already.*

натýра—*nature*

ширóкая натýра—*have a generous nature*

Игорь чáсто нас приглашáет в ресторáн; у негó ширóкая натýра. *Igor often takes us out to a restaurant—he has a generous nature.*

начáло—*beginning*

вести́ начáло—*descend; derive from someone*

Егó семья́ ведёт начáло от Ивáна Грóзного. *His family descends from Ivan the Terrible.*

на рáвных начáлах—*equitably; on a par with someone*

Мы с коллéгами раздели́ли рабóту на рáвных начáлах. *My colleagues and I divided the work equitably.*

начáть—*begin*

начáть своё—*be back at one's old tricks; start in on something all over again*

Не обращáя внимáния ни на когó, Пáвел нáчал своё. *Without regard for anyone, Pavel started in on his old tricks all over.*

не—*not*

быть не по себé—*feel extremely uncomfortable; be on edge*

Когдá хозя́ин с хозя́йкой пререкáлись, гостя́м бы́ло не по себé. *When the host and the hostess fell out with one another, the guests felt extremely uncomfortable.*

не ахти́ какóй—*nothing spectacular; not too pretty*

Не ахти́ какóй у нас дом. *Our house is nothing spectacular.*

не без тогó—*in all probability; with reasonable certainty*

«Твоя́ сестрá с мýжем приéдет?»—«Не без тогó!» *"Will your sister be coming with her husband?"—"In all probability."*

нé за что—*don't mention it*

Когдá я поблагодари́л егó за пóмощь, он отвéтил: «Нé за что.» *When I thanked him for his help, he answered, "Don't mention it!"*

нéбо—*sky*

витáть мéжду нéбом и землёй—*be (up) in the clouds*

Вы́играв в лотерéю, Мáша витáла мéжду нéбом и землёй. *When Masha won the lottery she was up in the clouds.*

возноси́ть (or **превозноси́ть**) **до небéс**—*praise someone to high heaven*

Áнна возноси́ла до небéс своегó возлю́бленного. *Anna praised her lover to high heaven.*

как нéбо и земля́; отличáются как нéбо и земля́—*be different as day and night; have nothing in common*

Мои́ два брáта как нéбо и земля́. *My two brothers are different as day and night.*

нéбо с овчи́нку показáлось—*be scared out of one's wits*

Когдá уви́дел пожáр, мне нéбо с овчи́нку показáлось. *I was scared out of my wits when I saw the fire.*

под откры́тым нéбом—*out in the open; outdoors*

Боя́сь землетрясéния, мы спáли под откры́тым нéбом. *We slept out in the open as we were afraid of an earthquake.*

невéдение—*ignorance*

быть (or **пребывáть) в блажéнном невéдении**—*live in a fool's paradise*

Не знáя реáльной жи́зни, Пётр пребывáет в блажéнном невéдении. *Peter doesn't know real life—he lives in a fool's paradise.*

невéстка—*daughter-in-law* (son's wife); *sister-in-law* (brother's wife)

невéстке в отмéстку—*even the score; pay in kind*

Лéна не поздрáвила Ни́ну с днём рождéния, и Ни́на, невéстке в отмéстку, отвéтила тем же. *Lena didn't congratulate Nina on her birthday so Nina, to even the score, did the same.*

невозмóжность—*impossibility*

до невозмóжности—*to the last* (or *nth) degree*

Он надоéл мне до невозмóжности. *I was fed up with him to the nth degree.*

нéжность—*tenderness*

теля́чьи нéжности—*sloppy sentimentality; sentimental slop*

Аркáдий цéнит нéжность, но реши́тельно отвергáет теля́чьи нéжности. *Arkady appreciates tenderness, but he decidedly rejects sloppy sentimentality.*

не́куда—*nowhere; no place*

дева́ть не́куда—*have more than enough; not to know what to do with something*

Де́нег у него́ так мно́го, что дева́ть не́куда. *He's got so much money, he doesn't know what to do with it.*

нелёгкая

нелёгкая его́ сюда́ несёт!—*What on earth* (or *the devil) is he doing here?*

Уви́дев пре́жнего му́жа, А́нна пробормота́ла: «Нелёгкая его́ сюда́ несёт!» *Seeing her ex-husband Anna murmured, "What on earth is he doing here?"*

нельзя́—*should not; could not*

как нельзя́ лу́чше—*couldn't be better; in the best possible way*

Ива́н вы́полнил зада́чу как нельзя́ лу́чше. *Ivan fulfilled his task in the best possible way.*

нельзя́ ли—*may I?; would you permit me?; would you mind if...*

Нельзя́ ли откры́ть окно́? *Would you mind if I opened the window?*

нельзя́ не—*can't help but*

Нельзя́ не любова́ться его́ тала́нтом. *You can't help but admire his talent.*

нельзя́ сказа́ть, что́бы—*something cannot be said; something can hardly be said; you can't exactly call someone something*

Нельзя́ сказа́ть, что́бы он был у́мным. *You can't exactly call him smart.*

немно́го—*a bit; a while*

немно́го погодя́—*after a while*

Он вдруг замолча́л, но немно́го погодя́ продо́лжил свой расска́з. *He fell suddenly silent, but after a while he continued telling his story.*

нерв—*nerve*

дéйствовать на нéрвы; игрáть на нéрвах—*get on someone's nerves*

Начáльник чáсто игрáет на нéрвах свои́х подчинённых. *The boss frequently plays on the nerves of the employees under him.*

несчáстье—*misfortune*

двáдцать два несчáстья—*a walking catastrophe*

Николáй—это двáдцать два несчáстья. С ним кáждый день что-то случáется. *Nikolay is a walking catastrophe—every day something happens to him.*

нет—*no; not*

нет как нет—*not a sign of*

Погóды нет как нет. *There's no sign of good weather.*

нет-нет да и—*every once in a while*

Егó нет-нет, да и неожи́данно придёт. *Every once in a while he arrives unexpectedly.*

нет (тогó) чтóбы—*1. be reluctant to do something 2. not to have the slightest inclination to do something; not to even think of something*

1. Нет тогó, чтóбы Сáша пошёл рабóтать. *Sasha is reluctant to go to work.*
2. Нет тогó, чтóбы они́ переселя́лись из Москвы́ в дерéвню. *They haven't the slightest inclination to move to the village from Moscow.*

своди́ть на нет—*totally to destroy; eliminate*

Муж Óльги свёл свой брак на нет. *Olga's husband totally destroyed his marriage.*

сойти́ на нет—*to go up in smoke; become nothing*

Нáша дрýжба сошлá на нет. *Our friendship went up in smoke.*

нетерпéние—*impatience*

ждать с нетерпéнием—*look forward to; eagerly to await*

Я жду с нетерпéнием нáшу встрéчу. *I am eagerly awaiting our meeting.*

сгорáть от нетерпéния—*be dying to do something*

Никúта сгорáет от нетерпéния встрéтиться с подрýгой. *Nikita is dying to meet his girlfriend.*

нечáянность—*unexpectedness*

по нечáянности—*accidentally*

По нечáянности я нарýшил прáвила ýличного движéния. *Accidentally I committed a traffic violation.*

нéчто—*something*

нéчто врóде—*a sort of; a kind of*

Егó положéние нéчто врóде ночнóго стóрожа. *His job is a sort of night watchman.*

ни—*not*

ни в какýю—*under no circumstances*

Я ни в какýю зáмуж за Борúса не вы́йду. *I won't marry Boris under any circumstances.*

ни с тогó, ни сегó—*without rhyme or reason; for no reason*

Ни с тогó, ни с сегó он нáчал кричáть. *He started to yell for no rhyme or reason.*

ни то, ни сё—*neither fish nor fowl*

Ивáн ужé не ребёнок и ещё не взрóслый—получáется ни то, ни сё. *Ivan is not a little boy anymore and neither is he a grownup—he is neither fish nor fowl.*

нúтка; нить—*thread*

бéлыми нúтками шúто—*be easily seen through; be too thin; be too obvious*

Егó объяснéние бéлыми нúтками шúто. *His explanation was too obvious.*

вы́мокнуть до (послéдней) нúтки—*get soaked to the bone* (or *through and through)*

Попа́в под дождь, Ива́н вы́мок до после́дней ни́тки. *Ivan got soaked to the bone in the rain.*

как ни́тка с иго́лкой—*be inseparable*

Мари́я с му́жем как ни́тка с иго́лкой. *Maria and her husband are inseparable.*

на живу́ю ни́тку—*hastily; anyhow; helter-skelter; haphazardly*

Не име́я вре́мени, Бори́с вы́полнил рабо́ту на живу́ю ни́тку. *Boris did a haphazard job for lack of time.*

обобра́ть до ни́тки—*strip someone of everything*

Взло́мщики обобра́ли нас до ни́тки. *The burglars stripped us of everything.*

проходи́ть (or **тяну́ться) кра́сной ни́тью**—*stand out; run through; run like thread through*

Его́ глубо́кая ве́ра в бо́га прохо́дит кра́сной ни́тью в жи́зни. *His deep faith in God runs like a thread through his life.*

ни́точка—*thread*

разобра́ть по ни́точке—SEE: **разбира́ть по ко́сточкам**

ничего́—*all right*

ничего́ подо́бного!—*no way! under no circumstances!*

«Попро́бовал нарко́тики?»—«Ничего́ подо́бного!» *"Have you tried drugs?"—"No way!"*

ничего́ себе́—*so-so; nothing special; not too bad*

Моя́ рабо́та ничего́ себе́. *My work is nothing special.*

нога́—*foot*

быть на коро́ткой ноге́—*be on friendly terms with one*

С пе́рвой мину́ты знако́мства я с ним на коро́ткой ноге́. *From the first moment we met we were on friendly terms.*

быть (or **стоя́ть) на ра́вной ноге́**—*regard* (or *treat*) *someone as an equal*

Дире́ктор со мной на ра́вной ноге́. *The director treats me as an equal.*

в нога́х пра́вды нет—*give one's feet a rest*

Хозя́ин сказа́л нам: «Сади́тесь, пожа́луйста, в нога́х пра́вды нет.» *"Sit down, give your feet a rest," the host said.*

вста́ть не с той ноги́; вста́ть с ле́вой ноги́—*get out of bed on the wrong side*

Сего́дня Ири́на всем недово́льна; ка́жется, что она́ вста́ла с ле́вой ноги́. *Irina is unsatisfied with everything today—seems she got out on the wrong side of the bed.*

жить на широ́кую но́гу—*live in grand style*

Получи́в насле́дство, Бори́с живёт на широ́кую но́гу. *Having gotten his inheritance, Boris is living in a grand style.*

идти́ (or **шага́ть**) **нога́ в но́гу**—*keep abreast of (or apace with) something*

С измене́нием мо́ды я иду́ нога́ в но́гу. *I keep abreast of the changing fashions.*

лиза́ть но́ги—*lick someone's boots* (or *feet*); *basely to flatter someone*

В интере́сах своего́ повыше́ния Пётр ли́жет но́ги своему́ нача́льнику. *In order to ensure his advancement, Peter is licking his boss's boots.*

меша́ться под нога́ми—*be in one's way*

Ко́шка всегда́ меша́ется под нога́ми у Ма́ши в ку́хне. *The cat's always in Masha's way in the kitchen.*

смотре́ть под но́ги—*watch one's step*

Смотри́ под но́ги, что́бы не упа́сть. *Watch your step so that you don't fall!*

спать без за́дних ног—*sleep like a log*

От уста́лости шахтёр спал без за́дних ног. *Exhausted, the miner slept like a log.*

тяжёл(ый) на́ ногу—*have trouble walking*

На ста́рости лет де́душка стал тяжёлым на́ ногу. *In his old age the grandfather had trouble with his walking.*

что ле́вая нога́ хо́чет (or **захо́чет**)—*whatever one pleases*

Что у избало́ванной де́вочки ле́вая нога́ захо́чет, роди́тели всё испо́лнят. *Whatever the spoiled little girl pleases, her parents do for her.*

но́готь—*nail*

от (or **с**) **молоды́х ногте́й**—*from early childhood on*

От молоды́х ногте́й Са́ша люби́л му́зыку. *Sasha has loved music from early childhood on.*

нож—*knife*

без ножа́ ре́зать (or **заре́зать**)—*get one into a fix; do someone in*

Арка́дий вложи́л де́ньги в фи́рму, и партнёр его́ без ножа́ заре́зал, присво́ив себе́ де́ньги. *Arkady invested money into the business. His partner expropriated it and thereby got Arkady into a fix.*

быть на ножа́х—*be at loggerheads; be bitterly at odds*

Мы поспо́рили и сейча́с на ножа́х. *We fell out with one another and now we are at loggerheads.*

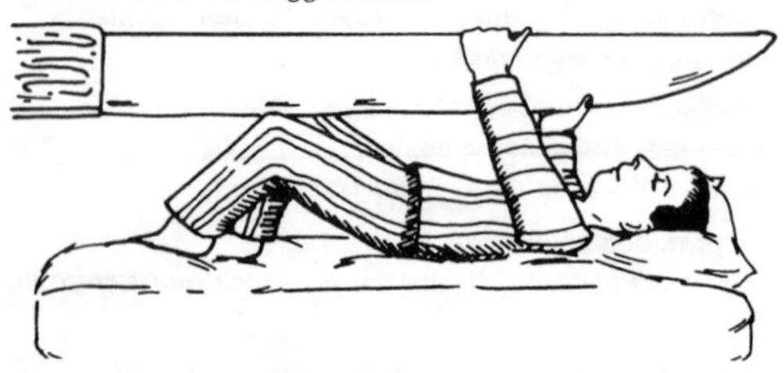

лечь под нож—*have an operation*

В го́спитале мне пришло́сь лечь под нож. *I had to have an operation in the hospital.*

ноль or **нуль**—*zero*

ноль без па́лочки—*a big zero; nobody; small fry*

Хотя́ мой нача́льник ду́мает высоко́ о себе́, он ноль без па́лочки. *Although my boss thinks very highly of himself, he's actually a big zero.*

свести́ к нулю́—*to destroy; reduce to nothing*

Полити́ческие собы́тия свели́ на́ши пла́ны к нулю́. *The political events reduced our plans to nothing.*

стричь под ноль—*give someone a close-cropped haircut*

Парикма́хер стриг под ноль во́лосы Ива́на. *The barber gave Ivan a close-cropped haircut.*

но́мер—*number*

на оди́ннадцатом но́мере; оди́ннадцатым но́мером—*on one's own two feet*

Так как у меня́ автомоби́ля нет, я езжу́ на оди́ннадцатом но́мере. *Since I have no car I travel on my own two feet.*

нос—*nose*

води́ть за́ нос—*lead one down the garden path; make a fool of someone*

Пётр не заме́тил, что его́ во́дят за́ нос. *Peter didn't notice that he was made a fool of.*

вороти́ть нос; крути́ть но́сом—*sneeze at; turn one's nose up at something*

Что я Ната́ше не предлага́ю, она́ кру́тит но́сом. *Whatever I offer Natasha, she turns her nose up at it.*

держа́ть нос по ве́тру—*know which way the wind is blowing*

Васи́лию при любо́й вла́сти хорошо́, потому́ что он уме́ет держа́ть нос по ве́тру. *Vasily does well under any rule whatsoever—he knows which way the wind is blowing.*

коро́че воробьи́ного но́са—*very short; very small*

Э́та исто́рия коро́че воробьи́ного но́са. *This is a very short story.*

на носу́—*close at hand; round the corner; face to face*

Её ро́ды на носу́. *Her time of delivery is close at hand.*

нóса не покáзывать—*not to show up; be a no-show*
На собрáнии Никúта нóса не покáзывал. *Nikita was a no-show at the meeting.*

нос к нóсу—*eyeball to eyeball*
Мы стоя́ли с врагóм нос к нóсу. *We were facing the enemy eyeball to eyeball.*

нос не дорóс—*be wet behind the ears*
Ещё нос не дорóс у мáльчика, а ужé женúться хóчет. *The boy is still wet behind the ears but he wants to get married already.*

нос с пу́говкой—*pug nose*
У дéвочки нос с пу́говкой. *The little girl has a pug nose.*

подня́ть нос—*put on airs*
Пóсле побéды чемпиóн подня́л нос. *The champion put on airs after his victory.*

чу́ять нóсом—SEE: **ню́хом чу́ять** (or **чу́вствовать)**

нóта—*note*

всё прошлó как по нóтам—*everything went A-OK (*or *swimmingly* or *smoothly)*
На венчáнии всё прошлó как по нóтам. *Everything went A-OK at the wedding.*

говорúть как по нóтам—*talk a blue streak*
По-рýсски Áнна говорúт как по нóтам. *Anna can talk a blue streak in Russian.*

ночь—*night*

всю ночь напролёт—*all night long*
Всю ночь напролёт мы гуля́ли на берегу́ мóря. *We were walking by the seaside all night long.*

нá ночь—*before going to bed*
Нá ночь я прúнял снотвóрную таблéтку. *I took a sleeping pill before going to bed.*

нюх—*smell*

ни за нюх табаку́; ни за поню́шку табаку́—*for nothing; senselessly; in vain*

Не ходи́ но́чью в парк, ина́че пропадёшь ни за поню́шку табаку́. *Don't walk in the park at night—otherwise you'll perish senselessly.*

ню́хом чу́ять (or **чу́вствовать); чу́ять но́сом**—*know* (or *realize) something instinctively*

При пе́рвой встре́че Васи́лий ню́хом почу́ял, что Пётр—нече́стный челове́к. *During their first encounter Vasily realized instinctively that Peter is a dishonest person.*

соба́чий нюх—*extraordinary nose for something; be able to sniff something out*

У не́которых полице́йских соба́чий нюх на престу́пников. *Some cops can sniff criminals out.*

О

обе́д—*dinner*

дома́шние обе́ды—*home-cooked meals*

В на́шем рестора́не продаю́тся дома́шние обе́ды. *Home-cooked meals are served in our restaurant.*

обе́дня—*mass*

испо́ртить (всю) обе́дню—*spoil someone's game; foil one's plot*

Заме́тив хи́трость продавца́, покупа́тель испо́ртил ему́ обе́дню. *The customer noticed the salesman's underhandedness and foiled his plot.*

оби́да—*insult*

не дать в оби́ду—*stand up for someone*

Мать не дала́ в оби́ду свои́х дете́й. *The mother stood up for her children.*

обиня́к

без обиняко́в—*in plain terms; without beating around the bush*

Ива́н всегда́ говори́т без обиняко́в. *Ivan always talks without beating around the bush.*

о́блако—*cloud*

быть (or **вита́ть) в облака́х; уноси́ться в облака́**—*be up in the clouds; be unrealistic; be a rainbow chaser*

Пётр ве́чно в облака́х. *Peter is always up in the clouds.*

(как) с облако́в—*like lightning out of the clear blue sky*

Я давно́ не слы́шал о Ма́ше, и вдруг она́ появи́лась как с облако́в. *I haven't heard about Masha for a long time, and suddenly she appeared like lightning out of the clear blue sky.*

о́бласть—*province; field*

отойти́ в о́бласть преда́ния (or **воспомина́ний)**—*be condemned to oblivion* (or *obscurity)*

И́мя а́втора э́тих стихо́в отошло́ в о́бласть преда́ния. *The name of the author of these poems has been condemned to obscurity.*

оборо́т—*turn; circulation*

пуска́ть де́ньги в оборо́т—*invest money*

Мой дя́дя—бога́тый фабрика́нт, но у него́ никогда́ нет де́нег, так как он пуска́ет их в оборо́т. *My uncle is a rich factory owner, but he never has any money because he keeps investing it.*

о́браз—*portrayal; kind*

каки́м о́бразом?—*how?*

Каки́м о́бразом вы попа́ли сюда́? *How did you ever get here?*

не́которым о́бразом—*to a certain degree; in a way; to a certain extent*

Ива́н не́которым о́бразом прав. *Ivan is right to a certain extent.*

никаки́м (or **нико́им) о́бразом**—*under no circumstances; by no means*

Никаки́м о́бразом я с ва́ми не согла́сен. *By no means do I agree with you.*

о́браз жи́зни—*way of life*

Мне о́чень нра́вится америка́нский о́браз жи́зни. *I am very pleased with the American way of life.*

потеря́ть (or **утра́тить) о́браз челове́ческий**—*drop out of the human race; behave like an animal*

От гне́ва Па́вел потеря́л о́браз челове́ческий. *In his anger Pavel behaved like an animal.*

таки́м о́бразом—*in that way; thus*

Он ве́рил в на́чатое де́ло и таки́м о́бразом дости́г це́ли. *He believed in the cause and thus he achieved his goal.*

обстоя́тельство—*circumstance*

гля́дя (or **смотря́) по обстоя́тельствам**—*according to the circumstances*

Поступа́й смотря́ по обстоя́тельствам. *Act according to the circumstances.*

о́бщий—*common*

в о́бщем (и це́лом)—*all in all; on the whole*

В о́бщем, наш разгово́р получи́лся прия́тный. *Our conversation was a pleasant one all in all.*

обя́занность—*duty*

как по обя́занности—*willy-nilly; reluctantly*

Он отвеча́л на мои́ вопро́сы, как по обя́занности. *He answered my questions willy-nilly.*

обыкнове́ние—*habit*

по обыкнове́нию—*as usual*

По обыкнове́нию мой дя́дя Ива́н встал ра́но. *As usual, my uncle Ivan got up early.*

овладе́ть—*take posssession*

овладе́ть собо́й—*get hold of oneself; pull oneself together*

Не ка́ждому дано́ овладе́ть собо́й в тру́дной ситуа́ции. *Not everyone can get hold of himself in a difficult situation.*

óвощ—*vegetables*

вся́кому óвощу своё врéмя—*there is a time to sow and a time to reap; everything in its own good time*

Зачéм торопи́ться с·жени́тьбой? Вся́кому óвощу своё врéмя. *Why rush into marriage? Everything in its own good time.*

овчи́нка—*sheepskin*

овчи́нка вы́делки не стóит—*not to be worth the effort* (or *trouble)*

Ремонти́ровать таку́ю стáрую маши́ну—овчи́нка вы́делки не стóит. *It's not worth the effort to repair such an old car.*

оглашéние—*publication*

не подлежáть оглашéнию—*confidential*

«Э́ти фáкты не подлежáт оглашéнию»—стрóго сказáл адвокáт. *"These facts are confidential," the lawyer said severely.*

огонёк—*(small) light*

с огонькóм—*with zest*

В отли́чие от други́х, Михаи́л всегдá рабóтает с огонькóм. *Unlike others, Mikhail always works with zest.*

огóнь—*fire*

боя́ться когó **как огня́**—*be scared to death of someone*

Пáвел бои́тся Бори́са как огня́. *Pavel is scared to death of Boris.*

готóв пойти́ в огóнь и в вóду—*be ready to go through fire and water*

За свои́х детéй О́льга готóва пойти́ в огóнь и в вóду. *Olga is ready to go through fire and water for her kids.*

из огня́ да в пóлымя—*out of the frying pan into the fire*

В результáте своегó вторóго брáка Михаи́л попáл из огня́ да в пóлымя. *With his second marriage, Mikhail jumped out of the frying pan and into the fire.*

мéжду двýх огнéй—SEE: **быть** (or **находи́ться** or **попáсть**) **мéжду мóлотом и наковáльней**

пройти́ сквозь ого́нь и во́ду (и ме́дные тру́бы)—*go through thick and thin; go through fire and water; to have seen a lot; have been through a lot*

За свою́ жизнь стари́к прошёл сквозь ого́нь и во́ду. *The old man has been through a lot in his lifetime.*

огорче́ние—*grief*

к моему́ вели́кому огорче́нию—*much to my regret*

К моему́ вели́кому огорче́нию на́ша пое́здка не состоя́лась. *Much to my regret, our trip fell through.*

одёжка—*clothes*

по одёжке протя́гивай но́жки—*cut your coat to fit your cloth; live within one's means*

Я не дам тебе́ бо́льше взаймы́, а посове́тую: по одёжке протя́гивай но́жки. *I won't loan you any more money and suggest that you cut your coat to fit your cloth.*

оди́н—*one; alone*

(все) как оди́н—*to a man*

Все как оди́н ста́ли на защи́ту ро́дины. *They rose to their country's defense to a man.*

оди́н (вслед) за други́м—*single file; in a queue*

Мы вошли́ в дом оди́н за други́м. *We entered the house single file.*

оди́н на оди́н—*face to face; privately; one on one*

Он ча́сто говори́т со мно́й оди́н на оди́н о свои́х пробле́мах. *He often talks to me about his problems face to face.*

оди́н-оди́н; оди́н-одинёшенек—*all alone*

По́сле сме́рти жены́ стари́к оста́лся оди́н-одинёшенек. *After his wife's death the old man remained all alone.*

оди́н про Фому́, друго́й про Ерёму—*be at cross-purposes*

Оди́н про Фому́, друго́й про Ерёму—так они́ друг дру́га не понима́ли. *They couldn't understand one another as they kept being at cross-purposes.*

одно́ и то же—*same thing*

Одно́ и то же он повторя́л без конца́. *He kept repeating the same thing without end.*

ожида́ние—*waiting; expectation*

сверх вся́ких ожида́ний—*beyond all expectations*

Сверх вся́ких ожида́ний Ива́н получи́л золоту́ю меда́ль. *Ivan won a gold medal beyond all expectations.*

о́ко—*eye*

о́ко за о́ко—SEE: **зуб за зуб**

окруже́ние—*environment; surroundings*

в окруже́нии—*accompanied by; in the company of; together with someone*

Мы провели́ ве́чер в окруже́нии друзе́й. *We spent the evening in the company of our friends.*

о́пера—*opera*

из (совсе́м) друго́й о́перы; не из той о́перы—*that's a horse of another color; that's (quite) a different matter; sing a different tune*

Вчера́ мы договори́лись, а то, что вы сейча́с говори́те, совсе́м из друго́й о́перы. *We had agreed yesterday—and now you're singing quite a different tune!*

о́пыт—*experience*

нау́ченный го́рьким о́пытом—*learned the hard way*

Нау́ченный го́рьким о́пытом, Бори́с стара́лся не де́лать оши́бок. *Boris made an effort not to commit the same errors he learned to avoid the hard way.*

опя́ть—*again*

опя́ть два́дцать пять!—*the same thing over and over again*

Де́душка говори́т о войне́—опя́ть два́дцать пять! *Grandpa is talking about the war—the same thing over and over again.*

орёл—*eagle*

орёл или ре́шка?—*heads or tails?*

Подбро́сив моне́ту, Оле́г сказа́л: «Орёл или ре́шка?» *Oleg tossed the coin and cried, "Heads or tails?"*

оре́х—*nut*

бу́дет (or **доста́нется) на оре́хи**—*be called on the carpet; be dragged over the coals*

Е́сли оте́ц узна́ет о мое́й прока́зе, бу́дет мне на оре́хи. *When Dad finds out about my mischief, I'll be called on the carpet.*

оре́шек (or **оре́х) не по зуба́м**—*hard nut to crack*

Э́та рабо́та оказа́лась для Ива́на оре́шком не по зуба́м. *This job seemed a hard nut to crack for Ivan.*

осёл—*donkey; ass*

как осёл упрётся—SEE: **как бара́н упрётся**

о́сень—*autumn; fall*

глубо́кая о́сень—*late fall*

Глубóкой óсенью погóда обы́чно прохлáдная. *The weather is usually cool in the late fall.*

оскóмина—*nausea*

наби́ть оскóмину—*be fed up with*

Свои́ми расскáзами Пáвел наби́л нам оскóмину. *We were fed up with Pavel's stories.*

основáние—*basis*

до основáния—*1. entirely 2. to the bottom of one's soul; deep down where it really counts*

1. До основáния мы уничтóжили врагá. *We wiped out the enemy entirely.*
2. Извéстие потряслó егó до основáния. *The events shook him to the bottom of his soul.*

на основáнии—*on the grounds; according to*

Правосýдие ведётся вообщé на основáнии закóнов. *In general, justice is supposed to be handed down according to the law.*

с пóлным основáнием—*with good reason; have a good reason to do something*

Он затрóнул вопрóс с пóлным основáнием. *He had a good reason to bring up the issue.*

основнóй—*basic*

в основнóм—*basically; by and large; mainly; on the whole*

В основнóм я с ним соглáсна. *On the whole I agree with him.*

осóба—*person*

своéй (сóбственной) осóбой—*in person*

Он предстáл пéред судóм своéй сóбственной осóбой. *He showed up in court in person.*

оставáться—*remain; stay*

счастли́во оставáться!—*take care!; good luck!*

При прощáнии Михаил сказáл: «Счастлúво оставáться!» *"Take care!" Mikhail said in parting.*

останóвка—*stop; stoppage*

останóвка за кем-лúбо; чем-лúбо—*nothing holds back one but...*

Я бы охóтно переселúлся в Австрáлию, но останóвка за рабóтой. *I would gladly move to Australia—nothing holds me back but my job.*

острóта—*sharpness; witticism*

отпускáть (or **сы́пать**) **острóты**—*crack jokes*

На вечерúнке мы отпускáли острóты. *We were cracking jokes during the evening party.*

удáчная острóта—*good joke*

Удáчная острóта развеселúла нас. *We were cheered up by a good joke.*

отбóй—*retreat*

отбóю (or **отбóя**) **нет**—*there's no end to something*

А́нна такáя красúвая, что отбóя нет от женихóв. *Anna is so beautiful that there's no end to the suitors.*

отвéт—*answer*

(быть) в отвéте; держáть отвéт—*be responsible; answer for something*

Кáждый дóлжен держáть отвéт за свои постýпки. *Everyone has to be responsible for his/her own actions.*

ни отвéта ни привéта—*there is no word from anybody*

Погостúв у нас, друзья уéхали—и ни отвéта ни привéта. *After staying with us as our guests, our friends left and there is no word from them.*

ответственность—*responsibility*

под ответственность—*let it be one's responsibility; one will answer for something*

Дайте Николаю ключи под мою ответственность. *Give Nikolay the keys, I'll answer for them.*

отвод—*leading; taking*

для отвода глаз—*in order to divert attention*

Для отвода глаз у Бориса была фирма, но в основном он занимался контрабандой. *Boris had a firm as a front, but in reality he was a smuggler.*

отказ—*refusal*

без отказа—*run smoothly* (or *perfectly*)

Мои новые часы работают без отказа. *My new watch runs perfectly.*

до отказа—*to capacity; to the bursting point*

Стадион был полон, народу было до отказа. *The stadium was filled with people to the bursting point.*

отказать—*refuse*

нельзя отказать в чём-либо—*you can't deny something*

Ивану нельзя отказать в природном таланте. *There's no denying that Ivan is talented.*

отказать наотрез—*refuse point-blank*

Пётр не хотел работать со мной и отказался наотрез от моего предложения. *Peter didn't want to work with me and so refused my proposal point-blank.*

отношение—*attitude; respect*

в некотором отношении—*in a way*; *in a certain respect*

В некотором отношении Игорь был прав. *Igor was right in a certain respect.*

халатное отношение—*carelessness*

Хала́тное отноше́ние к рабо́те нетерпи́мо. *Carelessness is not tolerated at work.*

оторва́ть—*tear off*

оторва́ть от себя́ (or **от се́рдца**)—*deprive oneself of something; forego something; tear off; tear away*

«От себя́ отрыва́ю!»—сказа́л Никола́й и протяну́л дру́гу после́днюю сигаре́ту. *"I'll forego this one," Nikolay said and handed his last cigarette to his friend.*

отста́вка—*dismissal, resignation*

дава́ть отста́вку—*give the axe; break up with someone*

За неде́лю до сва́дьбы Ле́на дала́ отста́вку своему́ жениху́. *One week before the wedding Lena gave her fiancé the axe.*

получа́ть отста́вку—*get the axe; get dumped*

Серге́й получи́л отста́вку от свое́й неве́сты за неве́рность. *Sergey was given the axe by his fiancée because of his infidelity.*

отсу́тствие—*absence*

блиста́ть свои́м отсу́тствием—*be conscpicuous by one's absence*

Зна́я, что его́ бу́дут критикова́ть, Са́ша блиста́л свои́м отсу́тствием на собра́нии. *Knowing he would be criticized, Sasha was conspicuous by his absence from the meeting.*

отчего́—*why*

отчего́ да почему́—*whys and wherefores*

По́сле несча́стного слу́чая мы задава́ли вопро́сы отчего́ да почему́. *We asked a lot of whys and wherefores after the accident.*

отчего́-то—*for some reason or (an)other*

Отчего́-то сего́дня Ири́на не в настрое́нии. *For some reason or another, Irina is in a bad mood today.*

отчёт—*account*

отдава́ть себе́ отчёт—*realize*

Мáльчик укрáл велосипéд, но бы́ло я́сно, что он так и не отдавáл себé отчёта в том, что сдéлал. *The little boy stole the bicycle, but it was evident that he didn't realize what he had done.*

охóта—*desire; inclination*

отби́ть охóту—*discourage*

Авиациóнная катастрóфа отби́ла у меня́ охóту летáть. *The air crash discouraged me from flying.*

охóта пýще невóли—*work isn't hard if you enjoy it.*

Меня́ всегдá удивля́ет, как мóжет Олéг выполня́ть такýю тяжёлую рабóту с огонькóм. Очеви́дно, охóта пýще невóли. *I was always surprised how Oleg can do such heavy work enthusiastically—evidently work isn't hard if you enjoy it.*

что за охóта?—*what's the use of something*

Что за охóта гуля́ть под дождём? *What's the use of walking in the rain?*

óчередь—*line; turn*

в свою́ óчередь—*in due course*

В свою́ óчередь Бори́с подари́л Áнне обручáльное кольцó. *Boris gave Anna an engagement ring in due course.*

стоя́ть на óчереди—*be on the waiting list*

Эмигрáнты стоя́ли на óчереди на получéние субсиди́рованной кварти́ры. *The immigrants were on the waiting list for subsidized apartments.*

очи́стка; очищéние—*cleaning*

для очи́стки (or **очищéния**) **сóвести**—*for conscience's sake; to set one's mind at ease*

Для очи́стки сóвести я передáл нáйденную сýмму в поли́цию. *For conscience's sake, I handed over the money I found to the police.*

очки́—*glasses*

втира́ть очки́—*pull the wool over one's eyes*

Свои́ми обеща́ниями Пётр втира́л мне очки́. *Peter pulled the wool over my eyes with his promises.*

смотре́ть сквозь ро́зовые очки́—*see* (or *look) through rose-colored glasses*

Ма́ша смотре́ла на жизнь сквозь ро́зовые очки́. *Masha was looking at life through rose-colored glasses.*

очко́—*point*

дава́ть де́сять очко́в вперёд—*outdo someone a great deal; beat someone by a mile*

Чемпио́н дал де́сять очко́в вперёд остальны́м шахмати́стам. *The champion beat the other chess players by a mile.*

П

па́ва—*peahen (*female of the peacock*)*

ни па́ва, ни воро́на—*neither fish nor fowl*

Как врач Бори́с сла́бый, как поэ́т он натала́нтлив—получа́ется ни па́ва, ни воро́на. *As a doctor Boris is poor; as a poet he's got no talent—it follows that he is neither fish nor fowl.*

пай—*share*

на пая́х—*on an equal footing; going shares*

Партнёры дели́ли при́быль фи́рмы на ра́вных пая́х. *The partners in the firm divided up the profits on an equal footing.*

па́лец—*finger*

вы́сосать из па́льца—*fabricate; dream* (or *make) something up*

Ле́на ча́сто выса́сывает исто́рии из па́льца, что́бы очерни́ть други́х. *Lena often makes up stories in order to denigrate others.*

гляде́ть (or **смотре́ть) сквозь па́льцы**—*turn a blind eye*
Ива́н смотре́л сквозь па́льцы на пробле́мы други́х. *Ivan turned a blind eye to the problems of others.*

зна́ть как свой пять па́льцев—*know like the palm of one's hand*
Бори́с го́род знал как свой пять па́льцев. *Boris knew the town like the palm of his hand.*

па́лец о па́лец не уда́рить; па́льцем не шевельну́ть; па́льца не разогну́ть—*not to stir* (or *lift) a finger*
Пётр па́лец о па́лец не уда́рил, что́бы оказа́ть по́мощь. *Peter didn't lift a finger to help.*

па́лец в рот не клади́—*watch your step with someone; be careful with someone*
Нача́льнику па́лец в рот не клади́. *Watch your step with the boss!*

попа́сть па́льцем в не́бо—*be way off the mark; miss the point by a mile*
«Где нахо́дится о́стров Гава́йи?»—«В А́фрике, коне́чно!»—«Попа́л па́льцем в не́бо!» *"Where are the Hawaiian islands?"—"Surely, in Africa."—"You're way off the mark!"*

па́лка—*stick*

вставля́ть па́лки в колёса—*put a spoke in the wheel; hinder someone* or *something*

Нача́льник ненави́дел Петра́ и всегда́ вставля́л ему́ па́лки в колёса. *Peter's boss hated him and he always put a spoke in his wheel.*

па́лка о двух конца́х—*double-edged sword*

Не́нависть—э́то па́лка о двух конца́х. *Hatred is a double-edged sword.*

перегиба́ть па́лку—*go too far*

Свои́ми тре́бованиями Ива́н перегиба́л па́лку, за что и поплати́лся. *Ivan went too far with his demands and so he had to pay for it.*

па́мять—*memory*

ве́чная па́мять—*may one's memory live forever*

Ве́чная па́мять геро́ям! *Eternal memory to the heroes!*

вы́лететь (or **вы́скочить**) **из па́мяти**—*slip one's memory*

Фами́лия э́того челове́ка вы́скочила у меня́ из па́мяти. *The surname of this man slipped my memory.*

де́вичья (or **кури́ная**) **па́мять**—*bad* (or *poor) memory*

У меня́ де́вичья па́мять. *I've got a poor memory.*

говори́ть по па́мяти; знать на па́мять—*recite* (or *know) by heart*

Актёр зна́ет на па́мять всего́ «Евге́ния Оне́гина.» *The actor can recite all of "Evgeny Onegin" by heart.*

заруби́ть в па́мяти—*memorize well; commit to memory thoroughly*

Я заруби́л в па́мяти са́мые ва́жные номера́ телефо́нов. *I memorized the most important telephone numbers.*

люби́ть без па́мяти—*be head over heels in love; be crazy about one*

Молодожёны люби́ли друг дру́га без па́мяти. *The newlyweds were head over heels in love with one another.*

на па́мять—*remember by something*

О́льга подари́ла мне на па́мять свою́ фотогра́фию. *Olga gave me a picture of herself to remember her by.*

по ста́рой па́мяти—*for old times' sake*

Проходя́ ми́мо витри́ны, по ста́рой па́мяти я посмотре́л игру́шечную желе́зную доро́гу. *Passing by I looked at the toy trains in the shop window for old times' sake.*

пан—*Polish landowner; gentleman*

ли́бо пан, ли́бо пропа́л; пан и́ли пропа́л—*all or nothing*

Когда́ И́горь взя́лся за сомни́тельное де́ло, он сказа́л: «Пан и́ли пропа́л». *When Igor started a dubious business, he said, "It's all or nothing!"*

пар—*steam*

на всех пара́х—*at full* (or *top) speed; at full steam*

У нас рабо́та идёт на всех пара́х. *Our work is progressing at full speed.*

па́ра—*pair*

па́ра пустяко́в—*a mere trifle; kid's play*

То, что мне тру́дно, друго́му мо́жет быть па́ра пустяко́в. *Things that are hard for me can be kid's play for someone else.*

педа́ль—*pedal*

нажима́ть на все педа́ли—*pull out all the stops; do one's utmost*

Ники́та нажима́л на все педа́ли, что́бы доби́ться це́ли. *Nikita pulled out all the stops in order to meet his objective.*

пелена́—*shroud*

как бы (or **сло́вно** or **то́чно**) **пелена́ с глаз упа́ла**—*scales fell from one's eyes*

Когда́ я узна́л от О́льги пра́вду, у меня́ то́чно пелена́ с глаз упа́ла. *The scales fell from my eyes when I learned the truth from Olga.*

пе́на—*foam; spume*

дока́зывать с пе́ной у рта—*argue* (or *insist on) furiously* (or *very aggressively)*

Йгорь дока́зывал свою́ правоту́ с пе́ной у рта. *Igor was insisting on being right very aggressively.*

пе́рвый—*first*

пе́рвый и после́дний—*the only one*

Мой брат Па́вел для меня́ пе́рвый и после́дний ро́дственник. *My brother Pavel is my only relative.*

пе́рво-на́перво—*first of all*

Прие́хав в го́род, мы пе́рво-на́перво ста́ли иска́ть гости́ницу. *When we hit town, first of all we looked for a hotel.*

перево́д—*translation; transfer*

нет перево́да (or **перево́ду**)—*there's no end to something*

Ско́лько рабо́ты мы ни де́лаем, ей нет перево́да. *We keep working all the time, yet there's no end to it.*

перекрёсток—*cross-road; crossing*

крича́ть на всех перекрёстках; крича́ть на вся́ком перекрёстке—*cry from the rooftops; divulge*

Йгорь крича́л на всех перекрёстках о свои́х успе́хах. *Igor was crying from the rooftops about his successes.*

переплёт—*binding*

попа́сть в переплёт—*get into a tight corner; get into a scrape*

Йз-за свое́й лжи он попа́л в переплёт. *He got into a tight corner because of his own lie.*

пе́рец—*pepper*

задава́ть пе́рцу—*give it someone hot; bawl someone out; let one have it*

Когда́ Па́вел серди́тый, он задаёт всем пе́рцу. *When Pavel is mad, he lets everyone have it.*

перó—*pen; feather*

вы́йти и́з-под перá—*be written by*

Ромáн «Войнá и мир» вы́шел и́з-под перá Толстóго. *The novel* War and Peace *was written by Tolstoy.*

рядúться в чужи́е пéрья—*adorn oneself with borrowed feathers*

Варвáра самá ничегó не умéет, а рядúтся в чужи́е пéрья. *Barbara doesn't know anything—she merely adorns herself with borrowed feathers.*

персóна—*person*

сóбственной персóной—SEE: **своéй (сóбственной) осóбой**

пéсенка—*song*

пéсенка спéта—*one's goose is cooked; one is done for*

Егó разоблачи́ли, егó пéсенка спéта. *He got exposed—his goose is cooked.*

пéсня—*song*

дли́нная (or **дóлгая**) **пéсня**—*long story*

О моéй жи́зни я расскажу́ потóм. Э́то дóлгая пéсня. *I'll talk about my life later—it's a long story.*

пéтля—*noose; buttonhole*

засу́нуть гóлову в пéтлю; лезть в пéтлю—*put one's neck into the noose; take risks*

Проси́вшись на передову́ю, мнóгие молоды́е солдáты добровóльно лéзли в пéтлю. *By asking to be sent to a forward position, many young soldiers voluntarily put their heads into the noose.*

надéть пéтлю на шéю—*hang a millstone around one's neck; carry an unwanted burden*

Приня́ть иждивéнца—знáчит надéть пéтлю себé на шéю. *To take in an unemployed man as a dependent is like hanging a millstone around one's neck.*

петýх—*rooster*

вставáть с петухáми—*rise with the chickens*

У Ивáна привы́чка вставáть с петухáми. *Ivan habitually rises with the chickens.*

до петухóв—*till the crack of dawn*

Мы рабóтали до петухóв. *We kept on working till the crack of dawn.*

от петухóв до петухóв—*around the clock*

Пожáрники рабóтали от петухóв до петухóв, чтóбы потуши́ть огóнь. *The firefighters worked around the clock to put out the fire.*

пусти́ть крáсного петухá—*set fire; commit arson*

Пáвел грози́лся пусти́ть крáсного петухá и уничтóжить моё предприя́тие. *Pavel threatened to destroy my business with arson.*

пусти́ть петухá—*let out a squeak (*on a high note*)*

Вчерá на концéрте сопрáно пусти́ла петухá на высóкой нóте. *During yesterday's concert the soprano let out a squeak on a high note.*

печáль—*grief; sorrow*

(вот) нé было печáли!—*That's all we needed!*

Вот нé было печáли! А тут дом сгорéл. *That's all we needed—now even the house has burned down.*

не твоя́ печáль!—*mind your own business; it isn't your concern* (or *business)*

Не твоя́ печáль занимáться мои́ми проблéмами. *Dealing with my problems isn't your concern.*

печáть—*press*

вы́йти из печáти—*appear in print; be published*

Моя́ пéрвая кни́га скóро вы́йдет из печáти. *My first book will soon be published.*

попáсть в печáть—*be mentioned in newspapers*

Свéдения о развóде извéстной актри́сы попáли и в печáть. *The news about the famous actress's divorce was mentioned even in the newspapers.*

пéчка—*stove*

пéчки—лáвочки—*this and that*

«О чём вы разговáривали весь вéчер?»—«Ни о чём, так—пéчки—лáвочки.» *"What were you talking about all night long?"—"This and that."*

писáть—*write*

не про когó-ли́бо пи́сано—*be way above one's head*

Изучи́ть япóнский язы́к не про меня́ напи́сано. *Learning Japanese is way above my head.*

пиши́ пропáло—*it's as good as lost; you can kiss it good-bye*

Одолжи́ Петру́ дéньги—пиши́ пропáло. *Lend Peter some money, and you can kiss it good-bye.*

пить—*drink*

как пить дать—*as sure as you're born*

Он снóва потеря́ет зóнтик, как пить дать. *He'll lose his umbrella again as sure as you're born.*

пла́стырь—*plaster*

прилипа́ть (or **пристава́ть**) **как пла́стырь**—SEE: **приста́ть** (or **привяза́ться**) **как ба́нный лист**

платфо́рма—*platform*

стоя́ть на платфо́рме—*be a supporter*

Ива́н стои́т на платфо́рме демокра́тии. *Ivan is a supporter of democracy.*

плева́ть—*spit*

плева́ть на всё—*not to give a damn; not to care a bit* (or *hoot*)

Мне плева́ть на всё, что лю́ди обо мне ду́мают. *I don't give a damn what people think of me.*

плечо́—*shoulder*

выноси́ть на свои́х плеча́х—*bear the responsibility* (or *burden*) *all alone*

По́сле сме́рти отца́ ста́рший брат вы́нес на свои́х плеча́х все забо́ты о семье́. *After the father's death the older brother bore the entire family burden.*

по плечу́—*be equal to a task*

Э́та зада́ча Бори́су не по плечу́. *Boris isn't equal to this task.*

сбро́сить (or **сложи́ть**) **с плеч** (**доло́й**)—*get rid of something*

Вы́платив за дом всю су́мму, Па́вел сбро́сил с плеч долги́. *Pavel got rid of his debts after paying up the loan on the house.*

с чужо́го плеча́—*hand-me-downs; used clothing; secondhand*

Костю́м Бори́су не по разме́ру, очеви́дно с чужо́го плеча́. *Boris's suit doesn't fit him—it's obviously a hand-me-down.*

плоть—*flesh*

войти́ в плоть и кровь—*become second nature; get it in one's bones*

Привы́чка чита́ть газе́ту за за́втраком вошла́ в его́ плоть и кровь. *It became his second nature to read the newspaper while having his breakfast.*

плю́нуть—*spit*

раз плю́нуть—*child's play; be a cinch; be a piece of cake for someone*

Така́я зада́ча Ива́ну раз плю́нуть. *A task like that is a piece of cake for Ivan.*

побо́ище—*slaughter; bloody battle*

заводи́ть мама́ево побо́ище—*stage a big quarrel; have a major falling out*

Из-за распределе́ния насле́дства семья́ завела́ мама́ево побо́ище. *The family had a major falling out because of the dividing up of the inheritance.*

поворо́т—*bend*

ле́гче на поворо́тах!—*watch your step! Hold your horses!*

Никола́й стал груби́ть, и я был вы́нужден сказа́ть ему́: «Поле́гче на поворо́тах!» *When Nikolay started to get rude, I had to tell him: "Hold your horses!"*

поговори́ть—*talk*

поговори́ть начистоту́—*speak one's mind; openly; without equivocation*

О́льга предложи́ла сы́ну-подро́стку поговори́ть начистоту́. *Olga advised her adolescent son to speak his mind.*

пого́да—*weather*

кака́я бы ни была́ пого́да—*rain or shine*

Кака́я бы ни была́ пого́да, на рабо́ту нельзя́ опа́здывать. *Rain or shine, you mustn't be late for work.*

поде́лать—*do; make; act*

ничего́ не поде́лаешь—*there's nothing to be done about something; it just can't be helped*

Мой оте́ц умира́ет от ра́ка, и ничего́ не поде́лаешь. *My father is dying of cancer, and there's nothing to be done about it.*

подело́м

подело́м ему!—*it serves him right!*

Па́вла посади́ли за воровство́, и подело́м ему́! *Pavel was sent to jail for stealing—serves him right!*

подма́зать—*grease*

не подма́жешь—не пое́дешь—*wheels don't run without oil*

Что́бы поступи́ть в университе́т в Росси́и, ну́жно дать взя́тку. «Не подма́жешь—не пое́дешь»—говоря́т лю́ди. *In order to get admitted to the university in Russia you have to grease someone's palm. "Wheels don't run without oil," people say.*

подмётка—*sole*

в подмётки не годи́ться—*cannot hold a candle to; not to be fit to lick one's boots*

Ири́на постоя́нно критику́ет ва́шу жену́, хотя́ она́ ей и в подмётки не годи́тся. *Irina constantly criticizes your wife, although she can't hold a candle to her.*

подо́бный—*similar; like*

и тому́ подо́бное (и т.п.)—*and the like; and so on; etc.*

Во вре́мя разгово́ра О́льга ча́сто повторя́ла: «И тому́ подо́бное, и тому́ подо́бное.» *During our talk Olga kept repeating "and the like, and the like."*

ничего́ подо́бного!—*no way! under no circumstances; absolutely not*

Заплати́ть миллио́н до́лларов за э́тот ста́рый дом? Ничего́ подо́бного! *To pay a million dollars for this old house? No way!*

пожáр—*fire*

не на пожáр—*there's no hurry; not to be urgent; there is no one chasing after you*

Почемý ты так бы́стро идёшь? Не на пожáр же ведь! *Why are you in such a hurry—there is no one chasing after you.*

поживáть—*get on*

поживём—уви́дим—*time will tell* (or *show)*

А как бýдет дáльше—никтó не знáет. Поживём—уви́дим. *How it will be later on, nobody knows, but time will tell.*

позволéние—*permission*

с позволéния сказáть—*if I may say so*

С позволéния сказáть, я вáшей рабóтой не óчень довóлен. *I'm not too pleased with your work, if I may say so.*

поздравля́ть—*congratulate*

с чем вас и поздравля́ю—*congratulations!* (ironically)

«Предстáвьте себé, за превышéние скóрости на дорóге мне прислáли штраф на двéсти дóлларов.» Васи́лий улыбнýлся и сказáл: «Ну, Алексéй, с чем вас и поздравля́ю!» *"Imagine, I got a $200 ticket for speeding." Vasily smiled and said, "Well, Aleksey, congratulations!"*

пои́ть—*give to drink*

пои́ть и корми́ть—*support someone; feed and keep someone*

Когдá Áнна приéхала в Амéрику, поначáлу рóдственники её пои́ли и корми́ли. *When Anna arrived in the States, she was supported by her relatives at the beginning.*

пойти́—*go; leave*

éсли (уж) на то пошлó; кóли на то пошлó—*speaking of something; since we are on the subject*

Éсли уж на то пошлó, что ты жени́лся, то будь счáстлив. *Since we are on the subject of your having gotten married, I wish you happiness.*

так не пойдёт!—*it won't do* (or *work)!*

«Так не пойдёт, ты меня не обма́нешь»—сказа́л нача́льник но́вому рабо́чему. *"This won't do—you can't cheat me!" the boss said to the new employee.*

поко́й—*rest; peace*

оста́вить в поко́е—*leave* (or *let) alone*

«Уходи́! Оста́вь меня́ в поко́е!»—сказа́л Ива́н серди́то. *"Get lost! Leave me alone!" Ivan said angrily.*

на поко́й—*time to turn in*

«Ребя́та, уже́ по́здно, пора́ на поко́й!»—сказа́л оте́ц. *"Kids, it's getting late... Time to turn in!" the father said.*

покори́тель—*subjugator*

покори́тель серде́ц—*lady-killer*

Молодо́й актёр был покори́телем серде́ц. *The young actor was a lady-killer.*

пола́—*skirt; flap*

продава́ть из-под полы́—*sell on the black market; sell under the counter*

Нарко́тики продаю́тся и́з-под полы́. *Drugs are sold on the black market.*

по́ле—*field; ground*

одного́ (or **своего́) по́ля я́года**—*be kindred spirits* (or *souls); be birds of a feather*

Вы с прия́телем—одного́ по́ля я́года. *You and your boyfriend are kindred spirits.*

па́вший на по́ле би́твы—*killed in action*

На пло́щади откры́ли па́мятник солда́там, па́вшим на по́ле би́твы. *They unveiled a memorial for the soldiers who were killed in action.*

полёт—*flight*

с пти́чьего полёта—*from a bird's-eye view*

Со 103-го этажа́ го́род ви́ден с пти́чьего полёта. *You can see the city from a bird's-eye view from the 103rd floor.*

полнота́—*plenitude; completeness*

от полноты́ се́рдца (or **души́**)—*with great love; with lots of affection*

Меня́ друзья́ поздравля́ли с днём рожде́ния от полноты́ се́рдца. *My friends congratulated me with great love on my birthday.*

по́лный—*full*

полны́м-полно́—*filled up to the bursting point*

Полны́м-полно́ бы́ло наро́ду на стадио́не. *The stadium was filled with people to the bursting point.*

положе́ние—*situation; condition*

быть в положе́нии—*be an expectant mother; be with child*

До́ктор сообщи́л, что моя́ жена́ в положе́нии. *The doctor informed us that my wife is expecting.*

войти́ в положе́ние—*put oneself in someone's shoes*

Зна́я мою́ фина́нсовую пробле́му, О́льга вошла́ в моё положе́ние, и дала́ мне сто до́лларов взаймы́. *Knowing my financial problems, Olga put herself in my shoes and loaned me $100.*

обще́ственное положе́ние—*walk of life; social standing*

В демонстра́ции принима́ли уча́стие лю́ди ра́зного обще́ственного положе́ния. *People of all walks of life participated in the demonstration.*

пи́ковое положе́ние—*a tight spot; dire straits; a pickle*

Когда́ ко́нчатся де́ньги, мы ока́жемся в пи́ковом положе́нии. *We'll be in a tight spot when our money runs out.*

положе́ние веще́й—*the lay of the land; state of affairs*

Как мы ни стара́лись, а положе́ние веще́й не измени́лось. *No matter how hard we tried, the state of our affairs didn't change.*

полусло́во or **полсло́ва**—*half of a word*

замолча́ть (or **останови́ться**) **на полусло́ве**—*stop in the middle of a sentence*

На допро́се Па́вел замолча́л на полусло́ве. *When Pavel was interrogated, he stopped in the middle of a sentence.*

мо́жно вас на полсло́ва?—*may I have a word with you?*

Ива́н подошёл ко мне и спроси́л: «Мо́жно вас на полсло́ва?» *Ivan came up to me and asked, "May I have a word with you?"*

оборва́ть на полусло́ве—*cut someone short*

Неве́жливо обрыва́ть на полусло́ве. *It's impolite to cut someone short.*

помо́и—*slop*

облива́ть помо́ями—*sling (*or *fling) mud at someone; besmirch one's reputation*

Во вре́мя разво́да Пётр и Ири́на облива́ли друг дру́га помо́ями. *At the time of their divorce, Peter and Irina were slinging mud at one another.*

понима́ние—*understanding; comprehension*

вы́ше понима́ния—*beyond one's grasp*

«Астроно́мия вы́ше моего́ понима́ния»—сказа́л учи́тель физкульту́ры. *"Astronomy is beyond my grasp," said the physical education teacher.*

понима́ть—*understand*

(вот) э́то я понима́ю!—*that's great!; you cannot beat that!; that's really something!*

Андре́й из горя́щего до́ма вы́нес ребёнка. Вот э́то я понима́ю! *Andrey rescued a child from inside the burning house. You can't beat that!*

пописáть—*write*

ничегó не попи́шешь—*it can't be helped; there is nothing one can do about it*

Ничегó не попи́шешь, жизнь óчень тяжёлая. *Life is very hard; it can't be helped.*

попы́тка—*attempt*

попы́тка не пы́тка—*nothing ventured, nothing gained*

Давáй кýпим áкции! Попы́тка не пы́тка. *Let's buy some shares! Nothing ventured, nothing gained!*

попя́тный—*backward*

пойти́ на попя́тный—*go back on one's word*

Хотя́ Игорь обещáл жени́ться на Лéне, он пошёл на попя́тный и эмигри́ровал в Амéрику. *Although Igor promised to marry Lena, he went back on his word and emigrated to the States.*

порá—*time*

в (сáмую) пóру; как раз в пóру—*just in time; at just the right time; the perfect moment*

Он приéхал в пóру сбóра урожáя. *He arrived just in time for the harvest.*

давнó порá—*it's high time*

Дéти, вам давнó порá на боковýю. *Come on kids, it's high time you went to bed.*

до поры́ до врéмени—*1. for the time being 2. up to a certain time; for a while; for a time*

1. До поры́ до врéмени мы проживáем в э́том гóроде. *For the time being, we'll stay and live in this town.*
2. До поры́ до врéмени я терплю́ мою́ рабóту. *I'll put up with my job for a while.*

мне порá—*I have got to go*

Пóсле обéда Ники́та встáл и сказáл: «Мне порá.» *After dinner Nikita stood up and said, "I've got to go."*

на пéрвых порáх—*at the beginning; at first*

На пе́рвых пора́х поживи́ у нас, пото́м бу́дет ви́дно. *Stay with us at the beginning—later we'll see what happens.*

с да́вних пор—*for ages; for a long time*
С да́вних пор мы друзья́. *We've been friends for ages.*

с тех пор не ма́ло воды́ утекло́—*since then a lot of water has flowed under the bridge*
Де́тство мы провели вме́сте, но с тех пор не ма́ло воды утекло́. *We spent our childhood together, but since then a lot of water has flowed under the bridge.*

поро́г—*threshold*

быть на поро́ге—*be coming very soon; be around the corner; be very close*
Весна́ уже́ на поро́ге. *Spring is coming very soon.*

по́рох—*gunpowder*

не хвата́ет по́роха (or **по́роху**)—*lack strength* (or *stamina* or *guts*); *be too weak for something*
У стари́ка не хвата́ет по́роха для физи́ческой рабо́ты. *The old man is too weak for physical work.*

па́хнуть по́рохом—*there's a threat of war in the air*
В на́шей стране́ бе́шеное вооруже́ние—па́хнет по́рохом. *There is a feverish arms race going on in our country—there's a threat of war in the air.*

поря́док—*order; arrangement; setup*

быть в поря́дке веще́й—*be quite natural; be a matter of course*
Я тебе́ помога́ю, э́то в поря́дке веще́й. *I'll help you—that's a matter of course.*

в пожа́рном поря́дке—*in great haste; posthaste*
Йз-за бомбёжки мы уе́хали из го́рода в пожа́рном поря́дке. *We left the city because of the bombardments posthaste.*

в поря́дке живо́й о́череди—*first come first served*

В билéтной кáссе обслýживание в порядке живóй óчереди. *Service at the ticket office is on a first-come-first-served basis.*

в чáстном порядке—*on the sly* (or *quiet); on the QT*

Контрáкт мы заключи́ли в чáстном поря́дке. *We concluded the contract on the quiet.*

идти́ свои́м поря́дком—*take it's normal course*

Пóсле óтпуска нáша жизнь идёт свои́м поря́дком. *Our life will take it's normal course after our vacation.*

ну и поря́дки!—*what a mess!*

Никтó ничегó не знáет—ну и поря́дки! *What a mess! Nobody knows anything!*

приводи́ть себя́ в поря́док—*clean* (or *tidy) oneself up*

Пóсле рабóты Áнна приводи́ла себя́ в поря́док. *Anna got all tidied up after work.*

пост—*position; duty*

стоя́ть на своём постý—*perform one's duties*

Он всегдá добросóвестно стоя́л на своём постý. *He always performed his duties conscientiously.*

пот—*perspiration, sweat*

рабóтать до седьмóго (or **кровáвого) пóта**—*work to the point of collapse*

Для благополýчия семьи́ отéц рабóтал до седьмóго пóта—*The father worked to the point of collapse for the sake of the family's well-being.*

потолóк—*ceiling*

брать с потолкá—*spin a yarn out of thin air; make something up*

Емý нельзя́ вéрить, он всё берёт с потолкá. *You can't believe him—he makes everything up.*

потóп—*deluge*

пóсле нас хоть потóп—*all hell can break loose; "après moi le déluge"*

Мы своё сдéлали, а пóсле нас хоть потóп. *We've done all we could—so let all hell break loose!*

потрохá—*bowels; entrails*

со всéми потрохáми—*lock, stock and barrel*

Бори́с прóдал свою́ фи́рму со всéми потрохáми. *Boris sold his firm, lock, stock and barrel.*

поцелу́й—*kiss*

посылáть возду́шный поцелу́й—*blow* (or *throw) a kiss to someone*

Уходя́, он послáл мне возду́шный поцелу́й. *He threw me a kiss as he left.*

пóчва—*soil; ground*

зонди́ровать пóчву—*test the ground; see how the land lies*

Прéжде всегó нам придётся зонди́ровать пóчву, а потóм решáть, что дéлать. *First we have to see how the land lies, and then we'll decide what to do next.*

подготóвить пóчву—*pave the way for something; lay the ground for something*

Недовóльство нарóда подготóвило пóчву для революции. *The people's dissatisfaction paved the way to the revolution.*

пóчва ушлá и́з-под ног—*flounder; become disoriented*

Когда́ Ива́на уво́лили с рабо́ты, по́чва ушла́ и́з-под его́ ног. *Ivan became all disoriented when he lost his job.*

теря́ть по́чву под нога́ми—*loose one's footing; slip; become disjointed*

По́сле сме́рти роди́телей А́нна потеря́ла по́чву под нога́ми. *Anna became all disjointed after her parents' death.*

пра́вда—*truth; right*

все́ми пра́вдами и непра́вдами—*by hook or by crook*

Пётр все́ми пра́вдами и непра́вдами стара́лся дости́чь свое́й це́ли. *Peter strove to achieve his objectives by hook or crook.*

говори́ть (or **ре́зать**) **пра́вду-ма́тку в глаза́**—*call a spade a spade; be outspoken; give it to one straight*

Ива́на уво́лили, потому́ что он ре́зал пра́вду-ма́тку в глаза́ нача́льнику. *Ivan was let go from his job, because he gave it to his boss straight.*

гляде́ть (or **смотре́ть**) **пра́вде в глаза́** (or **лицо́**)—*face up to the truth; be realistic*

В любо́м слу́чае ну́жно смотре́ть пра́вде в глаза́. *One has to face up to the truth under all circumstances.*

жить по пра́вде—*live an honest life*

Мои́ роди́тели жи́ли всю жизнь по пра́вде. *My parents have lived an honest life throughout their entire existence.*

по пра́вде говоря́ (or **сказа́ть**); **пра́вду говоря́** (or **сказа́ть**)—*to tell the truth*

По пра́вде говоря́, я не гото́вился к экза́мену. *I didn't study for this exam, to tell the truth.*

пра́вда глаза́ ко́лет—*truth hurts*

Оле́г оби́делся, когда́ я его́ обма́нщиком назва́л, ведь пра́вда глаза́ ко́лет. *Oleg got offended when I called him a cheat, but then truth hurts.*

что пра́вда, то пра́вда—*what's true is true*

Да, он в э́том де́ле невинова́т—что пра́вда, то пра́вда. *Yes, he's innocent in this matter—what's true is true.*

пра́вило—*rule; regulation*

положи́ть (or **поста́вить**) **(себе́) пра́вилом** (or **за пра́вило**)—*make it a rule to do something*

Я поста́вил себе́ за пра́вило принима́ть витами́ны пе́ред сном. *I made it a rule to take vitamins before going to sleep.*

пра́во—*right*

вступа́ть в свои́ права́—*come into one's own*

Когда́ весна́ вступа́ет в свои́ права́, ре́ки легко́ выхо́дят из берего́в. *When spring comes into its own, the rivers tend to flood.*

дать пра́во—*is good for something*

Э́тот биле́т даёт вам пра́во пересе́сть на друго́й маршру́т авто́буса. *This ticket is good for transfer to the other route of the bus line.*

жить на пти́чьих права́х—*live a precarious existence*

И́горь живёт с подру́гой на пти́чьих права́х. *Igor lives a precarious existence with his girlfriend.*

оста́вить за собо́й пра́во—*reserve the right*

Судья́ оста́вил за собо́й пра́во сказа́ть после́днее сло́во. *The judge reserved the right to have the last word.*

преде́л—*limit; end*

преде́л терпе́ния—*the last straw*

Хва́тит! Э́то уже́ преде́л терпе́ния! *Enough! That is the last straw!*

предме́т—*subject*

на предме́т—*for the purpose of something; in order to*

Бори́с прие́хал в Чика́го на предме́т жени́тьбы. *Boris came to Chicago in order to get married.*

на тот предме́т, е́сли—*in case, if*

На тот пре́дмет, е́сли дождь идёт, экску́рсия не состои́тся. *In case of rain, we'll cancel the excursion.*

предме́т постоя́нных насме́шек—*laughing stock*

Арка́дий одева́лся как кло́ун и был предме́том постоя́нных насме́шек. *Arkady became a laughing stock for dressing like a clown.*

предоставля́ть—*call upon*

быть предоста́вленным самому́ себе́—*be left on one's own*

По́сле ги́бели роди́телей в автомоби́льной катастро́фе ребёнок предоста́влен самому́ себе́. *After the parents died in a car accident, the child was left on his own.*

пре́сса—*press*

бульва́рная пре́сса—*yellow press*

Люби́мая те́ма бульва́рной пре́ссы—э́то сенса́ция. *Sensation mongering is the favorite topic of the yellow press.*

прести́ж—*prestige*

потеря́ть прести́ж—*lose face*

Бори́с потеря́л прести́ж, когда́ его́ разоблачи́ли. *Boris lost face when he was found out.*

спасти́ прести́ж—*save face*

Что́бы спасти́ прести́ж, Па́вел потра́тил мно́го де́нег. *Pavel spent a lot of money on saving face.*

прете́нзия—*claim*

быть в прете́нзии—*bear someone a grudge*

Ива́н ча́сто в прете́нзии к окружа́ющим. *Ivan often bears a grudge at those around him.*

приём—*admittance; welcome*

ока́зывать холо́дный приём—*give someone the cold shoulder*

А́нна оби́делась и оказа́ла Ива́ну холо́дный приём. *Anna got offended and gave Ivan the cold shoulder.*

прийти́сь—*to have to*

как придётся—*any way*

Поста́вьте ме́бель как придётся, а пото́м мы её расста́вим. *Just put the furniture down any way—we'll arrange it later.*

приме́р—*example*

брать приме́р—*follow one's example*

Сын брал приме́р со своего́ отца́. *The son followed his father's example.*

не в приме́р; невприме́р—*unlike*

Не в приме́р мно́гим, Са́ша отно́сится к себе́ крити́чески. *Unlike many others, Sasha takes a critical look at himself.*

не в приме́р лу́чше—*better by far*

Све́жие фру́кты не в приме́р лу́чше варе́нья. *Fresh fruit is far better than canned fruit.*

пода́ть (or **показа́ть) приме́р**—*set an example*

Он свое́й приле́жностью подава́л хоро́ший приме́р. *He set an example with his diligence.*

приня́ть—*accept; take*

э́то не при́нято—*it isn't done*

Пожа́луйста не чиха́йте в во́здух, э́то не при́нято. *Please stop sneezing around—it's not done!*

припа́рка—*poultice; fomentation*

как мёртвому припа́рки—*be needed like a hole in the head; be completely unnecessary*

Са́ше мои́ сове́ты нужны́ как мёртвому припа́рки. *Sasha needs my advice like a hole in the head.*

припева́ть—*troll (out)*

жить припева́ючи—*be in clover; live the life of Riley*

Получи́в насле́дство, Ива́н жил припева́ючи. *Ivan lived the life of Riley after he received his inheritance.*

припёк—*surplus*

сбóку припёка; сбóку припёку—*be unecessary; be a fifth wheel*

Мáша чáсто прихóдит к нам в дом и не замечáет, что онá сбóку припёку. *Masha comes to visit us often but doesn't notice that she is a fifth wheel.*

прúступ—*storm; rush; attack*

прúступу нет—*1. be (financially) out of reach*
2. be unapproachable

1. Цéны так повы́сились, что к нóвому дóму прúступа нет. *The prices rose so high that a new house is out of reach.*
2. Тепéрь Игорь такóй вáжный, что к немý прúступа нет. *Igor thinks of himself so highly that he's quite unapproachable.*

приходúть—*come*

приходúть некстáти—*come at the wrong time*

Гóсти пришлú к нам некстáти. *Our guests arrived at the wrong time.*

приходúться—*fit*

приходúться кстáти—*come at the perfect time; just what one needs at that time*

Её подáрок пришёлся мне кстáти. *Her present was just I needed at that time.*

прóба—*trial; test*

вы́сшей (or **высóкой**) **прóбы**—*of high quality*

Нáша фúрма купúла товáры вы́сшей прóбы úз-за границы. *Our firm bought goods of the highest quality from abroad.*

нúзшей (or **нúзкой**) **прóбы**—*the lowest* (or *worst) kind*

«Как ты мóжешь дружúть с Владúмиром, ведь он человéк нúзкой прóбы»—сказáл Олéг Пáвлу. *"How can you be friends with Vladimir? He is a person of the worst kind," said Oleg to Pavel.*

про́ба пера́—*first steps in literature*

Про́ба пера́ уже́ дала́ Ива́ну успе́х. *Already his first steps in literature brought Ivan success.*

про́бка—*cork*

про́бкой вы́лететь (or **вы́скочить**)—*shoot out of somewhere like a rocket*

Когда́ вошла́ больша́я соба́ка, Ники́та про́бкой вы́летел из ко́мнаты. *Nikita shot out of the room like a rocket when a big dog entered.*

продолже́ние—*continuation*

продолже́ние сле́дует—*to be continued*

На после́дней страни́це расска́за напи́сано: «Продолже́ние сле́дует.» *On the last page of the short story is written, "To be continued."*

пройти́—*walk through; go through*

пройти́ ми́мо—*overlook*

Я не могу́ пройти́ ми́мо ва́шего наха́льного поведе́ния. *I can't overlook your insolent behavior!*

про́клятый—*damned*

рабо́тать (or **занима́ться) как про́клятый**—*work like a possessed person*

Пе́ред сда́чей экза́менов Алексе́й занима́лся как про́клятый. *Aleksey worked like a possessed person before his examination.*

про́мах—*miss; slip*

дава́ть (or **де́лать) про́мах** (or **прома́шку)**—*make a big mistake* (or *blunder)*

Ли́за дала́ прома́шку, когда́ она́ упомяну́ла своего́ любо́вника пе́ред свекро́вью. *Lisa made a big blunder when she mentioned her lover in front of her mother-in-law.*

пропада́ть—*be missing; be lost*

где вы пропада́ли?—*where on earth have you been?*

Не ви́дев Оле́га до́лго, его́ спроси́ли: «Где вы пропада́ли?» *Since Oleg hadn't been seen for a long time, people were asking, "Where on earth have you been?"*

где на́ша не пропада́ла!; где на́ше не пропада́ло!—*take the risk; chance it*

И́горь реши́л внести́ дополни́тельную су́мму де́нег в фи́рму, а жена́ была́ про́тив, но И́горь сказа́л: «Где на́ша не пропада́ла!» *Igor wanted to invest a large sum of money in the firm, but his wife was against it. Then Igor said, "I will risk it!"*

про́рва—*a mass (of)*

как в про́рву—*wasted effort (*or *money); down the drain*

В прести́жном университе́те избало́ванный сын не занима́лся, и, таки́м о́бразом, де́ньги роди́телей шли как в про́рву. *The spoiled son at the prestigious university didn't study, and so the parents' money went down the drain.*

профо́рма—*formality*

для профо́рмы—*for appearance's sake*

Для профо́рмы Ле́на и Бори́с вме́сте пошли́ в го́сти, хотя́ они́ бы́ли в разво́де. *Lena and Boris went to the party together, although they were already in the midst of getting a divorce.*

прохо́д—*passage; isle*

не дава́ть прохо́да—*pester the life out of one; give one no peace*

Ната́ша му́жу прохо́да не дава́ла, что́бы он купи́л ей но́вую шу́бу. *Natasha was pestering the life out of her husband to buy her a new fur coat.*

пти́ца—*bird; poultry*

ва́жная пти́ца; пти́ца высо́кого (or **вы́сшего**) **полёта**—*big shot; big-wig*

Зако́нчив институ́т, Алексе́й стал ва́жной пти́цей. *Alex became a big shot after graduating from the university.*

жить как пти́ца небе́сная—*live an untroubled life*

Са́ша жил как пти́ца небе́сная, хотя́ вокру́г него́ лю́ди умира́ли от го́лода. *Sasha was living an untroubled life, although the people around him were dying of hunger.*

пу́говица—*button*

застёгнут(ый) на все пу́говицы—*be stiff*

С на́шим дире́ктором о́чень тру́дно обща́ться, он всегда́ застёгнут на все пу́говицы. *It is very difficult to be close to our boss—he is so stiff.*

пу́зо—*belly; paunch*

есть (or **нае́сться**) **от пу́за**—*eat one's fill*

Ли́за приде́рживалась дие́ты, но на сва́дьбе до́чери она́ разреши́ла себе́ есть от пу́за. *Lisa kept to her diet, but at her daughter's wedding she allowed herself to eat her fill.*

пузы́рь—*bubble*

ду́тый пузы́рь—*be a fake* (or *sham)*

По́сле изуче́ния книг разрекламированного в газе́тах специали́ста, Арка́дий по́нял, что э́то ду́тый пузы́рь. *After he read the book of the alleged specialist much advertised in the newspapers, Arkady realized that he was a fake.*

пуп—*navel*

мнить себя́ пу́пом земли́—*think of oneself as the hub* (or *navel) of the universe*

По поведе́нию Бори́са я́сно, что он мнит себя́ пу́пом земли́. *It is evident from Boris' behavior that he thinks of himself as the hub of the universe.*

путь—*way; path; journey*

держа́ть путь—*wend one's way toward*

Мы держа́ли путь в Москву́. *We were wending our way toward Moscow.*

обма́нным путём—*by false pretenses*

Обма́нным путём Ива́н уе́хал. *Ivan left by false pretenses.*

око́льным путём—*in a roundabout way; indirectly*

Я узна́л о про́шлом О́льги око́льным путём. *I found out about Olga's past in a roundabout way.*

проби́ть себе́ путь—*make a place in the sun for oneself; succeed*

Свои́ми уси́лиями Ники́та сам проби́л себе́ путь. *Nikita made his own place in the sun by his own efforts.*

счастли́вый путь! счастли́вого пути́!—*farewell! bon voyage!*

На проща́ние хозя́ева пожела́ли нам счастли́вого пути́. *When saying farewell our hosts wished us "bon voyage."*

пух—*down*

ни пу́ха, ни пера́!—*good luck!*

Пе́ред экза́меном обы́чно жела́ют ни пу́ха, ни пера́. *It is customary to wish one good luck before an exam.*

пу́шка—*cannon*

вы́лететь как из пу́шки—*fly* (or *tear) out like a bat out of hell*

Из кабине́та дире́ктора Ники́та вы́летел как из пу́шки. *Nikita tore out of the director's office like a bat out of hell.*

пыль—*dust*

в пылу́ гне́ва—*in a fit of anger*

В пылу́ гне́ва Ни́на уда́рила Петра́. *In a fit of anger Nina hit Peter.*

пыль столбо́м—*all hell has broken loose*

Во вре́мя разде́ла насле́дства семья́ ссо́рилась так, что пыль столбо́м стоя́ла. *When the inheritance was divided, the family quarrelled so hard that all hell broke loose.*

пуска́ть пыль в глаза́—*dazzle*

Свои́ми дороги́ми пода́рками Серге́й стара́лся пуска́ть пыль в глаза́ А́нны. *Sergey tried to dazzle Anna with his expensive gifts.*

с пы́лу, с жа́ру—*sizzling* (or *piping) hot*

Ба́бушка подала́ нам пиро́г на стол с пы́лу, с жа́ру. *Grandma served a sizzling hot pie.*

пядь—*span; inch*

семи́ пя́дей во лбу—*as wise as Solomon*

Будь он семи́ пя́дей во лбу, э́тот вопро́с не реши́л бы. *He could not solve this problem even if he were as wise as Solomon.*

пя́тка—*heel*

лиза́ть пя́тки—*lick someone's boots*

Трусли́вые лю́ди ча́сто ли́жут пя́тки нача́льнику. *Cowardly people often lick the boss's boots.*

пока́зывать пя́тки—*take to one's heels; show a clean pair of heels*

Уви́дев сто́рожа, ма́льчик с укра́денными фру́ктами в рука́х показа́л пя́тки. *When the boy saw the guard, he took to his heels with stolen fruit.*

пя́тница—*Friday*

семь пя́тниц на (одно́й) неде́ле—*keep changing one's mind*

Ива́ну нельзя́ ве́рить, у него́ семь пя́тниц на неде́ле. *You can't believe Ivan because he keeps changing his mind constantly.*

пятно́—*stain*

класть пятно́ на репута́цию—*besmudge* (or *besmirch) the reputation of somebody or something*

Манипуля́ции Петра́ кла́ли пятно́ на репута́цию на́шей фи́рмы. *Peter's manipulations besmirched the reputation of our company.*

пя́тый—*fifth*

расска́зывать (or **переска́кивать) с пя́того на деся́тое**—*tell a story in snatches; jump from one point to another*

Расска́з Ники́ты был непоня́тен, потому́ что он переска́кивал с пя́того на деся́тое. *It was not possible to understand Nikita's story because he kept jumping from one point to another.*

быть (or **находи́ться**) **под пято́й**—SEE: **быть под башмако́м**

Р

рабо́та—*work; job*

взя́ться за рабо́ту; стать на рабо́ту—*start working*

По́сле обе́да мы взя́лись за рабо́ту. *We started working after dinner.*

горе́ть на рабо́те—*be married to one's job; be a workaholic*

За́нятый с ра́ннего утра́ до по́зднего ве́чера свои́ми экспериме́нтами, профе́ссор Кузнецо́в гори́т на рабо́те. *Professor Kuznetsov is busy with his experiments from early in the morning till late at night—he is married to his job.*

иметь рабо́ты по го́рло—*have one's hands full*

Име́я всегда́ по го́рло рабо́ты, Ната́ша еще уме́ла уделя́ть внима́ние семье́. *Although she had her hands full, Natasha nevertheless was able to pay attention to her family.*

не пы́льная (рабо́та)—*not to have a tough job; have a cushy job*
У Никола́я рабо́та не пы́льная. *Nikolay has a cushy job.*

рабо́та кипи́т—*work is in full swing*
На стро́йке рабо́та кипи́т. *Work is in full swing on the construction site.*

рабо́тать над собо́й—*perfect* (or *improve) oneself*
Нам всем придётся постоя́нно рабо́тать над собо́й. *We all have to keep improving ourselves.*

устра́иваться на рабо́ту—*get a job*
Наконе́ц мой сын устро́ился на рабо́ту. *At long last my son got a job.*

рад—*glad*

и не рад; сам не рад—*regret; one wishes one hadn't done something*
Ива́н сам не рад, что рассказа́л Ири́не о свои́х чу́вствах. *Ivan wished he hadn't spoken to Irina about his feelings.*

рад не рад; хоть рад, хоть не рад—*willy-nilly; like it or not*
Рад не рад, но Бори́с согласи́лся на сотру́дничество. *Willy-nilly, Boris agreed to cooperate.*

раз—*time; once*

в са́мый раз—*just at the right time*
Обе́д поспе́л к прихо́ду госте́й в са́мый раз. *The dinner was ready just at the right time when the guests arrived.*

как раз—*just*
И́горь как раз собира́лся уходи́ть, когда́ зазвони́л телефо́н. *Igor was just about to leave when the phone started to ring.*

на э́тот раз—*for this once*
На э́тот раз я тебе́ дам де́ньги, но бо́льше у меня ничего́ не проси́. *For this once I'll give you money, but don't ask me anymore!*

ни ра́зу—*never*
Ни ра́зу я не был в Антаркти́де. *I have never been to Antarctica.*

раз гу́сто, раз пу́сто; ра́зом пу́сто, ра́зом гу́сто—*one day a feast, next day a famine*

Де́ньги мы получа́ем нерегуля́рно, так у нас раз гу́сто, раз пу́сто. *We don't get paid regularly, and so it's one day a feast, next day a famine.*

раз, два и обчёлся; оди́н, друго́й и обчёлся—*very few; you can count them on (the fingers of) one hand*

Ско́лько у него́ друзе́й? Раз, два и обчёлся. *"How many friends does he have?"—"You can count them on one hand!"*

раз за ра́зом—*time after time; again and again; over and over again*

Раз за ра́зом ве́тер захва́тывал кро́ну дере́вьев. *The wind shook the crown of the trees again and again.*

раз и навсегда́—*for good; once and for all*

Раз и навсегда́ Са́ша поко́нчил с куре́нием. *Sasha quit smoking once and for all.*

раз от ра́зу—*from case to case; each time*

Раз от ра́зу ма́льчик всё лу́чше игра́ет на роя́ле. *The boy plays the piano better each time.*

раз так—*if that is so; in that case; that being the case*

Раз так, я от тебя́ ухожу́. *I'll leave you if that's so.*

разга́р—*climax*

в по́лном разга́ре—*in full swing; in* (or *at*) *the height of*

Ле́на вы́шла за́муж в по́лном разга́ре ле́та. *Lena got married at the height of the summer.*

разгово́р—*conversation; talk; discussion*

друго́й разгово́р—*that's a different story*

А́нна вы́шла за́муж за Петра́ из-за де́нег. Е́сли бы по любви́, то был бы друго́й разгово́р. *Anna married Peter for money; if she had done it for love, that would be a different story.*

задуше́вный разгово́р; разгово́р по душа́м—*heart-to-heart talk*

Ма́ша и А́нна провели́ ве́чер в задуше́вном разгово́ре. *Masha and Anna spent the evening with a heart-to-heart talk.*

разгово́р о пустяка́х—*small talk*

Па́вел не те́рпит разгово́ров о пустяка́х. *Pavel can't stand small talk.*

ра́зница—*difference*

кака́я ра́зница?—*what difference does it make?*

Ну, кака́я ра́зница? Е́сли сего́дня не мо́жете, то позвони́те мне за́втра. *Well, what difference does it make? If you can't call me today, call me tomorrow!*

разреше́ние—*permission*

с ва́шего разреше́ния (or **позволе́ния**)—*if you don't mind; with your permission*

С ва́шего разреше́ния я сейча́с уйду́ домо́й. *I'm leaving for home now, if you don't mind.*

ра́зум—*mind; intelligence*

жить свои́м ра́зумом—*stick to one's convictions* (or *views*)

И́горь жил свои́м ра́зумом и стал кло́уном. *Igor stuck to his own views and became a clown.*

набра́ться ра́зума—*one should come to one's senses; one should get some sense into one's head*

Ты совершенноле́тний, пора́ уже набира́ться ра́зума! *You're a grown-up—it's time you came to your senses!*

наводи́ть на ра́зум—*bring someone to his senses*

Свои́ми аргуме́нтами отцу́ удало́сь навести́ сы́на на ра́зум. *The father succeeded in bringing his son to his senses with his arguments.*

ум за ра́зум захо́дит—*one's mind is going around in circles; be at one's wit's end*

У Бори́са уже́ ум за ра́зум захо́дит, но пробле́му реши́ть он не мо́жет. *Boris is already at his wit's end—still he hasn't found the solution to the problem yet.*

разуме́ться—*be self-explanatory*

само́ собо́ю разуме́ется—*it goes without saying; it stands to reason*

Само́ собо́ю разуме́ется, что де́вушки лю́бят комплиме́нты. *It goes without saying that girls like compliments.*

разуме́ние—*understanding*

по моему́ разуме́нию—*in my opinion; to my mind*

По моему́ разуме́нию, класси́ческое иску́сство красиве́е совреме́нного. *In my opinion classical art is more beautiful than modern art.*

рай—*heaven; paradise*

отпра́вить в рай—*send someone to kingdom come; do in someone*

Чле́ны ма́фии уже́ давно́ хотя́т отпра́вить Па́вла в рай. *The members of the Mafia have been wanting to do Pavel in for a long time.*

рак—*crawfish; cancer*

когда́ рак (на горе́) сви́стнет—*when hell freezes over; never*

Бори́с нам де́ньги вернёт, когда́ рак сви́стнет. *Boris will pay us our money back when hell freezes over.*

показа́ть, где ра́ки зиму́ют—*show someone what's what*

Оби́женный учи́тель реши́л показа́ть гру́бым ученика́м, где ра́ки зиму́ют. *The offended teacher decided to show the rude students what's what.*

ра́но—*early*

ра́но или по́здно—*sooner or later*

Ра́но и́ли по́здно, но и́стина всегда́ проясни́тся. *Sooner or later, but the truth will always out.*

раны́м-рано́—*at the crack of dawn; very early in the morning*

У Ива́на привы́чка встава́ть раны́м-рано́. *Ivan is in the habit of getting up at the crack of dawn.*

расположе́ние—*disposition; inclination*

расположе́ние ду́ха—*frame of mind; mood; humor*

По́сле еды́ его́ расположе́ние ду́ха всегда́ изменя́ется к лу́чшему. *After a meal his frame of mind always changes for the better.*

распу́тье—*crossroad(s)*

быть (or **стоя́ть) на распу́тье** (or **распу́тьи)**—*face a tough choice; be at a crossroads*

Мы стои́м на распу́тье: жени́ться и́ли расстава́ться? *We are at a crossroads: shall we get married or stop seeing each other?*

расте́ние—*plant*

оранжере́йное (or **тепли́чное) расте́ние**—*hothouse plant* (or *flower); mimosa*

С ним ну́жно делика́тно обраща́ться—он чувстви́тельный, как оранжере́йное расте́ние. *You must treat him with kid gloves—he is as sensitive as a hothouse plant.*

расхо́д—*expense*

брать на себя́ расхо́ды; нести́ расхо́ды—*bear* (or *cover) expenses*

В семье́ он оди́н нёс все расхо́ды. *He alone bore the expenses in the whole family.*

вводи́ть в расхо́ды—*run up a bill; cost a* (or *one) bundle*

Образова́ние на́шего сы́на вводи́ло нас в расхо́ды. *Our son's education has cost us a bundle.*

учáствовать в расхóдах—*go Dutch; share expenses*

В ресторáне все мои коллеги учáствовали в расхóдах. *All of my colleagues went Dutch in the restaurant..*

расцвéт—*bloom; blossoming*

в расцвéте сил—*in the prime of one's life; in one's prime*

Борúс стал чемпиóном по плáванию в расцвéте сил и энéргии. *Boris became a swimming champion in the prime of his life.*

расчёт—*calculation; computation*

быть в расчёте—*be even with someone; be even Steven*

Чтóбы быть с ним в расчёте, остáлось вы́платить ты́сячу дóлларов. *We had to pay $1,000 in order to be even with him.*

рéдко—*seldom*

рéдко да мéтко—*do something seldom, but to the point*

Мой отéц говорúт рéдко да мéтко. *My father doesn't talk much but when he says something it's to the point.*

рéдко когдá—*once in a blue moon; rarely*

Рéдко когдá из престýпника бýдет свящéнник. *Only once in a blue moon does a criminal become a priest.*

рéдкость—*rarity; curiosity*

музéйная рéдкость—*museum piece*

Корóна царя́ тепéрь музéйная рéдкость. *The czar's crown is now a museum piece.*

на рéдкость—*extraordinarily; unusually*

Моя́ сестрá на рéдкость красúвая. *My sister is unusually beautiful.*

рельс—*rail; truck*

постáвить на рéльсы—*get started; get something going*

Дав хорóшее образовáние дéтям, родúтели постáвили их на рéльсы. *By giving their children a good education, the parents gave them a good start in life.*

ре́па—*turnip*

дешёвле па́реной ре́пы—*dirt-cheap; a real bargain*

Э́то пла́тье сто́ит дешёвле па́реной ре́пы. *This dress is dirt-cheap.*

про́ще па́реной ре́пы—*child's* (or *kid's*) *play; a piece of cake*

Така́я рабо́та про́ще па́реной ре́пы. *This kind of work is easier than child's play.*

репута́ция—*reputation*

дурна́я репута́ция—*bad name; one's name is mud*

По́сле его́ растра́ты о нём пошла́ дурна́я репута́ция. *After his embezzlement his name was mud.*

име́ть незапя́тнанную репута́цию—*have a clean record*

На́ша шко́ла име́ет незапя́тнанную репута́цию. *Our school has a clean record.*

па́чкать репута́цию—*defame one's character; besmirch one's reputation*

Свои́ми де́йствиями он сам себе́ па́чкал репута́цию. *He besmirched his own reputation with his actions.*

речь—*speech; conversation*

вести́ речь—*drive at something; aim one's talk at something*

Он ведёт речь о приба́вке. *His talk is aimed at getting a raise.*

выступа́ть с ре́чью; держа́ть речь; произноси́ть речь—*deliver* (or *make*) *a speech*

Депута́т хоте́л вы́ступить с ре́чью пе́ред избира́телями. *The deputy wanted to make a speech in front of the electorate.*

и ре́чи быть не мо́жет—*be out of the question*

Тра́тить твои́ де́ньги на сигаре́ты? Об э́том и ре́чи быть не мо́жет. *To squander your money on cigarettes? It's out of the question.*

речь идёт—*talk about something; be a question of something*

У нас речь чáсто идёт об эколóгии окружáющей среды́. *We often talk about the protection of the environment.*

решéние—*solution; decision*

принимáть решéние; приходи́ть к решéнию—*make a decision; make up one's mind*

Дирéктор при́нял решéние и заяви́л о банкрóтстве. *The director made up his mind and declared bankruptcy.*

решётка—*bars*

посади́ть за решётку—*put someone into prison*

За взлом Ники́ту посади́ли за решётку. *Nikita was sent to jail for the robbery.*

сидéть за решёткой—*be* (or *stay) in prison*

Престýпник ужé год сиди́т за решёткой. *The criminal has been in jail for a year already.*

Ри́га—*Riga*

поéхать в Ри́гу—*vomit; throw up*

Пóсле оби́льного ýжина Игорь поéхал в Ри́гу. *Igor threw up after the ample dinner.*

риск—*risk*

на свой риск; на свой страх и риск—*at one's own risk*

Нóвый дирéктор при́нял решéние на свой страх и риск. *The new director made a decision at his own risk.*

рог—*horn*

наставля́ть рогá—*make a cuckold of someone; cuckold someone*

Невéрная женá настáвила мýжу рогá. *The unfaithful wife cuckolded her husband.*

сбить рогá—*clip one's wings*

Чтóбы Пётр знал своё мéсто, емý придётся сбить рогá. *Peter needs to have his wings clipped so he will know his place.*

род—*family; kin; birth; origin*

без рóду, без плéмени; без рóду и плéмени—*without kith or kin*

Бездóмный был без рóду и плéмени. *The homeless person was without kith or kin.*

в нéкотором рóде—*to some* (or *certain) degree* (or *extent)*

Ивáн в нéкотором рóде прав. *Ivan is right to a certain extent.*

в своём рóде—*in one's (own) way*

Э́та пьéса замечáтельна в своём рóде. *This play is remarkable in its own way.*

еди́нственный в своём рóде—*unique*

Талáнт Бори́са еди́нственный в своём рóде. *Boris's talent is unique in its own way.*

из рóда в род—*from generation to generation*

Музыкáльный талáнт в семьé Бáха передавáлся из рóда в род. *Musical talent in the Bach family was inherited from generation to generation.*

óт роду—*years of age; years old*

Я встрéтил старикá 102 лет óт роду. *I met an old man who was 102 years old.*

на роду́ напи́сано—*it's in the cards* (or *stars); it was preordained*

Ему́ бы́ло на роду́ напи́сано стать извéстным. *It was in the cards for him to become famous.*

ни рóду ни плéмени—*have not a* (or *one) soul left*

Пóсле смéрти жены́ у старикá не остáлось ни рóду ни плéмени. *After his wife's death the old man didn't have a soul left.*

рóдственник—*relative; relation*

рóдственник до вторóго (трéтьего) колéна—*cousin twice (thrice...) removed*

Ивáн мне рóдственник до вторóго колéна. *Ivan is my cousin twice removed.*

рожóн—*pointed rod; pointed stick*

лезть на рожóн—*ask for trouble; kick against the pricks*

Лýчше жить спокóйно, чем лезть на рожóн. *It's better to live quietly than to be asking for trouble.*

перéть прóтив рожнá—*swim against the tide*

«Я признаю́ твою́ правотý, но совéтую не перéть прóтив рожнá»—сказáл коллéга Никúте. *"I agree that you're right, but I suggest that you don't swim against the tide," Nikita's colleague said to him.*

роль—*part; role*

войтú в роль—*get adjusted to one's role; grow into one's role*

Николáй бы́стро вошёл в свою́ роль адвокáта. *Nikolay quickly grew into his role as a lawyer.*

выступáть (or **явля́ться**) **в рóли**—*assume the role of*

Во врéмя спóра Ивáн выступáл в рóли умиротворúтеля. *Ivan assumed the role of peacemaker during the quarrel.*

знать свою́ рóль—*know what one's duty* (or *task) is; know what to do*

В любóй ситуáции он знáет свою́ роль. *He knows what to do in any situation.*

игрáть пéрвую роль—*1. play the leading part 2. play first fiddle*

1.В нóвой пьéсе извéстный актёр игрáет пéрвую роль. *A famous actor plays the leading role in the new play.*

2. В нáшей фúрме он игрáет пéрвую роль. *He plays the first fiddle in our firm.*

на вторы́х роля́х—*be in a subordinate position; play a supporting role*

Талáнт актрúсы не был замéчен, и онá остáлась на вторы́х роля́х. *The actress's talent wasn't recognized and so she was left to do supporting roles.*

на пéрвых роля́х—*be in a key position*

Специалúсты по компью́теру в нáшей фúрме на пéрвых роля́х. *Computer specialists at our firm are in a key position.*

не игра́ет никако́й ро́ли—*it doesn't matter at all; it hardly matters*

Сентимента́льные вопро́сы не игра́ют никако́й ро́ли в на́шем фина́нсовом прое́кте. *Sentimentality hardly matters in our financial projects.*

рома́н—*novel; romance*

крути́ть рома́н—*fool around with someone*

Ле́на всё вре́мя крути́ла рома́н с ке́м-то. *Lena was always fooling around with someone.*

роси́нка—*dewdrop*

ни (ма́ковой) роси́нки не дать (or **получи́ть**)—*not to give (*or *get) a blessed thing*

Всю́ мою́ жизнь от мое́й бога́той тёти я не получи́л ни ма́ковой роси́нки. *All my life I never got a blessed thing from my wealthy aunt.*

рост—*growth; increase*

отдава́ть (or **пуска́ть**) **де́ньги в рост**—*lend money on interest*

Он разбогате́л за счёт того́, что отдава́л свои́ де́ньги в рост. *He got rich by lending his money on interest.*

рот—*mouth*

держа́ть рот на замке́—*keep one's mouth shut; not to reveal a secret*

Миха́йлу мо́жно расска́зывать секре́ты, он де́ржит рот на замке́. *You can tell Mikhail secrets—he keeps his mouth shut.*

зама́зывать рот—*bribe someone to keep one's mouth shut; pay hush money*

Кру́пная су́мма ему́ зама́зала рот. *The huge sum bribed him and he shut his mouth.*

ми́мо рта пролете́ть (or **пройти́**)—*forego something; miss the opportunity to do something*

Возмóжность дёшево купи́ть дом пролетéла у меня́ ми́мо рта. *I missed the opportunity to buy a cheap house.*

не брáть в рот—*not to (even) touch something*
Пётр вóдку в рот не берёт. *Peter won't even touch vodka.*

не лéзет в рот—*not to be able to eat a single bite*
От волнéния мне ничегó не лéзет в рот. *I am so excited I can't eat a single bite.*

разжевáть и в рот положи́ть—*spell something out for someone*
Емý нáдо всё разжевáть и в рот положи́ть. *You must spell everything out for him.*

смотрéть (or **глядéть**) **в рот**—*listen spellbound to someone*
Дéти смотрéли расскáзчику в рот. *The children were listening to the story teller spellbound.*

рубáха; рубáшка—*shirt; Russian blouse*

роди́ться в рубáшке (or **сорóчке**)—*be born with a silver spoon in the mouth; be born under a lucky star*
Олéг роди́лся в рубáшке и емý всё удаётся в жи́зни. *Oleg succeeds at everything in life—he was born under a lucky star.*

рубáха-пáрень—*regular guy; outgoing fellow*
Мой брат общи́тельный, рубáха-пáрень. *My brother is a friendly, outgoing fellow.*

своя́ руба́ха (or **руба́шка**) **бли́же к те́лу**—*self comes first; charity begins at home*

«Своя руба́ха бли́же к те́лу»—ду́мал дире́ктор и дал себе́ са́мое высо́кое повыше́ние зарпла́ты во всей фи́рме. *"Charity begins at home," the director thought, and gave himself the biggest raise in the whole company.*

рука́—*hand*

брать себя́ в ру́ки—*get control of oneself*

Возьми́ себя́ в ру́ки! Переста́нь крича́ть! *Stop yelling! Control yourself!*

быть на́ руку—*suit; be convenient; just what one needs*

Так как Ива́н зи́му не лю́бит, э́та пое́здка на юг ему́ на́ руку. *Since Ivan dislikes the winter, this field trip to the south suits him just fine.*

вы́рвать из рук сме́рти—*rescue from death; save one's life*

Хиру́рг вы́рвал больно́го из рук сме́рти. *The surgeon saved the patient's life.*

греть ру́ки—*feather one's nest; line one's pocket*

Бори́с нагре́л ру́ки на растра́те зарпла́ты рабо́чих. *Boris feathered his nest by embezzling the workers' salaries.*

здоро́ваться за́ руку—*shake hands*

При встре́че мы здоро́вались за́ руку. *We shook hands when we met.*

наложи́ть на себя́ ру́ки—*commit suicide*

От го́ря Ири́на наложи́ла на себя́ ру́ки. *Irina committed suicide in her grief.*

на́ руку не чи́ст(ый)—*have sticky fingers*

Осторо́жно с ним, он на́ руку не чи́стый. *Watch out for him—he's got sticky fingers!*

не поднима́ется рука́—*can't bring himself to do something against someone*

У меня́ не поднима́ется рука́ нанести́ ему́ боль. *I can't bring myself to cause him pain.*

отбива́ться рука́ми и нога́ми—*resist definitely; refuse vehemently*

Он рука́ми и нога́ми отбива́лся от физи́ческой рабо́ты. *He vehemently refused to do physical labor.*

оторва́ть с рука́ми—*sell like hot cakes*

Кни́ги о короле́вской семье́ с рука́ми отрыва́ют. *Books about the royal family sell like hot cakes.*

рабо́тать не поклада́я рук—*to work like crazy; work tirelessly*

Пе́ред ука́занным сро́ком мы рабо́тали не поклада́я рук. *We worked like crazy before the deadline.*

рука́ не дро́гнет—*have no scruples; not hesitate to do something*

У него́ рука́ не дро́гнет причини́ть неприя́тности. *He has no scruples about causing others trouble.*

ру́ки не отва́лятся—*doing something won't kill you*

Не бо́йся, от небольшо́й рабо́ты ру́ки не отва́лятся. *Don't be afraid, a little work won't kill you!*

ру́ки про́чь!—*hands off!*

Ру́ки про́чь от чужи́х де́нег! *Hands off the money of others!*

ру́чка—*little hand; handle*

довести́ до ру́чки—*drive someone to the deep end*

Свои́ми спекуля́циями Ива́н довёл на́шу фи́рму до ру́чки. *Ivan drove our company to the deep end with his speculations.*

ры́ба—*fish*

би́ться, как ры́ба об лёд—*struggle desperately*

Мы бьёмся, как ры́ба об лёд, что́бы вы́браться из долго́в. *We're struggling desperately to get out of debt.*

ни ры́ба ни мя́со—*neither fish, nor fowl*

Он не демокра́т и не республика́нец, получа́ется ни ры́ба ни мя́со. *He is neither a democrat, nor a republican—he is neither fish nor fowl.*

рыбák—*fisherman*

рыбák рыбáка вúдит издалекá—*birds of a feather flock together*

Богáтая прéемница вы́шла зáмуж за миллионéра—рыбák рыбáка вúдит издалéка. *The rich heiress married a millionaire—birds of a feather flock together.*

ряд—*row; line*

из ря́да вон (выходя́щий)—*outstanding; exceptional*

Егó знáния из ря́да вон выходя́щие. *His knowledge is outstanding.*

цéлый ряд—*a lot; many*

Чтóбы купúть себé плáтье по размéру, онá обошлá цéлый ряд магазúнов. *She visited a lot of stores in order to buy herself a dress in the right size.*

С

сáжа—*soot*

делá—как сáжа белá—*things are an awful mess; in a very bad way*

«Как дела?»—«Как сáжа белá.» "How are things going?"—*"They're an awful mess."*

чёрный, как сáжа—*black as pitch*

У Натáши вóлосы чёрные, как сáжа. *Natasha's hair is black as pitch.*

сам—*myself; yourself; himself; herself*

сам не свóй—*not to be* (or *feel like) oneself*

Сегóдня как-то я сам не свóй. *Today I am somehow not myself.*

самó собóй—*by itself*

Проблéма решúлась самá собóй. *The problem got solved by itself.*

са́мый—*very; most*

в са́мом де́ле—*really; indeed; actually*

Вам, в са́мом де́ле, сто лет? *Are you really a hundred years old?*

в са́мый раз—*1. at the best possible time; just the right moment 2. as if it was made to order; be a perfect fit*

1. Он пришёл в са́мый раз к обе́ду. *He arrived for dinner at the best possible time.*
2. Э́тот жаке́т ему́ в са́мый раз. *This jacket fits him as if it was made to order.*

на са́мом де́ле—*actually; in fact; really*

На са́мом де́ле я не собира́лся е́хать, но меня́ сро́чно вы́звали. *Actually, I didn't want to go on a trip, but I was urgently summoned.*

э́то то же са́мое (де́ло)—*be all the same; amount to the same thing*

Покупа́ть о́вощи на ры́нке, э́то то же са́мое де́ло, что и в магази́не. *It amounts to the same thing if you buy your vegetables in a store or at the market.*

сапо́г—*boot*

два сапога́—па́ра—*two of a kind; they make a pair; be well matched*

Ива́н и Ле́на два сапога́—па́ра. *Ivan and Lena are quite well matched.*

сапоги́ всмя́тку—*rubbish; sheer nonsense*

Что Бори́с говори́т, э́то одни́ сапоги́ всмя́тку. *What Boris says is sheer nonsense.*

сапо́жник—*shoemaker*

сапо́жник без сапо́г—*the shoemaker's child goes barefoot*

Он архите́ктор, а у них до́ма нет—сапо́жник без сапо́г. *He is an architect but they have no house—the shoemaker's child goes barefoot.*

пья́н(ый) как сапо́жник—*be drunk as a sailor*

Он лежа́л на полу́, пья́ный как сапо́жник. *He lay on the floor, drunk as a sailor.*

са́хар—*sugar*

не са́хар—*not all milk and honey*

Моя жизнь с ней—не са́хар. *My life isn't all milk and honey with her.*

сва́дьба—*wedding*

бриллиа́нтовая (or **алма́зная**) **сва́дьба**—*75th wedding anniversary*

Мои́м сосе́дям уже́ недалеко́ до алма́зной сва́дьбы. *It's not too long before my neighbors' diamond jubilee.*

до сва́дьбы заживёт—*one will survive it; one will be just fine*

Пла́чущего ма́льчика ма́ма успоко́ила: «Твоя́ ра́на несерьёзна, до сва́дьбы заживёт.» *The mother comforted the crying little boy, "Your wound is not serious, you're going to be just fine."*

(как) на Мала́ньину сва́дьбу—*enough to feed an army*

На мой день рожде́ния мы напекли́ сто́лько пирого́в, как на Мала́ньину сва́дьбу. *We baked so many pies for my birthday that it was enough to feed an army.*

сват—*father of a son-in-law* (or *daughter-in-law)*

ни сват, ни брат—*no relation of one's; no kith or kin of one*

Как он сме́ет вме́шиваться в мою́ ли́чную жизнь? Он мне ни сват, ни брат. *How does he dare interfere with my personal life? He's no kith or kin of mine.*

све́дение—*information*

к ва́шему све́дению—*you might want to know; for your information*

К ва́шему све́дению, пи́сьменный экза́мен бу́дет за́втра. *For your information, the written examination will take place tomorrow.*

приня́ть к све́дению—*take into consideration* (or *account)*

Олéг прúнял моё мнéние к свéдению. *Oleg took my opinion into consideration.*

свéжесть—*freshness*

не пéрвой свéжести—*1. not quite fresh 2. not very clean 3. not very young; past her prime*

1. Óвощи бы́ли не пéрвой свéжести. *The vegetables weren't quite fresh.*
2. Постéль былá не пéрвой свéжести. *The bedding was not very clean.*
3. Невéста былá не пéрвой свéжести. *The bride was past her prime.*

свéрху—*from above*

свéрху дóнизу—*1. from top to bottom 2. to the core*

1. Я обыскáл квартúру свéрху дóнизу, но ключéй не нашёл. *I searched my apartment from top to bottom, but couldn't find my keys.*
2. Он был плохóй человéк свéрху дóнизу. *He was a man rotten to the core.*

смотрéть свéрху вниз—*look down on someone*

На людéй Николáй смотрéл свéрху вниз, бýдучи самоувéренным. *Being very self-assured, Nikolay looked down on people.*

свет—*light*

чуть свет—*crack of dawn*

Чуть свет Ивáн приéхал. *Ivan arrived at the crack of dawn.*

свет—*world*

выпускáть в свет—*publish*

Мою кнúгу вы́пустили в свет год томý назáд. *My book was published a year ago.*

выходúть в свет—*be published*

Но́вый журна́л выхо́дит в свет два ра́за в ме́сяц. *The new journal will be published twice a month.*

люби́ть свет—*enjoy society*

Она́ жизнера́достная, лю́бит свет. *She enjoys society as she is full of joie de vivre.*

на бе́лом све́те—*in the wide world*

Тако́й ма́тери, как моя́, нет на бе́лом све́те. *There isn't another mother like mine in the whole wide world!*

ни за что на све́те—*not for the life of one; not for anything in the world*

Ни за что на све́те я э́ту та́йну не расскажу́. *I won't give this secret away for anything in the world.*

переверну́ть весь свет—*leave no stone unturned; move heaven and earth*

Что́бы доказа́ть свою́ невино́вность, он переверну́л весь свет. *He left no stone unturned in order to prove his innocence.*

по всему́ све́ту—*high and low; everywhere*

Ива́н иска́л Ве́ру по всему́ све́ту. *Ivan was looking for Vera everywhere.*

руга́ть кого́ **на чём свет стои́т**—*call someone every name in the book*

Ива́н руга́л Никола́я на чём свет стои́т. *Ivan called Nikolay every name in the book.*

тот свет—*the other* (or *next*) *world*

Он до́лго не возвраща́лся с войны́, и мы счита́ли, что он уже́ на том све́те. *He didn't return from the war for a long time, so we thought he was already in the other world.*

яви́ться на свет; уви́деть свет (or **мир**)—*be born*

Моя сестра́ появи́лась на свет три го́да тому́ наза́д. *My sister was born three years ago.*

свида́ние—*meeting; appointment*

до ско́рого свида́ния!; до ско́рого!—*see you soon!*

«До скóрого свидáния!»—сказáл Сергéй уходя́. *"See you soon," Sergey said as he was leaving.*

свидéтель—*witness*

быть (or **служи́ть) живы́м свидéтелем**—*be a living monument*

Руи́ны цéркви бы́ли живы́м свидéтелем войны́. *The church ruins were a living monument to the destructiveness of the war.*

свинья́—*pig; hog*

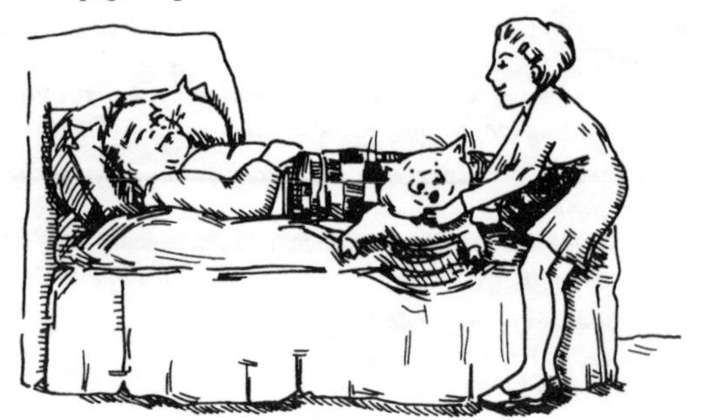

подложи́ть свинью́—*play a dirty* (or *mean) trick on someone*

Лéна подложи́ла Пáвлу свинью́ тем, что на свидáние пришлá с пáрнем. *Lena played a dirty trick on Pavel by showing up on their date with another young man.*

подложи́ть свинью́ самомý себé—*throw a stone in one's own garden*

Приня́в на рабóту растрáтчика, он подложи́л свинью́ самомý себé. *He threw a stone in his own garden by hiring an embezzler.*

посади́ свинью́ за стол, онá и нóги на стол—*give him an inch and he will take a mile*

Оле́г не зна́ет грани́цы—посади́ свинью́ за стол, она́ и но́ги на стол. *Oleg doesn't know the limits—give him an inch and he will take a mile.*

свой—*one's own*

на свои́х (на) двои́х—*on foot*

Он хо́дит на рабо́ту на свои́х двои́х. *He goes to work on foot.*

по-сво́йски—*free and easy*

Ива́н с на́ми обраща́лся по-сво́йски. *Ivan behaved free and easy in our company.*

сда́ча—*surrender; change*

дать сда́чи—*answer* (or *pay back) in kind*

Ну́жно уме́ть дать сда́чи, е́сли тебя́ оби́дят. *Insults should be paid back in kind.*

себя́—*myself; yourself*

быть вне себя́—*be beside oneself*

Оле́г был вне себя́ от го́ря. *Oleg was beside himself with grief.*

не по себе́—*be ill at ease; be uneasy*

Ле́не бы́ло не по себе́ в семье́ му́жа. *Lena felt ill at ease in her husband's family.*

уйти́ в себя́—*lost in thought; be pensive; withdrawn into oneself*

Он ушёл в себя́ и не заме́тил, когда́ я вошёл в ко́мнату. *Withdrawn into himself, he didn't notice when I entered the room.*

уйти́ к себе́—*withdraw to one's quarters; go to one's office*

По́сле ссо́ры с жено́й И́горь ушёл к себе́. *After the fight with his wife, Igor withdrew to his quarters.*

у себя́—*in; at home*

Да, Са́ша у себя́, он сейча́с подойдёт к телефо́ну. *Yes, Sasha's in; he'll come to the phone in a minute.*

сего́дня—*today*

не сего́дня—за́втра—*one of these days; any time* (or *moment*) *now*

Не сего́дня—за́втра мо́гут прие́хать ро́дственники. *One of these days our relatives may be arriving.*

сезо́н—*season*

ба́рхатный сезо́н—*the warm autumn months*

Мы взя́ли о́тпуск в ба́рхатный сезо́н. *We took our vacation during the warm autumn months.*

секре́т—*secret*

под стро́гим (or **строжа́йшим** or **больши́м**) **секре́том**—*in strict confidence*

Ива́н рассказа́л о свое́й жи́зни под стро́гим секре́том. *Ivan talked about his life in strict confidence.*

секу́нда—*second*

одну́ (or **сию́**) **секу́нду!**—*just a moment!; wait a moment!*

Одну́ секу́нду, я верну́сь. *I'll be back in just one moment...*

секу́нда в секу́нду—*on the dot; at the precise time; right on time*

Я был уве́рен, что он рабо́ту вы́полнит секу́нда в секу́нду. *I was convinced that he'd complete his work on the dot.*

сентя́брь—*September*

смотре́ть сентябрём—*have a long face on; look morose*

По́сле похоро́н отца́ Ники́та смотре́л сентябрём. *Nikita looked morose after his father's funeral.*

се́рдце—*heart*

(бли́зко) принима́ть к се́рдцу—*take to heart*

Ни́на всё бли́зко принима́ет к се́рдцу, а пото́м не́рвничает. *Nina takes everything to heart, and then she gets nervous.*

брать за се́рдце—*move deeply*

Трагéдия сироты́ меня́ брала́ за сéрдце. *The tragedy of the orphan has moved me deeply.*

лежáть на сéрдце—*weigh heavily on one's mind*

Судьба́ угнетённых нарóдов лежи́т на сéрдце у меня́. *The fate of oppressed peoples weighs heavily on my mind.*

от всегó сéрдца—*with all one's heart*

От всегó сéрдца я поздрáвил мать с днём рождéния. *I congratulated my mother on her birthday with all my heart.*

по сéрдцу (or **душé**)—*to one's liking; please one; something appeals to someone*

Извéстно, что лесть всем по сéрдцу. *It is well known, that flattery pleases everyone.*

сéрдце замирáет—*one's heart sinks* (or *skips a beat)*

Когдá я получи́л счетá из больни́цы, у меня́ сéрдце зáмерло. *My heart sank when I received the bill from the hospital.*

сéрдце (or **душá) не лежи́т**—*have no liking for; something doesn't appeal to one*

У меня́ сéрдце не лежи́т к совремéнной мýзыке. *I have no liking for modern music.*

сéрдце не на мéсте—*be anxious* (or *uneasy); be sick at heart; be worried sick*

Когдá дéти больны́, у мáтери сéрдце не на мéсте. *When her children are sick, the mother is sick at heart.*

сéрдце отхóдит—*calm down*

Мáша легкó раздражáется, но её сéрдце бы́стро отхóдит. *Masha becomes excited very easily, but she also cools down just as fast.*

скрепя́ сéрдце—*reluctantly*

Скрепя́ сéрдце Лéна позвони́ла кредитóру, чтóбы объясни́ть, почемý онá не мóжет плати́ть. *Reluctantly Lena phoned her creditor to explain why she couldn't pay.*

с лёгким сéрдцем—*without anxiety; lightheartedly*

Оле́г при́нял но́вый пост с лёгким се́рдцем. *Oleg assumed his new post without anxiety.*

середи́на—*middle*

золота́я середи́на—*happy middle; golden mean*

В жи́зни лу́чше всего́ держа́ться золото́й середи́ны. *It is best to keep to the golden mean in life.*

си́ла—*strength*

быть не под си́лу—*be too much for one; be more than one can handle*

Учёба э́тому ма́льчику не под си́лу. *Studying is too much for this boy.*

вступа́ть в (зако́нную) си́лу—*become effective*

Че́рез ме́сяц но́вые зако́ны всту́пят в си́лу. *New laws will become effective within a month.*

крича́ть и́зо всех сил—*cry* (or *shout) at the top of one's voice* (or *with all one's might)*

От бо́ли Арка́дий крича́л и́зо всех сил. *Arkady was shouting at the top of his voice with pain.*

не рассчита́ть свои́х сил—*overestimate one's strength*

Не рассчита́в свои́х сил, он заболе́л. *He overestimated his strength and became ill.*

оста́ться в си́ле—*be effective; hold good*

На́ши реше́ния оста́лись в си́ле на до́лгое вре́мя. *Our decisions were effective for a long time.*

сказа́ть—*tell; say; talk*

как вам сказа́ть?—*how shall I put it?*

Ну как вам сказа́ть? Мне ка́жется, что вы с тако́й рабо́той не спра́витесь. *How shall I put it? It seems to me that this kind of work is not really for you.*

к сло́ву сказа́ть; кста́ти сказа́ть—*by the way*

Кста́ти сказа́ть, я за́втра уезжа́ю. *By the way—I'm off tomorrow on a trip.*

не́чего сказа́ть!—*I must say!*

Серге́й прав. Не́чего сказа́ть! *I must say—Sergey is right!*

ничего́ не ска́жешь—*one can't deny; one has to admit that*

Дом про́чно постро́ен, ничего́ не ска́жешь. *The house is solidly built—one has to admit that!*

так сказа́ть—*so to speak*

Мы, так сказа́ть, уже́ реши́ли э́ту пробле́му. *We have solved this problem already, so to speak.*

ска́терть—*tablecloth*

ска́тертью доро́га—*good riddance!*

Мо́жешь уходи́ть, ска́тертью тебе́ доро́га! *You may go! Good riddance!*

скла́д—*stamp; mould*

ни скла́ду, ни ла́ду—*neither rhyme nor reason*

В расска́зе Ники́ты ни скла́ду, ни ла́ду. *There's no rhyme or reason to Nikita's story.*

склад ума́—*mentality; way of thinking*

Э́то не по его́ скла́ду ума́ де́ло. *This is not a matter that corresponds to his way of thinking.*

ско́лько—*how much*

ско́лько уго́дно—*to one's heart's content; as much as you want*

Ку́шайте, ско́лько уго́дно! *Eat to your heart's content!*

ско́рый—*quick; fast*

скоре́е всего́—*most likely; probably*

Скоре́е всего́, дождя́ не бу́дет. *It is most likely that it won't rain.*

ску́ка—*bore*

зелёная ску́ка—*unbearable* (or *intolerable) boredom*

Э́та кни́га—зелёная ску́ка. *This book is unbearable boredom.*

наводи́ть ску́ку—*bore to death*

Арка́дий наводи́л ску́ку на меня́ свои́ми расска́зами. *Arkady bored me to death with his stories.*

сла́ва—*glory*

входи́ть в сла́ву—*win fame; become famous*

Получи́в Но́белевскую пре́мию, поэ́т вошёл в сла́ву. *The poet became famous after he won the Nobel Prize.*

сла́ва бо́гу—*thank God*

Сла́ва бо́гу мы жи́вы и здоро́вы. *Thank God, we're alive and healthy.*

на сла́ву—*excellent(ly); really well*

Рабо́ту мы вы́полнили на сла́ву. *We have really done our job well.*

след—*mark*

его́ и след просты́л—*vanish into thin air*

Его́ и сле́д просты́л, когда́ он заме́тил полице́йского. *He vanished into thin air when he saw the policeman.*

слеза́—*tear*

до слёз—*be extremely upset* (or *hurt* or *offended,* etc.)

До слёз бо́льно, что я напра́сно труди́лся. *It hurts to think that I have labored in vain.*

облива́ться слеза́ми—*dissolve in tears*

На похорона́х Ната́ша облива́лась слеза́ми. *Natasha dissolved in tears at the funeral.*

осуши́ть слёзы—*dry one's tears; comfort someone*

Тёплыми слова́ми И́горь осуши́л слёзы О́льге. *Igor comforted Olga with his compassionate words.*

отолью́тся слёзы—*will have to pay for*

Хотя́ Анато́лий оби́делся на Арка́дия, он ничего́ не сказа́л, но ду́мал: отолью́тся слёзы. *Although Anatoly got offended at*

Arkady, he didn't say anything and just thought, "He will have to pay for it."

сло́во—*word*

без да́льних (or **ли́шних**) **слов**—*without further ado*

Без да́льних слов, Михаи́л попроси́л меня́ оста́вить его́ в поко́е. *Without further ado, Mikhail asked me to leave him alone.*

брать сло́во—*deliver a speech*

На собра́ниях Са́ша ча́сто брал сло́во. *Sasha frequently delivered speeches at the meetings.*

брать сло́во с кого́—*make one promise*

Я уже́ не раз брал с Ники́ты сло́во, что он бро́сит кури́ть. *I made Nikita promise more than once that he would quit smoking.*

броса́ть слова́ на ве́тер—*1. waste words 2. speak* (or *talk) at random*

1. Ты лишь броса́ешь слова́ на ве́тер, когда́ даёшь ему́ сове́ты. *You'll just waste your words by giving him advice.*
2. Не поду́мав, Пётр броса́л слова́ на ве́тер. *Peter was talking thoughtlessly and at random.*

ве́рить на́ слово—*take one at one's word*

Че́стному челове́ку мо́жно ве́рить на́ слово. *You can take an honest person at his word.*

в двух слова́х; в коро́тких слова́х—*in a nutshell; briefly*

В двух слова́х я объясни́л Са́ше ситуа́цию. *I explained the situation to Sasha in a nutshell.*

двух слов связа́ть не мочь—*not to be able to put two words together*

И́горь постоя́нно хва́стался зна́нием францу́зского языка́, но когда́ пришло́сь говори́ть по-францу́зски, он двух слов связа́ть не мог. *Igor kept bragging about his knowledge of French, but when it came to having to speak French, he was unable to put two words together.*

держáть (своё) слóво—*be as good as one's word; stick to one's word*

Я обещáл Пáвлу держáть слóво. *I promised Pavel that I'd stick to my word.*

к слóву (сказáть)—*by the way; incidentally*

К слóву сказáть, в расскáзе Ивáна ни кáпли йстины нет. *By the way, there wasn't a shred of truth in Ivan's story.*

нет слов; слов нет—*there's no doubt*

Ивáн прав, слов нет. *There is no doubt that Ivan is right.*

слóво в слóво (or **до слóва**)—*word by word; word for word*

Слóво в слóво Грйша передáл мой указáния. *Grisha transmitted my directives word by word.*

слóвó зá слово—*one word led to another*

Слóво зá слово, и вéчер прошёл. *One word led to another and the evening passed by.*

стоять на своём слóве—*be as good as one's word*

В любóй ситуáции Борйс стоял на своём слóве. *Boris was as good as his word in every situation.*

черкнýть нéсколько слов—*drop a line*

Я черкнýла Сáше нéсколько слов о встрéче на зáвтра. *I dropped Sasha a line about our meeting tomorrow.*

чéстное слóво!—*upon my word!; word of honor!*

Чéстное слóво, я э́то сдéлаю! *I'll do this—word of honor!*

словцó—*word*

крáсно словцó—*clever* (or *apt*) *remark*

Йгорь слáвился тем, что умéл встáвить крáсное словцó. *Igor was famous for his clever remarks.*

слóжность—*complication*

в óбщей слóжности—*in sum; in all*

В óбщей слóжности вéчер прошёл приятно. *In sum, the evening went by pleasantly.*

слон—*elephant*

(как) слон в посу́дной ла́вке—*(like) a bull in a china shop*

Игорь на катке́, как слон в посу́дной ла́вке. *On a skating rink Igor is like a bull in a china shop.*

слона́ не приме́тить—*overlook the obvious*

В тако́м разнообра́зии това́ров да́же слона́ мо́жно не приме́тить. *In such an abundance of goods, one can easily overlook the obvious.*

слон на́ ухо наступи́л—SEE: **медве́дь на́ ухо наступи́л**

слу́жба—*service; work; favor*

дви́гаться (or **повыша́ться) по слу́жбе**—*get a promotion*

Андре́й бы́стро дви́гался по слу́жбе. *Andrey got a fast promotion.*

не в слу́жбу, а в дру́жбу—*for friendship's sake; do someone a favor*

Не в слу́жбу, а в дру́жбу за́втра подмени́ меня́ на рабо́те. *Please stand in for me at work tomorrow, for friendship's sake!*

сослужи́ть слу́жбу—*do a favor*

Сослужи́те мне слу́жбу, вы́зовите врача́! *Do me a favor and call the doctor, won't you?*

слух—*hearing*

ни слу́ху, ни ду́ху—*there's no news whatsoever*

По́сле отъе́зда Ле́ны о ней ни слу́ху, ни ду́ху. *There was no news from Lena whatsoever after she had left.*

обрати́ться (or **преврати́ться**) **в слух; навостри́ть** (or **насторожи́ть**) **слух**—*be all ears*

Когда́ выступа́л президе́нт, Фёдор весь обрати́лся в слух. *When the President appeared on the stage, Fedor was all ears.*

слу́чай—*case; occasion; accident*

в кра́йнем слу́чае—*if worst comes to worst*

В кра́йнем слу́чае, нам придётся отказа́ться от пое́здки. *If worst comes to worst we'll just have to cancel our trip.*

в лу́чшем слу́чае—*in the best of cases; in an optimal scenario*

В лу́чшем слу́чае Ива́на вы́берут президе́нтом. *In an optimal scenario, Ivan might be elected president.*

во вся́ком слу́чае—*in any case* (or *rate*)

Во вся́ком слу́чае позвони́ мне по́сле прие́зда. *Give me a ring once you've arrived, at any rate.*

на вся́кий слу́чай—*just in case*

На вся́кий слу́чай оста́вь свой но́мер телефо́на. *Give your phone number, just in case.*

ни в ко́ем слу́чае—*under no circumstances*

Ни в ко́ем слу́чае не продава́й дом. *Don't sell the house under any circumstances!*

от слу́чая к слу́чаю—*from time to time*

От слу́чая к слу́чаю Па́вел приезжа́л к нам в го́сти. *Pavel would visit us from time to time.*

при слу́чае—*on occasion; when opportunity offers; when you get a chance*

При слу́чае напиши́ подро́бное письмо́. *Write me a detailed letter when you get a chance!*

удо́бный слу́чай—*the right time; (if* or *when we get) a chance*

При удо́бном слу́чае мы поговори́м о твое́й пробле́ме. *We'll talk about your problem when we get a chance.*

смерть—*death*

до сме́рти хо́чется—*is dying for something; want something very much*

Петру́ до сме́рти хо́чется купи́ть я́хту. *Peter is dying to buy a yacht.*

смерть как люби́ть—*just love; love to distraction; be crazy about something*

Смерть как люблю́ слу́шать расска́зы Ве́ры. *I just love to listen to Vera's stories.*

умере́ть свое́й сме́ртью—*die a natural death*

На войне́ солда́т ре́дко умира́ет свое́й сме́ртью. *Soldiers seldom die a natural death in a war.*

смех—*laugh*

ката́ться (or **па́дать**) **со́ смеху; па́дать от сме́ха**—*roll with laughter*

От шу́ток Арка́дия мы ката́лись со́ смеху. *We were rolling with laughter from Arkady's jokes.*

ло́паться от сме́ха (or **со́ смеху**)—*burst with laughter*

Когда́ Степа́н расска́зывал анекдо́ты, мы про́сто ло́пались от сме́ха. *We simply burst with laughter when Stepan told us his jokes.*

поднима́ть на́ смех—*make a laughing stock of someone; make fun of someone*

Оле́г ча́сто поднима́л меня́ на́ смех. *Oleg often made me into a laughingstock.*

смотре́ть—*look; see*

смотре́ть в о́ба—*be on one's guard; be on alert; keep one's eyes open*

Э́тот челове́к—опа́сный банди́т, с ним ну́жно смотре́ть в о́ба. *This fellow is a dangerous criminal—keep your eyes open when he's around.*

смотри́(те)—*be sure*

Смотри́те, не забу́дьте вы́ключить свет. *Be sure not to forget to turn the light out!*

смотря́ как—*depending on*

«Мы поéдем в Нью-Йорк?»—«Смотря́ как вы бу́дете себя́ вести́.» *"Are we going to New York?"—"We'll see; depends on how well you behave yourselves."*

смысл—*meaning; sense*

в не́котором смы́сле—*in a way*

В не́котором смы́сле Ива́н прав. *Ivan is right—in a way.*

в перено́сном смы́сле сло́ва—*figuratively; in the figurative sense of the word*

Э́то я сказа́л в перено́сном смы́сле сло́ва. *I said this in the figurative sense of the word.*

в по́лном смы́сле сло́ва—*in the full* (or *true*) *sense of the word*

Фёдор был в по́лном смы́сле сло́ва счастли́вым челове́ком. *Fedor was a happy man, in the true sense of the word.*

снег—*snow*

как (бу́дто or **сло́вно** or **то́чно) снег на го́лову**—*like a bolt from the blue; out of the clear blue sky; out of nowhere*

Мы до́лго не ви́дели А́нну, и вдруг она́ появи́лась, бу́дто снег на го́лову. *We hadn't seen Anna for a long time when she appeared like a bolt from the blue.*

ну́жен, как прошлого́дний снег—*someone needs something like a hole in the head*

Э́ти расхо́ды мне нужны́, как прошлого́дний снег. *I need these expenses like a hole in the head.*

собáка—*dog*

вéшать всех собáк—*blame somebody for everything*

Я ужé привы́к, что брáтья вéшают всех собáк на меня́. *I am used to the fact that my brothers blame me for everything.*

вот где собáка зары́та—*that's where the shoe pinches; that's where the trouble lies; that's the root of the matter*

«Вот где собáка зары́та»—сказáл проверя́ющий, когдá закóнчил ревúзию в бухгáлтерских докумéнтах. *"That's where the trouble lies," said the supervisor when he finished the checking of the ledgers.*

как собáка на сéне—*like a dog in the manger*

Петру́ велосипéд не ну́жен, а другúм не даёт; тóчно как собáка на сéне. *Peter doesn't want the bicycle and yet he won't give it to anyone else—like a dog in the manger.*

любúть как собáка пáлку—*love as a horse loves the whip*

Васúлий лю́бит свою́ рабóту как собáка пáлку. *Vasily loves his work like a horse loves the whip.*

ну́жен, как собáке пя́тая ногá—*need as a fifth wheel* (or *like a hole in the head)*

Мне егó дру́жба нужнá, как собáке пя́тая ногá. *I need his friendship like a fifth wheel.*

собáке собáчья смерть—*a cur's death to a cur!*

Олéг всех обману́л, а сейчáс и сам попáл в лову́шку. Собáке собáчья смерть. *Oleg cheated everyone, but now he fell into his own trap. A cur's death to a cur!*

собáку съéсть—*be an old hand; know something inside out*

В компью́терном дéле Ѝгорь собáку съел. *Igor is an old hand when it comes to the computer.*

сóвесть—*conscience*

лежáть на сóвести—*have pangs of conscience*

Ошúбки, сдéланные в ю́ности, до сих пор лежáт на сóвести Аркáдия. *The mistakes Arkady made in his youth are still giving him pangs of conscience.*

по со́вести сказа́ть—*honestly speaking; to tell you the truth*

По со́вести сказа́ть, я о́чень го́лоден. *I am very hungry, to tell you the truth.*

со споко́йной со́вестью—*with a clear conscience; without a guilt complex*

Ири́на плохо́го ничего́ не сде́лала, она живёт со споко́йной со́вестью. *Since Irina hadn't done anything wrong, she lives with a clear conscience.*

хва́тит со́вести—*have the cheek; have the gall; have the nerve*

У Са́ши хвати́ло со́вести проси́ть у нас де́ньги. *Sasha had the nerve to ask us for money.*

совсе́м—*completely; entirely*

совсе́м бы́ло—*just about*

Я совсе́м бы́ло реши́л уе́хать в о́тпуск. *I've just about made up my mind to take a vacation trip.*

совсе́м наоборо́т—*just the other way around*

Я ду́мал, что о́бувь хоро́шего ка́чества, а оказа́лось совсе́м наоборо́т. *I thought that the shoes were of good quality, but it was just the other way around, as it turned out.*

совсе́м нет—*1. not in the least; not at all 2. out of the question*

1. У него́ совсе́м нет угрызе́ний со́вести за свои́ отрица́тельные посту́пки. *He has no guilty conscience in the least on account of his misdeeds.*
2. «Ты мо́жешь пойти́ с на́ми в теа́тр?»—«К сожале́нию, совсе́м нет.» *"Can you come with us to the theater?"—"Unfortunately, it's out of the question."*

сожале́ние—*regret*

к вели́кому моему́ сожале́нию—*much to my regret*

К вели́кому моему́ сожале́нию, я до́лжен уе́хать из го́рода. *Much to my regret, I must leave town.*

к сожале́нию—*unfortunately*

К сожале́нию, тепе́рь я не могу́ вам верну́ть мой долг. *Unfortunately, I cannot repay my debt to you just now.*

соль—*salt*

сы́пать соль на рáну—*rub it in*

Капитали́ст Михаи́л горди́лся, что у негó есть Мерседéс и не пóльзуется городски́м трáнспортом. «Не сыпь мне соль на рáну!»—сказáл обанкрóтившийся друг. *Mikhail was bragging that he has a Mercedes and doesn't use public transport. "Don't rub it in!" said his friend who suffered bankruptcy.*

сон—*sleep; dream*

ни сном ни дýхом (не виновáт)—*be not guilty at all*

Вы́яснилось, что подсуди́мый ни сном ни дýхом не виновáт. *It became clarified that the accused wasn't guilty at all.*

прия́тного сна!—*sleep well!; sleep tight*

«Прия́тного сна!»—сказáла мать дéтям. *"Sleep tight," the mother said to her children.*

сон в рýку—*the dream has come true*

Натáша вы́шла зáмуж за миллионéра—сон в рýку. *Natasha's dream came true—she married a millionaire.*

сон (в гóлову) не идёт—*be unable to sleep; be unable to catch any z's*

Из-за волнéния мне сон в гóлову не идёт. *I can't catch any z's because of all the excitement.*

сор—*rubbish*

выноси́ть сор из избы́—*wash one's dirty linen in public*

У Лéны былá плохáя привы́чка выноси́ть сор из избы́. *Lena had the bad habit of washing her dirty linen in public.*

сорóчка—*shirt*

роди́ться в сорóчке—SEE: **роди́ться в рубáшке**

состáв—*composition; staff*

в пóлном состáве—*in a body; as one man; in its entirety*

На заседáние нáша фи́рма появи́лась в пóлном составе. *Our firm appeared in its entirety at the session.*

сóус—*sauce; gravy*

ни под каки́м сóусом—SEE: **ни в кóем слу́чае**

спаси́бо—*thanks*

большóе спаси́бо—*thanks a lot; many thanks*

Большóе спаси́бо за окáзанную мне пóмощь. *Many thanks for the help you gave me.*

и на том спаси́бо; спаси́бо и на э́том—*one should be thankful at least for that*

Мы у́чимся на тру́дностях жи́зни, и на том спаси́бо. *We learn from the difficulties of life—one should be thankful at least for that.*

сдéлать за однó спаси́бо—*do something for love* (or *for free of charge)*

Óльга сдéлала мне мнóго услу́г за однó спаси́бо. *Olga did me many favors for love.*

спи́ца—*knitting needle; spoke*

послéдняя спи́ца в колесни́це—*be a tiny cog in a machine; be a small fry*

Почему́ Пётр такóй самодовóльный? Ведь он послéдняя спи́ца в колесни́це на своéй фи́рме. *Why is Peter so impressed with himself, when he is but a tiny cog in the machine at the firm?*

пя́тая спи́ца в колесни́це—SEE: **пя́тое колесó в телéге**

срéдство—*means; way*

жить не по срéдствам—*live beyond one's means*

Покупáя бóльше плáтьев, чем ей ну́жно, сестрá живёт не по срéдствам. *By buying far more clothes than she needs, my sister lives beyond her means.*

зарабáтывать срéдства на жизнь—*earn one's living*

Мы зараба́тываем сре́дства на жизнь больши́м трудо́м. *We earn our living with great difficulty.*

не по сре́дствам—*not to be able to afford something*

Предложи́ли дорого́й автомоби́ль, но мне э́то не по сре́дствам. *I was offered an expensive car, but I just can't afford it.*

срок—*date; time*

к сро́ку—*on time*

Наве́рно, мы не поспе́ем к сро́ку. *We probably won't make it on time.*

ста́рость—*old age*

дожи́ть до глубо́кой ста́рости—*live to be very old*

Де́душка дожи́л до глубо́кой ста́рости и никогда́ не боле́л. *Grandpa lived to be very old and was never sick.*

на ста́рости лет—*in one's old age*

На ста́рости лет Степа́н на́чал интересова́ться садово́дством. *Stepan began to cultivate an interest in gardening in his old age.*

стать—*stand; become; begin*

во что бы то ни ста́ло—*at any price*

Во что бы то ни ста́ло, Ири́на хо́чет стать актри́сой. *Irina wants to become an actress at any price.*

ни стать ни сесть—*there is no room at all; no room to (even) drop a needle*

На конце́рте изве́стной поп-звезды́ в за́ле ни стать ни сесть. *There is no room at all at the famous pop singer's concert.*

ни стать ни сесть не уме́ть—*be uncultured*

Как он пойдёт на диплома́тический приём? Он ни стать ни сесть не уме́ет. *How will he attend the diplomatic reception—he is so uncultured!*

стена́—*wall*

жить стена́ в стену́—*live next door to someone*

Мы с подру́гой живём стена́ в стену́. *I live next door to my girlfriend.*

лезть на сте́ну—*be beside oneself with something; get mad*

От гне́ва Бори́с лез на сте́ну. *Boris was beside himself with fury.*

стол—*table*

ложи́ться на стол—*have surgery*

По́сле дли́тельного обсле́дования вы́яснилось, что Петру́ придётся лечь на стол. *After a lengthy examination it turned out that Peter had to have surgery.*

писа́ть на стол (or **в я́щик**)—*write for the desk drawer*

Стихи́ тала́нтливой поэте́ссы не издава́ли и она́ писа́ла на стол. *The talented poetess's verses didn't get published—she wrote for the desk drawer.*

сади́ться за оди́н стол—*sit down at the negotiating table*

Представи́тели бо́рющихся сторо́н наконе́ц се́ли за оди́н стол. *The representatives of the warring parties finally sat down at the negotiating table.*

столб—*pole*

стоя́ть столбо́м—*stand like a statue; stand dumb and motionless*

Когда́ преподава́тель спра́шивал Арка́дия, он стоя́л столбо́м. *When the teacher asked Arkady, he stood dumb and motionless.*

сто́ить—*cost*

не сто́ит (чего́-либо)—*don't mention it!*

Когда́ я поблагодари́л Па́вла, он отве́тил: «Не сто́ит благода́рности.» *When I thanked Pavel, he said, "Don't mention it!"*

ничего́ не сто́ит—*be like kid's play; be easy to handle* (or *take care of*)

Петру́ ничего́ не сто́ит отремонти́ровать автомоби́ль. *It's kid's play for Peter to repair the car.*

сто́ит то́лько мигну́ть—*all one has to do is snap one's fingers*

Мне сто́ит то́лько мигну́ть, и О́льга тут же вернётся ко мне. *All I have to do is snap my fingers and Olga comes running back to me.*

сторона́—*side; part; land*

брать (or **держа́ть** or **принима́ть**) **сто́рону**—*side with someone; be on someone's side*

Тёща Ива́на всегда́ держа́ла сто́рону свое́й до́чери. *Ivan's mother-in-law was always on her daughter's side.*

друга́я (or **оборо́тная**) **сторона́ (меда́ли)**—*other side of the coin; the downside of something; on the negative side of something*

У́мной же́нщине трудне́е вы́йти за́муж—вот оборо́тная сторона́ (меда́ли)! *The downside of being a smart woman is that it is harder to get married.*

лицева́я сторона́ до́ма—*front of the house*

Лицева́я сторона́ на́шего до́ма смо́трит на се́вер. *The front of our house faces north.*

с мое́й стороны́—*for my part*

С мое́й стороны́ что тре́буется—я сде́лаю. *For my part, I'm doing all that's required.*

с одно́й стороны́ ... с друго́й стороны́—*on the one hand... on the other hand*

С одно́й стороны́ И́горь на́ши усло́вия не зна́л, с друго́й стороны́ он и не хоте́л их знать. *On the one hand, Igor didn't know our circumstances; on the other, neither did he want to.*

узна́ть сторonóй—*learn from hearsay; through the grapevine; (from the) scuttlebutt*

Сторonóй я узна́л, что О́льга вы́шла за́муж за моего́ дру́га. *I heard through the grapevine that Olga married my friend.*

стра́сть—*passion*

стра́сть как—*very much; intensely; passionately; be crazy about something*

Стра́сть как люблю́ путеше́ствовать. *I am crazy about traveling.*

стра́сть ско́лько—*very many; a dreadful quantity of; a huge amount*

Стра́сть ско́лько люде́й собрало́сь на пля́же. *There were dreadfully many people on the beach.*

стра́сть как хо́чется—*be dying to do something*

Стра́сть как Петру́ хо́чется уе́хать в Австра́лию. *Peter is dying to go to Australia.*

строй—*system; order*

войти́ в строй—*start to function; begin production; go into operation*

Но́вая фа́брика вошла́ в строй. *The new factory began production.*

вы́йти из стро́я—*1. go bad 2. become dysfunctional; break down; be out of order*

1. Бори́с сто́лько пья́нствовал, что его́ пе́чень вы́шла из стро́я. *Boris drank so much that his liver went bad.*
2. В на́шем до́ме лифт сно́ва вы́шел из стро́я. *The elevator has broken down again in our building.*

вы́вести из стро́я—*put out of action*

Жильцы́ до́ма вы́вели из стро́я водопрово́д. *The tenants put the water pipe out of action.*

стул—*chair*

сиде́ть ме́жду двух сту́льев—*sit on the fence; to equivocate*

Ма́ша сиде́ла ме́жду двух сту́льев, не зна́я что де́лать: вы́йти за́муж и́ли поступи́ть в университе́т. *Masha didn't know whether to get married or attend the university—she was sitting on the fence.*

стыд—*shame*

как вам не сты́дно—*aren't you ashamed (of yourself) for doing something?*

Как вам не сты́дно так вражде́бно клевета́ть на колле́г? *Aren't you ashamed of yourself for badmouthing your colleagues so maliciously?*

нет стыда́ в глаза́х—*have no shame at all*

О́льга нам нагруби́ла и на сле́дующий день опя́ть пришла́. У неё про́сто стыда́ в глаза́х нет. *Olga offended us, yet next day she came to see us again. She has no shame at all.*

суд—*court; trial*

отдава́ть под суд; привлека́ть к суду́; предава́ть суду́—*put on trial; take to court*

За уби́йство его́ отда́ли под суд. *He was put on trial for murder.*

судьба́—*fate*

благодари́ть судьбу́—*thank one's lucky stars*

За мои́ успе́хи я благодарю́ судьбу́. *I thank my lucky stars for my success.*

искуша́ть судьбу́—*fly into the face of providence; tempt fate*

Свои́ми отрица́тельными де́йствиями Бори́с искуша́л судьбу́. *Boris was tempting fate with his thoughtless actions.*

каки́ми судьба́ми?—*what good wind brings you here? how on earth did you get here?*

Каки́ми судьба́ми ты яви́лся в наш университе́т? *How on earth did you get to our university?*

не судьба́—*not to be in the cards* (or *stars*)

Не судьба́ нам жени́ться. *It's not in the cards for us to get married.*

реша́ть судьбу́—*seal one's fate*

Случа́йная встре́ча реши́ла их судьбу́. *The accidental encounter sealed their fate.*

сумасше́ствие—*madness*

доводи́ть до сумасше́ствия—*drive someone mad*

Шум дете́й доводи́л нас до сумасше́ствия. *The noise of the kids was driving us mad.*

су́мма—*amount; sum*

кру́глая (or **кру́гленькая**) **су́мма**—*a pretty penny; a lot of money*

Кругосве́тное путеше́ствие обошло́сь нам в кру́гленькую су́мму. *Our trip around the world has cost us a pretty penny.*

существо́—*essence; being*

по существу́ (говоря́)—*in substance; basically; in essence*

Серге́й, по существу́, и́скренний челове́к. *Sergey is, basically, a sincere person.*

су́щность—*essence*

в су́щности (говоря́)—SEE: **по существу́ (говоря́)**

сча́стье—*happiness; luck*

име́ть сча́стье—*be honored; have the honor*

Я име́ю сча́стье прочита́ть ва́шу кни́гу. *I am honored to be reading your book.*

сча́стье измени́ло—*one's luck's run out*

По́сле мно́гих лет бога́тства, сча́стье нам измени́ло. *After many years of riches, our luck (finally) ran out.*

счёт—*bill; account*

в два счёта—*in a jiffy*

Я за́втрак пригото́влю в два счёта. *I'll fix the breakfast in a jiffy.*

в коне́чном (or **после́днем**) **счёте**—*finally; in the end*

В конéчном счёте всё хорошó получи́лось в моéй жи́зни. *In the end, everything has turned out OK in my life.*

для рóвного счёта—*make it even*

Для рóвного счёта мы прибáвили по два дóллара, чтóбы купи́ть подáрок для секретáрши. *To make it even, we all chipped in $2 so we can buy a present for the secretary.*

относи́ть (or **принимáть) на свой счёт**—*take something personally*

Мы говори́ли о знакóмом, а Пáвел отнёс э́то на свой счёт. *We were talking about an acquaintance, but Pavel took it personally.*

сын; сынóк—*son*

мáменькин сынóк—*mother's darling*

Éсли мáменькин сынóк попадáет в áрмию, то емý óчень тяжелó прихóдится. *When a mother's darling enters the military, he'll have a real rough time.*

сыр—*cheese*

катáться, как сыр в мáсле—*live off the fat of the land; be in clover*

Вы́играв в лотерéю, они́ катáлись как сыр в мáсле. *They were in clover when they won the lottery.*

T

тáйна—*secret*

открывáть тáйну—*reveal a secret*

Я случáйно откры́л тáйну о прóшлом моéй жены́. *I've accidentally revealed a secret about my wife's past.*

посвящáть в тáйну—*let someone into a secret*

Я не кáждого посвящáю в свои́ тáйны. *I don't let just anyone into my secrets.*

храни́ть в та́йне—*keep something a secret*

Своё разочарова́ние Ива́н бо́льше не мог храни́ть в та́йне. *Ivan could no longer keep his disappointment a secret.*

так—*so*

и так да́лее (и т.д.)—*etc.; and so on*

Ири́на уме́ет шить, вяза́ть, вышива́ть, и так да́лее. *Irina knows how to sew, knit, embroider, and so on.*

и так—*as it is; in the first place; to begin with*

Де́нег и так нет, а ты ещё тра́тишь на косме́тику. *As it is, there's no money—and yet you keep spending on cosmetics!*

так и́ли ина́че—*1. in any case 2. one way or (an)other*

1. Так и́ли ина́че, мне придётся изуча́ть языки́. *I must study languages in any case.*
2. Так или ина́че, я узна́ю пра́вду. *One way or another, I will learn the truth.*

так как—*because; since*

Так как бы́ло уже по́здно, мы пое́хали домо́й. *We went home, because it was late already.*

так себе́—*1. so-so 2. just passable; nothing special*

1. «Как вы себя́ чу́вствуете?»—«Так себе́.» *"How are you?—"So-so."*
2. Но́вый рестора́н так себе́. *The new restaurant is just passable.*

так то́чно—*yes, exactly!; that's right!; yes Sir* (or *Madam)!*

«Вы написа́ли ра́порт?»—«Так, то́чно, това́рищ полко́вник!» *"Did you write the report?"—"Yes, exactly, Comrade Colonel!"*

так что—*so*

Я уже́ купи́л тебе́ биле́т, так что мо́жешь е́хать в о́тпуск. *I bought your ticket already, so you can leave for your vacation.*

тала́нт—*talent*

зары́ть (or **закопа́ть**) **тала́нт в зе́млю**—*waste one's talent; hide one's light under a bushel*

О́льга зары́ла музыка́льный тала́нт в зе́млю, занима́ясь то́лько дома́шним хозя́йством. *Olga was wasting her musical talent by doing nothing except housekeeping.*

там—*there*

там ви́дно бу́дет—*we shall see when the time comes; we shall see when we get to it*

Там ви́дно бу́дет, как нам с на́шим прое́ктом пойти́ да́льше. *We'll see when the time comes how to proceed with this project.*

там же—*in the same place*

Бори́с рабо́тает там же, где его́ оте́ц. *Boris works at the same place as his father.*

там и тут; там и сям—*here and there and everywhere; every which way*

Там и тут бы́ли разбро́саны ве́щи в кварти́ре по́сле о́быска. *After the house search things lay strewn around here and there and everywere.*

там хорошо́, где нас нет—*the grass is (always) green(er) on the other side of the fence*

Ни́на ду́мает, что мне живётся лу́чше, чем ей. Там хорошо́, где нас нет. *Nina thinks that I do much better than she—the grass is always greener on the other side of the fence.*

таре́лка—*plate*

быть не в свое́й таре́лке—*be not quite oneself; feel ill at ease*

Среди́ чужи́х Ната́ша была́ не в свое́й таре́лке. *Natasha felt ill at ease among the strangers.*

теа́тр—*theater*

зелёный теа́тр—*open air theater*

Ле́том мы хо́дим в зелёный теа́тр. *We frequent the open air theater in the summer.*

телегра́мма—*telegram*

телегра́мма-мо́лния—*express telegram*

В день рождéния я получи́л телегрáмму-мóлнию. *I received an express telegram for my birthday.*

телефóн—*phone*

(часáми) висéть (or **пови́снуть) на телефóне**—*be on the phone for an excessively long time* (or *for ages*)

Нáши дéти часáми вися́т на телефóне. *Our kids are on the phone for ages.*

тем—*instrumental form of* **тот**

мéжду тем как—*whereas; while*

Я ужé пообéдал, мéжду тем как онá ещё не сéла за стол. *I already had my dinner, whereas she didn't even sit down yet.*

тем бóлее—*the more so; all the more*

Будь осторóжен, тем бóлее, что ты бóлен. *Take care of yourself—all the more, as you're sick!*

тем не мéнее—*nevertheless*

Имéя проблéмы, тем не мéнее мы сча́стливы. *Although we have some problems, we are, nevertheless, happy.*

тем ху́же—*so much the worse*

Ивáн до сих пор не знáет англи́йский, тем ху́же для негó. *Ivan still speaks no English—so much the worse for him!*

тéма—*subject; topic*

быть не по тéме—*be beside the point*

Егó аргумéнты не по тéме. *His arguments are beside the point.*

говори́ть по тéме—*keep to the point*

В свои́х выступлéниях И́горь всегдá говори́т по тéме. *Igor always keeps to the point with his comments.*

темп—*tempo; rate; speed*

в тéмпе—*posthaste; real fast*

Порабóтай в тéмпе, а потóм пойдём в ресторáн. *Work real fast and then we'll go to a restaurant.*

тень—*shade*

наводи́ть тень на плете́нь (or **я́сный день**)—*confuse matters; fog* (or *cloud*) *the issue*

Пётр рассказа́л о Никола́е так, как ему́ бы́ло вы́годно. Э́тим он наводи́л тень на плете́нь. *Peter spoke about Nikolay as it was favorable to himself—thereby he confused the matter.*

терпе́ние—*patience*

выводи́ть из терпе́ния—*try someone's patience*

Ученики́ ча́сто выво́дят из терпе́ния учителе́й. *Students often try the teachers' patience.*

вы́йти из терпе́ния—*lose patience*

Дискути́руя с Бори́сом, я стара́лся не вы́йти из терпе́ния. *I tried not to lose my patience while talking to Boris.*

терпе́ние ло́пается—*one's patience is* (or *gets*) *exhausted*

Бори́с так мно́го говори́л, что моё терпе́ние ло́пнуло. *Boris talked so much that my patience got exhausted.*

тече́ние—*current*

в тече́ние—*during; in the course of something*

В тече́ние ле́та Са́ша объе́здил всю страну́. *Sasha traveled all over the country during the summer.*

с тече́нием вре́мени—*in time; eventually; as time goes by*

С тече́нием вре́мени все невзго́ды уля́гутся. *All troubles go away as time goes by.*

това́р—*goods; merchandise.*

хо́дкий това́р—*goods in great demand*

Ле́гче всего́ продава́ть хо́дкий това́р. *The easiest to sell are goods in great demand.*

толк—*sense; use*

с то́лком—*properly; sensibly*

Нача́льник от нас потре́бовал вы́полнить рабо́ту с то́лком. *The boss demanded of us that we do our work properly.*

то́лько—*only; but; just*

то́лько и всего́—*(that's) all; nothing more*

Он подари́л мне одну́ ро́зу—то́лько и всего́. *All he gave me was a rose.*

то́лько что—*1. just 2. no sooner than*

1. Я то́лько что прие́хал из командиро́вки. *I just arrived back from my business trip.*
2. Са́ша то́лько что прие́хал, а его́ вы́звали обра́тно. *No sooner had Sasha arrived than he was called back.*

то́лько что не—*just short of; almost*

Пётр говори́л так гро́мко, то́лько что не крича́л. *Peter spoke so loudly, it was just short of shouting.*

тон—*tone; tune*

впада́ть в шу́точный тон—*speak in a funny* (or *joking* or *teasing) manner; assume a humorous manner*

По́сле посеще́ния конце́рта изве́стного юмори́ста, И́горь впал в шу́точный тон. *After the famous humorist's performance, Igor assumed a humorous manner himself.*

задава́ть тон—*set the tone*

В кругу́ друзе́й Ната́ша всегда́ задаёт тон. *It's always Natasha who sets the tone in her circle of friends.*

попада́ть в тон—*strike the right tone*

У Миха́йла тала́нт попада́ть в тон собесе́днику. *Mikhail has the talent to strike the right tone with the person he's speaking to.*

тот; то—*that*

до того́—*to such a degree; to the point where*

Он до того́ напи́лся, что не мог подня́ться с ме́ста. *He got drunk to the point where he couldn't get up from his seat.*

не без того́—*one could say that; one cannot deny*

Я челове́к неуравнове́шенный, во вре́мя бесе́ды могу́ сорва́ться, не без того́. *One cannot deny that I am not well balanced and that I can explode during a conversation.*

несмотря́ на то, что—*in spite of the fact that*

Несмотря́ на то, что была́ плоха́я пого́да, мы пое́хали в го́ры. *In spite of the fact that the weather was bad, we took off for the mountains.*

не то, чтобы—*not exactly*

Ми́ша не то, чтобы ге́ний, но о́чень у́мный. *Misha is not exactly a genius, but he's rather smart.*

по́сле того́, как—*after*

По́сле того́, как мы пожени́лись, мы кру́пно поссо́рились. *Just after we had tied the knot we had a terrible fight.*

то́ есть—*that is*

Мы добира́лись до Вене́ции во́дным путём, то́ есть на корабле́. *We reached Venice by water—that is, by boat.*

то́чка—*dot; point*

дойти́ до мёртвой то́чки—*come to a stop; come to a halt; be interrupted*

Из-за нехва́тки фина́нсов стро́ительство на́шей да́чи дошло́ до мёртвой то́чки. *Because of the finances the building of our summer cottage came to a halt.*

и то́чка!—*period!*

Ма́льчик заяви́л, что не вернётся в шко́лу, и то́чка. *The boy declared that he refuses to go back to school, period.*

попа́сть в то́чку—*hit the nail right on the head*

Свои́м выска́зыванием он попа́л в то́чку. *He hit the nail right on the head with his statement.*

ста́вить то́чки над «и»—*dot the "i's" and cross the "t's"; finish the fine detail; complete*

По́сле дли́тельных перегово́ров мы поста́вили то́чки над «и». *After extended negotiations we dotted the "i's" and crossed the "t's."*

то́чка в то́чку—*exactly; to a "T."*

Мне́ния А́нны и Никола́я совпада́ют то́чка в то́чку. *Anna's and Nikolay's opinions match to a "T."*

то́чка зре́ния—*point of view*

Па́вел ве́рит то́лько свое́й то́чке зре́ния. *Pavel only believes in his own point of view.*

трава́—*grass*

траво́й поросло́—*gone and all forgotten; gone with the wind*

На́ши ю́ные мечты́ уже́ траво́й поросли́. *The dreams of our young years are all gone and forgotten.*

труба́—*pipe*

вы́лететь в трубу́—*go bankrupt; go broke*

Мы всё потеря́ли и вы́летели в трубу́. *We lost everything and went bankrupt.*

спуска́ть в трубу́—*waste; squander*

Ива́н спусти́л в трубу́ всё своё иму́щество. *Ivan squandered his whole inheritance.*

труд—*work; difficulty*

брать (or **приня́ть) на себя́ труд; дать себе́ труд**—*take the trouble*

Профе́ссор взял на себя́ труд дать мне сове́т, как улу́чшить мою́ рабо́ту. *The professor took the trouble to make suggestions how to improve my work.*

не пожале́ть труда́—*spare no effort to do something*

Что́бы дости́чь успе́хов, Ники́та не пожале́л труда́. *Nikita spared no effort to achieve success.*

не сто́ит труда́—*it's not worth the trouble*

Не сто́ит труда́ стара́ться убеди́ть Петра́, он нам всё равно́ не ве́рит. *It's not worth trying to convince Peter—he won't believe us anyway.*

с трудо́м—*hardly be able to manage; barely to succeed doing something*

Во вре́мя бу́ри мы с трудо́м перебира́лись на другу́ю сто́рону доро́ги. *We could hardly manage to reach the other side of the road in the storm.*

с трудо́м перебива́ться—*live from hand to mouth*

На свою́ скро́мную зарпла́ту на́ша семья́ с трудо́м перебива́ется. *Our family lives from hand to mouth on a modest income.*

туда́—*there*

ни туда́, ни сюда́—*be stuck; be unable to move left or right*

С та́кой репута́цией Петру́ в по́иске рабо́ты—ни туда́, ни сюда́. *With such a reputation Peter is stuck on the job market.*

туда́ и обра́тно—*there and back*

Мы ежедне́вно е́здим туда́ и обра́тно на авто́бусе. *Every day we go by bus there and back.*

туда́ и сюда́—*back and forth; to and fro; up and down*

От волне́ния Ма́ша ходи́ла туда́ и сюда́ по ко́мнате. *Masha was pacing back and forth in the room in her excitement.*

тупи́к—*dead-end street*

быть в тупике́; зайти́ в тупи́к—*be at a loss; reach a dead end*

Мы до́лго обсужда́ли э́тот вопро́с, пока́ не зашли́ в тупи́к. *We discussed the problem at great length until we reached a dead end.*

ста́вить в тупи́к—*stump someone; corner someone*

Профе́ссор свои́ми вопро́сами поста́вил студе́нта в тупи́к. *The professor stumped the student with his questions.*

тут—*here*

при чём тут я?—*what business of mine is it?*

Е́сли Арка́дий провали́лся на экза́мене, то при чём тут я? *What business of mine is it if Arkady flunked his exam?*

тут же—*at once; immediately*

Гром загреме́л, и тут же пошёл дождь. *There was loud thunder and immediately it started to rain.*

тут как тут—*there one is; there they are*

Я то́лько поду́мал о Ната́ше, и вдруг она́ тут как тут! *I was just thinking of Natasha, and suddenly there she was!*

тут чего́-то не так—*something is wrong here*

Рассма́тривая счета́, я заме́тил, что тут чего́-то не так сде́лано. *I noticed that something was wrong here as I went through the account.*

я тут ни при чём—*I'm innocent; I've got nothing to do with something*

Меня́ обвиня́ли в кра́же докуме́нтов, но я тут ни при чём. *I was accused of theft, but I've got nothing to do with it.*

ту́ча—*cloud*

ту́ча-ту́чей—*1. in a swarm 2. morose; gloomy*

1. Ле́том на берегу́ о́зера комары́—ту́ча ту́чей. *In the summer there are swarms of mosquitoes on the lakeshore.*
2. По́сле ухо́да А́нны Бори́с стал ту́ча-ту́чей. *After Anna's departure, Boris became morose.*

ты—*you*

быть (or **говори́ть** or **обраща́ться) на ты**—*be on first name terms; "thee-and-thou" someone*

Он со все́ми был на ты *or* Он ко все́м обраща́лся на ты. *He was on first name terms with everybody.*

тяп

тяп да ляп; тяп-ляп—*anyhow; in a slipshod way; haphazardly*

Дома́шнее зада́ние де́вочка сде́лала тяп да ляп. *The girl did her homework haphazardly.*

убеждéние—*persuasion; belief*

приходи́ть к убеждéнию—*arrive at a conclusion*

Коми́ссия пришлá к убеждéнию, что бухгáлтер присвóил дéньги. *The committee arrived at the conclusion that the bookkeeper stole the money.*

уби́йство—*murder*

уби́йство и́з-за углá—*treacherous murder*

Уби́йства и́з-за углá не бывáют случáйными. *Treacherous murders don't happen accidentally.*

уби́ть—*kill*

хоть убéй—*for the life of me*

Хоть убéй, я не знáю, где твои́ ключи́! *For the life of me, I don't know where your keys are!*

убы́ток—*loss*

продавáть (or **торговáть**) **себé в убы́ток**—*sell oneself off* (or *trade) at a loss*

Обанкрóтившаяся фи́рма продавáла себé в убы́ток. *After it went bankrupt, the firm sold itself off at a loss.*

увели́чить—*increase*

увели́чить вдвóе—*double*

Мы суméли увели́чить дохóд вдвóе за счёт нóвой технолóгии. *Thanks to the new technology we succeeded in doubling our income.*

увéренный—*assured; certain*

бýдьте увéрены!—*you can rest assured*

Вы дости́гнете своéй цéли, бýдьте увéрены! *You'll reach your goal, you can rest assured!*

уговóр—*persuasion; agreement*

уговóр дорóже дéнег—*a promise is a promise*

Éсли я обещáл, то сдéлаю—уговóр дорóже дéнег. *If I promise something, I'll do it, too. A promise is a promise.*

угоди́ть—*please; oblige*

на всех не угоди́шь—*you can't please everyone*

Старáйся как мóжешь, но на всех не угоди́шь. *You can try as hard as you want—you can't please everyone.*

ýгол; уголóк—*corner*

дéйствовать и́з-за углá—*be underhanded; act dishonestly* (or *treacherously)*

Тóлько хи́трый дéйствует и́з-за углá. *Only sly people act underhandedly.*

загоня́ть (or **прижимáть) в ýгол**—*be driven into a corner*

Зáгнанный в ýгол И́горь признáлся в своéй винé. *Driven into a corner, Igor confessed.*

под углóм зрéния—*from the point of view; from the vantage point of*

Бори́с всё рассмáтривает под свои́м углóм зрéния. *Boris looks at everything from his own point of view.*

срéзать ýгол—*take a shortcut*

Чтóбы быстрée приéхать, мы срéзали ýгол. *We took a shortcut in order to get there faster.*

уголкóм глáза—*out of* (or *from) the corner of one's eye*

Онá смотрéла на меня́ уголкóм глáза. *She looked at me from the corner of her eye.*

шептáться (or **шушýкаться) по углáм**—*talk in secret* (or *in whispers)*

Девчóнки, как обы́чно, шептáлись по углáм. *The girls, as usual, were talking in whispers.*

у́голь—*coal*

быть (or **сиде́ть), как на угля́х** (or **уго́льях)**—*be* (or *sit) on pins and needles*

Ожида́я звонка́, Еле́на сиде́ла, как на у́глях. *Elena was sitting on pins and needles while she waited for the phone call.*

уда́р—*blow; stroke*

быть в уда́ре—*be in great form*

Сего́дня ве́чером Ива́н был в уда́ре. *Tonight Ivan was in great form.*

у́дочка—*fishing rod*

подде́ть (or **пойма́ть) на у́дочку**—*dupe; trick; outwit*

Ей каза́лось, что она́ мо́жет подде́ть меня́ на у́дочку. *It seemed to her that she might be able to outwit me.*

у́жас—*fright; horror*

до у́жаса—*terribly; an awful lot*

Я люблю́ сла́дости до у́жаса. *I like sweets an awful lot.*

прийти́ в у́жас—*be horrified*

Уви́дев мёртвого, я пришёл в у́жас. *I was horrified when I saw the dead body.*

узда́—*bridle*

держа́ть в узде́—*keep in check; hold in leash*

Полице́йский держа́л в узде́ престу́пника, освободи́вшегося на пору́ки. *The police officer kept the parolee in check.*

узело́к—*small knot*

завя́зывать узело́к (на па́мять)—*make sure that one won't forget something*

Она́ завяза́ла узело́к, что́бы не забы́ть меня́ поздра́вить с днём рожде́ния. *She made sure that she wouldn't forget to congratulate me on my birthday.*

у́йма—*load; heap*

име́ть у́йму вре́мени—*have all the time in the world*

А́нна до́лго говори́ла по телефо́ну, бу́дто име́ла у́йму вре́мени. *Anna spoke so long on the phone as if she had all the time in the world.*

уйти́—*leave*

не уйдёт—*it can wait; one can do it later*

Ты пока́ отложи́ э́ту рабо́ту, она́ не уйдёт. *Put this work on the side for a while—you can do it later.*

уйти́ ни с чем—*go away empty-handed*

По́сле разво́да муж ушёл ни с чем. *The husband left empty-handed after the divorce.*

у́лица—*street*

бу́дет на на́шей у́лице пра́здник—*our day will come*

Не грусти́, бу́дет и на на́шей у́лице пра́здник. *Don't be sad—our day will come!*

выноси́ть на у́лицу—*make something public*

У Ни́ны была́ привы́чка выноси́ть семе́йные пробле́мы на у́лицу. *Nina was in the habit of making family matters public.*

на у́лице—*outside; in the street*

Сего́дня о́чень хо́лодно на у́лице. *Today it's very cold outside.*

улыба́ться—*smile*

улыба́ться кому́-ли́бо—*appeal to someone; please someone*

Никола́ю улыбну́лось пое́хать в Аме́рику. *Nikolay was pleased by the thought of going to the States.*

ум—*mind*

бра́ться за ум—*become reasonable; come to one's senses*

Преподава́тель сказа́л ученика́м, что пора́ бра́ться за ум. *The teacher said to the students that it was time to come to their senses.*

быть без умá—*be charmed; be enthused about somebody or something; be crazy about something*

Женúх без умá от богáтства невéсты. *The groom is enthused about the bride's wealth.*

быть не в своём умé—*be off the rails; be out of one's mind*

Егó поведéние говорúт о том, что он не в своём умé. *His behavior indicated that he is out of his mind.*

в своём умé—*in one's right mind*

Тóлько лю́ди не в своём умé дýмают, что, запóлнив билéт, онú тут же вы́играют в лотерéю. *Only people not in their right mind think that just by filling out a slip they've already won the lottery.*

зáдним умóм крéпок—*be wise after the event; hindsight is 20-20*

Éсли бы я знал вчерá, что Йгорь своегó слóва не сдéржит, то я бы на негó не рассчúтывал. Человéк всегдá зáдним умóм крéпок. *If I had known yesterday that Igor wouldn't keep his word, I wouldn't have counted on him. One is always wise after the event.*

на ум не идёт—*won't even enter one's mind*

Петрý на ум не идёт рабóта. *Working doesn't even enter Peter's mind.*

сойтú с умá—*go off one's head; go mad*

У меня́ стóлько забóт, что я с умá сойдý. *I've got so much to worry about that I'm going mad.*

умá палáта—*very wise; have a lot of brains*

У моегó мýжа умá палáта. *My husband is very wise.*

что на умé, то и на языкé—*be frank; not to beat around the bush*

Ивáн не хóдит вокрýг да окóло, а что на умé, то и на языкé. *Ivan doesn't beat about the bush, he is frank.*

упóр—*rest; stop*

глядéть (or **смотрéть) в упóр**—*stare at someone or something in a fixed gaze*

Никола́й гляде́л на меня́ в упо́р. *Nikolay stared at me in a fixed gaze.*

сказа́ть в упо́р—*say something to someone's face* (or *point-blank)*

Я сказа́л в упо́р, что я о нём ду́маю. *I told him straight to his face what I thought of him.*

ура́—*hurrah*

на ура́—*haphazardly; by the seat of one's pants; on luck alone*

Экза́мен Степа́н сдал на ура́. *Stepan passed his exam by the seat of his pants.*

уро́к—*lesson; homework; class*

извле́чь уро́к—*learn a lesson*

Ива́н извлёк уро́к из свои́х оши́бок. *Ivan learned from his own mistakes.*

ус—*mustache*

и в ус (себе́) не дуть—*not to give a damn*

Срок отда́чи фо́рмы для но́вой рабо́ты уже прошёл, а Ники́та и в ус не дул. *The deadline for the application for a new job had passed already, but Nikita didn't give a damn.*

са́ми с уса́ми—*not to be a babe in the woods; have got brains, too*

Нас не обма́нешь, мы са́ми с уса́ми. *You can't cheat us—we're no babes in the woods either!*

усло́вие—*condition*

в настоя́щих усло́виях—*in these* (or *under the) circumstances*

В настоя́щих усло́виях тру́дно воспи́тывать дете́й. *It is a daunting task to bring up kids under the present circumstances.*

уста́—*mouth; lips*

быть на уста́х у всех—*be the talk of the town; be on everybody's lips*

Нóвые скандáлы извéстной актрúсы на устáх у всех. *The famous actress's newest scandals are the talk of the town.*

из уст в устá—*by word of mouth*
Нóвости о побéде нáшей комáнды передавáлись из уст в устá. *The news of our team's victory was spreading by word of mouth.*

ýтка—*duck*

пустúть ýтку—*spread false rumors*
Противобóрствующие пáртии пустúли ýтку о своéй побéде. *The opposing parties spread false rumors about their respective victories.*

ýхо; ýшко—*ear*

быть пó уши в долгáх—*be up to one's ears* (or *neck) in debts*
Олéг жáловался, что он пó уши в долгáх. *Oleg complained that he's up to his ears in debt*

быть пó уши в рабóте—*be up to the eyes in work*
Андрéй постоя́нно пó уши в рабóте. *Andrey is always up to the eyes in work.*

влюбúться пó уши—*be head over heels in love; be madly in love*
Ужé на пéрвой встрéче Пáвел влюбúлся в Áнну пó уши. *Pavel fell head over heels in love with Anna at first sight.*

говорúть нá ухо—*whisper into one's ear*
Сергéй говорúл Ирúне нá ухо о своéй любвú. *Sergey whispered into Irina's ear about his love.*

держáть ýхо востró—*watch one's step with someone; be on one's guard with someone*
С такúм человéком слéдует держáть ýхо востró! *One has to watch one's step with such a person.*

доходúть до ушéй—*come to one's knowledge; become aware of*
Дошлó до моúх ушéй, что бухгáлтер присвóил капитáл фúрмы. *I became aware of the fact that the bookkeeper expropriated the company's funds.*

крéпкий (or **тугóй) нá ухо**—*hard of hearing*
Бáбушка крепкá нá ухо. *Grandma is hard of hearing.*

навострúть ýши—*prick up one's ears*
Когдá онú нáчали говорúть обо мне, я навострúл ýши. *I pricked up my ears when they started to talk about me.*

покраснéть до ушéй—*blush to the roots of one's hair*
От смущéния Лéна покраснéла до ушéй. *Lena blushed to the roots of her hair in her embarrasment.*

прожужжáть все ýши—*din into one's ears*
Своúми трéбованиями Натáша прожужжáла мýжу все ýши. *Natasha dinned into her husband's ears with her demands.*

сказáть на ýшко—*whisper into someone's ear*
Э́то секрéт, но я тебé на ýшко скажý. *This is a secret but I'll whisper it into your ear.*

ýшки на макýшке—*be all ears; perk up one's ears*
Когдá мáма читáла скáзку о Зóлушке, у Мáши ýшки бы́ли на макýшке. *When Mother read the story about Cinderella, Masha was all ears.*

учёный—*learned; academic*

не учú учёного—*don't teach your grandmother; don't teach your father how to make a child*
Я и без тебя́ всё знаю. Не учú учёного! *I know everything even without you—don't teach your grandmother!*

фавóр—*favor*

быть в фавóре—*be in one's good graces*
Я в фавóре у жены́ дирéктора. *I am in the good graces of the director's wife.*

фасо́н—*fashion; style*

держа́ть фасо́н—*show off; put on the dog*

Ле́на держа́ла фасо́н не по средства́м. *Lena put on the dog beyond her means.*

фигу́ра—*figure*

кру́пная фигу́ра—*important person*

В на́шей фи́рме Ива́н—кру́пная фигу́ра. *Ivan is an important person at our firm.*

флаг—*flag*

под фла́гом—*1. in the name of 2. in the guise of*

1. Под фла́гом зако́на ста́линская кли́ка соверша́ла преступле́ния. *Stalin's clique committed crimes in the name of the law.*
2. Под фла́гом нужды́ в гуманита́рной по́мощи нече́стное прави́тельство тра́тило де́ньги на себя́. *The dishonest regime spent the money for its own purposes in the guise of humanitarian help.*

фо́кус—*trick*

выки́дывать фо́кус—*play a trick*

Пётр вы́кинул очередно́й фо́кус, что́бы заня́ть мою́ до́лжность. *Peter played all sorts of dirty tricks in order to take over my job.*

фра́за—*sentence*

отде́лываться о́бщими фра́зами—*fob something off*

Па́влу не́чего сообщи́ть, поэ́тому он отде́лывается о́бщими фра́зами. *Peter doesn't have anything real to say, so he fobs off the matter with empty phrases.*

фрукт—*fruit*

ну и фрукт!—*he is a rotten apple!; a bad egg*

Ну и фрукт! С ним не бу́дем дружи́ть. *We won't associate with him—he's a rotten apple.*

фунт—*pound*

вот так фунт!—*what a mess!*

Когда́ лифт останови́лся ме́жду двумя́ этажа́ми, мы воскли́кнули: «Вот так фунт!» *"What a mess!" we cried, when the elevator got stuck between two floors.*

не фунт изю́му!—*it isn't to be sneezed at! it isn't a trifle; be no easy matter*

Написа́ть рома́н—э́то не фунт изю́му! *It's no easy matter to be writing a novel!*

фуфу́

на фуфу́—*carelessly; thoughtlessly*

Бродя́га всю жизнь прожи́л на фуфу́. *The vagabond lived his entire life thoughtlessly.*

Х

хам—*cad; boor*

из ха́ма не быва́ет па́на—*you cannot make a silk purse out of a sow's ear*

Как Илья́ ни стара́лся вести́ себя́ культу́рно, но из ха́ма не быва́ет па́на. *Ilya did all he could to behave like a cultured person, but then you can't make a silk purse out of a sow's ear.*

хара́ктер—*disposition; temper; nature*

выде́рживать хара́ктер—*be firm; not to give in*

Во всех ситуа́циях Ива́н выде́рживает хара́ктер. *Ivan stays firm in all situations.*

не сойти́сь хара́ктером—*not to get along*

Ири́на и Никола́й, как ни стара́лись, всё-таки не сошли́сь хара́ктером. *No matter how hard Irina and Nikolay tried, they just didn't get along.*

хáта—*peasant house*

моя́ (твоя́ ...) хáта с крáю—*it's none of my (your...) business* (or *concern)*

Когдá Васи́лий попроси́л Сáшу быть свидéтелем во врéмя судá, он отказáлся, сказáв: «Моя хáта с крáю.» *When Vasily asked Sasha to be a witness at court, Sasha refused him by saying, "It's none of my business."*

хватáть—*have enough*

хвáтит!—*1. stop! 2. that'll do!; enough of that!*

1.«Хвáтит болтáть!»—сказáла преподавáтельница. *"Stop chattering!" the teacher said.*

2. Хвáтит бездéльничать, порá занимáться дéлом! *Enough of the loitering! Let's get down to work!*

хвáтит на сегóдня—*let's call it a day*

К вéчеру начáльник сказáл: «Хвáтит на сегóдня». *Toward evening the boss said, "Let's call it a day!"*

хвати́ть чéрез край—*exaggerate a bit*

Пётр хвати́л чéрез край в своём расскáзе. *Peter exaggerated a bit in his account.*

с меня́ хвáтит—*I've had enough; be fed up with something*

Э́та кни́га—зелёная скýка. С меня́ хвáтит! *This book is boredom incarnate. I'm all fed up with it.*

хвост—*tail; rear*

стоя́ть в хвостé—*stand in line; queue up*

Мы стоя́ли в хвостé за билéтами на концéрт поп-мýзыки. *We stood in line to buy a ticket for the pop concert.*

хвóстик—*little tail*

с хвóстиком—*1. and (a little) more; plus 2. with (an) additional family member(s)*

1. Ей сóрок лет с хвóстиком. *She is forty-something.* 2. Он женúлся на жéнщине с хвóстиком. *He married a woman with an additional family member.*

хлеб—*bread; grain*

быть на хлебáх—*be kept* (or *supported) by someone else; be a boarder*

В мой студéнческие гóды я был на хлебáх у дя́ди. *During my student years I was a boarder at my uncle's.*

водúть хлеб-соль—*be friends; exchange frequent visits*

Мы вóдим хлеб-соль с сосéдями. *We are friends with our neighbors.*

встречáть хлéбом-сóлью—*give a warm welcome*

Нас рóдственники встречáли хлéбом-сóлью. *Our relatives gave us a warm welcome.*

есть чужóй хлеб—*live at someone else's expense; be a free-loader*

Никúта не рабóтает, а ест чужóй хлеб. *Nikita lives like a free-loader—he's got no job.*

зарабáтывать себé на хлеб—*earn one's living*

На хлеб Сáша себé всегдá зарабáтывал. *Sasha has always earned his own living.*

хлебнýть лúшнего—*have a drop too much; have one too many*

На свáдьбе дóчери Ивáн хлебнýл лúшнего. *Ivan had one too many at his daughter's wedding.*

хлеб с мáслом—*live well; have enough to live on*

Пётр зарабáтывает себé на хлеб с мáслом. *Peter makes a good living.*

хлóпоты—*trouble*

хлопóт (or **забóт) пóлон рот**—*have one's hands full*

У Ле́ны больша́я семья́, хлопо́т по́лон рот. *Lena has a large family—she's got her hands full.*

ход—*motion; course*

быть в (большо́м) ходу́—*be in (great) demand*

Кроссо́вки везде́ в большо́м ходу́. *Sneakers are in great demand everywhere.*

знать все ходы́ и вы́ходы—*know the ropes; know all the ins and outs*

Ива́н в э́том де́ле знал все ходы́ и вы́ходы. *Ivan knew all the ropes of this business.*

по́лным хо́дом—*in full swing; at top speed*

Рабо́та идёт по́лным хо́дом на на́шей фа́брике. *Work is in full swing at our factory.*

пуска́ть в ход—*1. get started 2. use*

1. Заво́д пу́стят в ход то́лько по́сле капита́льного ремо́нта. *The factory will get started only after a major overhaul.*
2. Ива́н пусти́л все свя́зи в ход, что́бы дости́гнуть свое́й полити́ческой це́ли. *Ivan used all of his connections in order to reach his political goals.*

ход конём—*decisive step*

Эмигра́ция в Аме́рику—это был ход конём в мое́й жи́зни. *Emigration to the States was the decisive step in my life.*

хозя́ин—*owner; host; master*

быть хозя́ином положе́ния—*have the upper hand; be master of the situation*

Бори́с как адвока́т был хозя́ином положе́ния в перегово́рах. *Being a lawyer Boris had the upper hand during the negotiations.*

быть хозя́ином своего́ сло́ва—SEE: **быть господи́ном своего́ сло́ва**

сам себе́ хозя́ин—SEE: **сам себе́ голова́**

хóлод—*cold*

áдский (or **собáчий**) **хóлод**—*bitter cold*

В áдский хóлод мы поéхали в лес за ёлкой. *We went to the forest for a Christmas tree in the bitter cold.*

обдáть хóлодом—*turn a cold shoulder to someone*

С ним неприя́тно; он обдаёт всех хóлодом. *It's unpleasant to be with him—he turns a cold shoulder to everyone.*

хорóший—*good*

всегó хорóшего!—*best of luck!*

«Всегó хорóшего!»—сказáл Ники́та прощáясь. *"Best of luck!" Nikita said as we parted.*

что хорóшего?—*what's the news?*

Ещё с порóга Сáша спроси́л: «Что хорóшего?» *Sasha asked already from the threshhold, "What's the news?"*

хотéть—*want; wish*

хóчешь, не хóчешь—*like it or not; willy-nilly*

Хóчешь, не хóчешь, но в шкóлу идти́ нýжно. *Like it or not, you must go to school!*

хоть—*though; even; at least*

хóть бы—*1. I wish 2. the least (one can do)*

1. Хóть бы Николáй меня́ пóнял! *I wish Nikolay would understand me!* 2. Хóть бы Ивáн подари́л бéдной Мáше букéт роз! *The least Ivan could give poor Masha is a bouquet of roses!*

хоть и—*although*

Хоть и богáтый, Аркáдий жáлуется, как ни́щий. *Although Arkady is rich, he is poor-mouthing like a beggar.*

хоть какóй—*no matter what kind; any kind*

«Мне бы муж, хоть какóй!»—сказáла Мáша, не знáя, какáя онá наи́вная. *"May I have a husband, any kind!" said Masha, not knowing how naive she was.*

хоть куда́!—*splendid!*

Ива́н па́рень хоть куда́! *Ivan is a splendid guy.*

хотя́—*although*

хотя́ бы—*even if*

Приезжа́йте к нам, хотя́ бы на денёк. *Come and visit us, even if only for a short day.*

Христос—*Christ*

Христа́ ра́ди—*for God's sake.*

Христа́ ра́ди, переста́нь пла́кать! *For God's sake, stop crying!*

Христо́с воскре́с!—*Christ has arisen! (*greeting on Easter Sunday*)*

При встре́че в Све́тлое Воскресе́нье Пётр приве́тствовал нас: «Христо́с воскре́с!»—«Воистину воскре́с!»—отве́тили мы. *Peter greeted us by saying, "Christ has arisen!" when we met on Easter Sunday. "Indeed He is risen!" we answered.*

Ц

цвет—*flower; bloom*

во цве́те лет—*in the prime of one's life*

Ива́н да́же во цве́те лет не дости́г призна́ния. *Ivan didn't get any recognition, not even in the prime of his life.*

загоре́ться как ма́ков(ый) цвет—*blush crimson*

Когда́ мы уличи́ли его́ во лжи, Па́вел загоре́лся, как ма́ковый цвет. *Pavel blushed crimson when we proved him a liar.*

целико́м—*whole; entirely*

целико́м и по́лностью—*completely; utterly and completely; without reservations*

Я ему́ доверя́ю целико́м и по́лностью. *I believe him utterly and completely.*

це́лый—*whole*

це́л(ый) и здоро́в(ый)—*alive and kicking; safe and sound*

Никола́й верну́лся по́сле кругосве́тного путеше́ствия цел и здоро́в. *Nikolay returned from his round-the-world trip safe and sound.*

цель—*goal; objective*

бить в цель—*achieve one's aim*

Бори́с сде́лал всё, что́бы бить в цель. *Boris did all he could in order to achieve his aim.*

бить ми́мо це́ли—*go astray; not to have any impact*

Но́вый дире́ктор бил ми́мо це́ли свои́ми чересчу́р честолюби́выми пла́нами. *The new director went astray with his over-ambitious plans.*

не отвеча́ть це́ли—*serve no purpose*

Безделу́шки на комо́де не отвеча́ли никако́й це́ли. *The knick-knacks in the credenza served no (useful) purpose.*

с како́й це́лью?—*what for?*

С како́й це́лью вы посыла́ете мне цветы́?—спроси́ла Ири́на. *"What are you sending me flowers for?" asked Irina.*

цена́—*price; value*

загну́ть це́ну—*charge an exorbitant price*

Хозя́ин магази́на загну́л та́кую це́ну за шу́бу, что мне бы́ло не по карма́ну. *The owner of the store charged such an exorbitant price for the fur coat that I just couldn't afford it.*

знать себе́ це́ну—*know one's own value*

Во всех ситуа́циях жи́зни Ири́на зна́ла себе́ це́ну. *Irina knew her own value in all situations of life.*

любо́й ceно́й—*at all costs; by hook or by crook*

Любо́й ceно́й Серге́й добива́лся свое́й це́ли. *Sergey strove to achieve his goals at all costs.*

нет цены́—*invaluable*

Ста́рым ру́кописям нет цены́. *The old manuscripts are invaluable.*

сбить це́ну (or **це́ны**)—*lower the price*

В конце́ сезо́на магази́ны сбива́ют це́ну на шу́бы. *At season's end stores lower the price of fur coats.*

цыплёнок—*chicken*

цыпля́т по о́сени счита́ют—*don't count your chickens before they're hatched*

Устро́ившись на рабо́ту, я уже́ мечта́л, что ско́ро бу́ду дире́ктором, но Ле́на напо́мнила мне, что цыпля́т по о́сени счита́ют. *When I got the job I dreamt that soon I'd be the director, but Lena reminded me not to count my chickens before they're hatched.*

Ч

чадра́—*chador*

(с)бро́сить чадру́—*become emancipated*

Же́нщины в на́шем ве́ке сбро́сили чадру́. *The women became emancipated during the course of the present century.*

ходи́ть под чадро́й—*pretend; hide one's real face*

Мы не зна́ли её и́стинные чу́вства, потому́ что Ната́ша ходи́ла под чадро́й. *We didn't know Natasha's true sentiments—she kept hiding her real face.*

чай—*tea*

гоня́ть чай—*spend one's time drinking tea*

По вечера́м мы с дру́гом гоня́ем чай. *My friend and I spend our time drinking tea in the evenings.*

дава́ть на чай (or **на чаёк**)—*give a tip*

Официа́нту в рестора́не мы всегда́ даём на чай. *We usually give the waiter a tip in the restaurant.*

час—*time; o'clock; hour*

би́тый час—*a whole hour; a good hour*

Мы жда́ли авто́буса би́тый час. *We were waiting a whole hour for the bus.*

в до́брый час!—*good luck!*

«Наконе́ц я устро́ился на рабо́ту.»—«В до́брый час!» *"I got a job at long last!"—"Good luck!"*

вся́кий час—*constantly; incessantly*

Гро́мкая му́зыка сосе́да меша́ла мне вся́кий час. *My neighbor's loud music kept bothering me constantly.*

в (or **че́рез) час по (ча́йной) ло́жке**—*1. in dribs and drabs 2. very slowly*

1. Ста́рая коро́ва дала́ молока́ в час по ча́йной ло́жке. *The old cow gave milk in driblets.* 2. Све́дения о землетрясе́нии мы получа́ли в час по ча́йной ло́жке. *We received news of the earthquake only very slowly.*

не в до́брый час—*in an evil hour; in an unlucky moment*

О́льга и Арка́дий познако́мились не в до́брый час. *It was in an evil hour that Olga and Arkady got acquainted.*

не ровён час—*who knows (*what may happen*)*

Хотя́ со́лнце све́тит, но хо́лодно. Не ровён час, мо́жно простуди́ться. *Although the sun is shining, it's cold. Who knows, one may catch a cold.*

стоя́ть на часа́х—*stand on guard; keep watch*

Пе́ред короле́вским дворцо́м охра́на стои́т на часа́х. *The guards keep watch in front of the royal palace.*

с час—*about an hour*

Никола́й занима́лся уро́ком с час. *Nikolay spent about an hour at his homework.*

с ча́су на час—*every moment*

Пассажи́ры, потерпе́вшие кораблекруше́ние, с ча́су на час поджида́ли спасе́ния. *The shipwrecked passengers expected to be rescued at any moment.*

час в час—*right on time*

Самолёт приземли́лся час в час. *The plane landed right on time.*

час-друго́й—*(for) an hour or two*

Мы побесе́довали час-друго́й. *We chatted for an hour or two.*

час о́т часу не ле́гче—*things are going from bad to worse*

«Ва́ша пробле́ма решена́?»—«Нет, совсе́м наоборо́т, час о́т часу не ле́гче.» *"Did your problem get resolved?"—"No, things are actually going from bad to worse."*

часы́ пик—*rush hour*

В часы́ пик тру́дно добира́ться на рабо́ту. *It's very difficult to get home during the rush hour.*

ча́ша—*cup; bowl*

перепо́лнить ча́шу (терпе́ния)—*be the last straw (that breaks the camel's back)*

Гру́бость Петра́ перепо́лнила ча́шу терпе́ния. *Peter's rudeness was the last straw that broke the camel's back.*

челове́к—*man; person*

все до одного́ челове́ка—*to a man; to the last person*

Все до одного́ челове́ка бы́ли со мной согла́сны. *Everybody agreed with me to the last person.*

полтора́ челове́ка—*very few people*

На заседа́нии бы́ло полтора́ челове́ка. *There were very few people at the meeting.*

с челове́ка—*a* (or *per) person; a head*

Они́ должны́ плати́ть за обе́д 10 до́лларов с челове́ка. *They have to pay $10 a person for dinner.*

у́зкий челове́к—*narrow-minded person*

С у́зким челове́ком тру́дно говори́ть о поли́тике. *It's very hard to discuss politics with a narrow-minded person.*

челове́к на все ру́ки—SEE: **ма́стер на все ру́ки**.

челове́к с вы́вертом—*eccentric man*

С Са́шей тру́дно дружи́ть, он челове́к с вы́вертом. *It's difficult to be friends with Sasha; he is an eccentric person.*

челове́к с и́менем—*well-known person*

В на́шей дере́вне ещё никогда́ не было челове́ка с и́менем. *There has never been a well-known person in our village.*

чепуха́—*nonsense*

чепуха́ на по́стном ма́сле—SEE: **ерунда́ на по́стном ма́сле**

червячо́к—*small worm*

замори́ть червячка́—*take a bite; take the edge off one's appetite*

Мы то́лько замори́ли червячка́ не име́я вре́мени обе́дать. *Since we had no time to eat dinner, we just had a bite to take the edge off our hunger.*

чересчу́р—*too*

э́то уже́ чересчу́р!—*that's going a bit too far*

У вас тако́е плохо́е мне́ние о Петре́? Э́то уже́ чересчу́р! *Do you have such a bad opinion about Peter? That's going a bit too far.*

чёрт—*devil; damn*

иди́ к чёрту!—*go to hell!*

Не мешáй мне, идú к чёрту! *Don't bother me! Go to hell!*

на кой чёрт?—*why the hell?*

На кой чёрт мне нужны́ долгú? *Why the hell do I need debts?*

ни к чёрту не годúтся—*not to be worth a damn*

Егó обещáния ни к чёрту не годя́тся. *His promises aren't worth a damn.*

у чёрта на кулúчках—*at the back of beyond; in a godforsaken place*

Онú живýт у чёрта на кулúчках. *They live in a godforsaken place.*

чёрт знает—*the devil only knows*

Чёрт знáет, что Сергéй дéлает пóсле рабóты. *The devil only knows what Sergey is doing after work.*

что за чёрт!—*what the hell!*

Что за чёрт! Кáжется, я снóва потеря́л ключú. *What the hell! It looks as if I lost my keys again!*

чертá—*line*

в глáвных (or **óбщих** or **основны́х**) **чертáх**—*in outline; roughly; in a general way*

Обрисýй мне положéние вещéй в óбщих чертáх. *Give me the lowdown in a rough outline.*

честь—*honor*

нáдо (or **порá**) **и честь знать**—*it's time to call it quits*

Уже пóздно, порá и честь знать. *It's late—it's time to call it quits.*

числó—*number; date*

без числá—*in (great) numbers; countless; more than one can count*

На демонстрáции людéй—без числá. *There were countless people at the demonstration.*

в числé—*among*

В числе́ слу́шателей бы́ло мно́го специали́стов. *There were many specialists among the audience.*

в том числе́—*including*

Мно́гие бы́ли про́тив забасто́вки, в том числе́ и я. *Many were against the strike, including me.*

нет и числа́—*innumerable; countless*

Мои́м забо́там нет и числа́. *I've got countless worries.*

превосходи́ть число́м—*outnumber*

Же́нщины в на́шей фи́рме превосхо́дят число́м мужчи́н. *The men at our firm are outnumbered by the women.*

чих—*sneeze*

на вся́кий чих не наздра́вствуешься—*don't pay any attention*

Почему́ ты так расстро́ился по́сле разгово́ра с ним, ты же зна́ешь его́. На вся́кий чих не наздра́вствуешься. *Why were you so down after you had talked to him? You know him; don't pay any attention.*

что—*what*

не́ за что—*don't mention it*

«Спаси́бо!»—сказа́л Оле́г. «Не́ за что»—отве́тила Ма́ша. *"Thanks!" Oleg said. "Don't mention it!" Masha answered.*

не что ино́е, как—*nothing but*

Для не́которых люде́й жизнь—не что ино́е, как ра́дость. *Life is nothing but happiness for some people.*

что́ ли—*perhaps; maybe*

Су́дя по шу́му, там вертолёт пролете́л, что ли? *Judging from the noise, maybe a helicopter was flying by.*

что слы́шно?—*any news? what's new? what's the news?*

Что слы́шно у вас? *What's the news with you?*

что там тако́е?—*what's the matter?*

Почему́ ты пла́чешь? Что там тако́е? *Why are you crying? What's the matter?*

ýвство—*sense*

чýвство лóктя—*feeling of comradeship* (or *solidarity)*

Во врéмя войны́ чýвство лóктя средú солдáт бы́ло осóбенно вáжно. *During the war a feeling of comradeship among the soldiers was especially important.*

уть—*hardly; scarcely*

чуть не—SEE: **едвá не**

Ш

шаг—*step*

в двух шагáх—*a few steps away; a stone's throw away; near by*

Кинó в двух шагáх от нáшего дóма. *The cinema is just a few steps away from our house.*

éхать шáгом—*go slowly: at a slow pace*

В густóм тумáне мы éхали шáгом. *We drove at a slow pace in the thick fog.*

на каждóм шагý—*at every turn*

В цéнтре города на кáждом шагý магазúн. *There is a shop at every turn in the city.*

напрáвить шагú—*head in a certain direction*

Мы напрáвили шагú на мировóе сотрýдничество. *We were headed toward peaceful cooperation.*

ни шáгу!—*stay put!*

Ни шáгу! Я за тобóй придý. *I'll come and get you right away. Stay put!*

шаг за шáгом—*step by step; little by little*

Он шаг за шáгом докáзывал своó теóрию. *He proved his theory step by step.*

шагну́ть—*take a step*

шагну́ть не дать—*be unable to budge; be all squeezed in; b cornered*

Актри́се фоторепортёры шагну́ть не даю́т. *The paparazzi kee hounding the actress—she's all squeezed in.*

шёлковый—*silk*

стать шёлковым—*become as meek as a lamb*

Я ему́ моё мне́ние вы́сказал, и тепе́рь он стал шёлковым. *I gav him a piece of my mind—he's become as meek as a lamb.*

шерсть—*wool*

гла́дить по ше́рсти—*flatter; compliment*

Дире́ктор привы́к, что́бы его́ гла́дили по ше́рсти. *The directo got used to being flattered.*

гла́дить про́тив ше́рсти—*ruffle someone else's feathers*

Мы постара́лись не гла́дить Са́шу про́тив ше́рсти. *We tried no to ruffle Sasha's feathers.*

ше́я—*neck*

жить на ше́е—*be a burden; live off*

Ива́н живёт свои́ми пробле́мами на ше́е у меня́. *Ivan with hi problems is a burden to me.*

Хотя́ Бори́с уже́ взро́слый, он ещё живёт на ше́е роди́телей *Although Boris is a grown-up, he is still living off his parents.*

по ше́ю—*up to the neck*

Никола́й и Ири́на в долга́х по ше́ю. *Nikolay and Irina are up t the neck in debt.*

сверну́ть ше́ю—*break one's neck; run afoul; fall down on*

На э́той пробле́ме да́же специали́ст мо́жет сверну́ть ше́ю. *Eve an expert can fall down on this problem.*

ши́ворот—*collar*

ши́ворот-навы́ворот—*topsy-turvy; the wrong way round*

Ивáн дéлает всё шúворот-навы́ворот. *Ivan does everything topsy-turvy.*

шить—*sew*

шúто-кры́то—*quietly; on the sly; on the QT*

У Никúты всегдá всё шúто-кры́то, но все знáют, что он занимáется грязными делáми. *Nikita handles everything on the QT—yet everyone knows that he is up to no good.*

шиш—*fig*

ни шишá нет—*not to have a thing*

Тепéрь на счетý Борúса ни шишá нет дéнег в бáнке. *There isn't a thing in Boris' bank account.*

шúшка—*cone*

большáя (or **вáжная**) **шúшка**—SEE: **вáжная птúца**

шкýра—*skin; hide*

быть в шкýре—*be in someone's shoes*

Я не хотéл бы быть в твоéй шкýре. *I wouldn't like to be in your shoes*

драть (or **сдирáть**) **семь шкур**—*exploit*

Начáльник сдирáет семь шкур с подчинённых. *The boss is exploiting his employees.*

штýка—*piece; thing*

вот так штýка!—*1. that's great! 2. what a blow!*

1. Он стал чемпиóном—вот так штýка! *He became a champion! That's great!*
2. У меня́ укрáли дéньги—вот так штýка! *My money was stolen! What a blow!*

в тóм-то и штýка!—*that's just the point!*

Прерывáя аргументáцию Лéны, Ивáн воскли́кнул: «Вот в тóм-то и штýка!» *Interrupting Lena's argument in the middle, Ivan cried out, "That's just the point!"*

шум—*noise; racket*

мно́го шу́ма из ничего́—*much ado about nothing*

Он уме́ет создава́ть мно́го шу́ма из ничего́. *He can make much ado about nothing.*

шу́тка—*joke; joking*

в шу́тку—*in jest; not seriously*

Не обижа́йся! Я сказа́л э́то то́лько в шу́тку. *Don't be offended! I was just saying that in jest.*

не до шу́ток—*1. not to be a laughing matter 2. one is in no mood for joking*

Когда́ в ба́нке не ока́зывается де́нег на счету́, то тут не до шу́ток. *When one has no money in one's bank account, it's nothing to laugh about.*

Сего́дня Бори́су не до шу́ток. *Boris is in no mood for joking today.*

отпуска́ть шу́тки—*crack a joke*

Он люби́л иногда́ отпуска́ть шу́тки в кругу́ друзе́й. *Among his friends, he liked to crack a joke every now and then.*

шу́тки в сто́рону! шу́тки прочь!—*joking aside*

Шу́тки в сто́рону, дава́й займёмся де́лом. *Joking aside, come and let's start working.*

шу́тку (or **шу́тки**) **шути́ть**—*kid someone; fool around*

Вы действи́тельно вы́играли миллио́н, и́ли шу́тку шу́тите? *Have you really won a .nillion, or are you just kidding me?*

Щ

щека́—*cheek*

есть (or **упи́сывать**) **за о́бе щеки́**—*gulp down something; stuff oneself with something*

Своё люби́мое блю́до Ва́ня всегда́ упи́сывает за о́бе щеки́. *Vanya always gulps down his favorite food.*

ще́пка—*kindling*

худо́й, как ще́пка—*skinny as a toothpick*

По́сле боле́зни Ма́ша ста́ла худа́я, как ще́пка. *After her illness, Masha was as skinny as a toothpick.*

щит—*shield*

подня́ть на щит—*praise to high heaven* (or *to the skies*)

Газе́ты подня́ли на щит но́вого президе́нта. *The newspapers praised the new president to high heaven.*

Э

экра́н—*screen*

вы́пустить на экра́н—*release a motion picture*

Э́тот фильм вы́пустили на экра́н в про́шлом году́. *This motion picture was released last year.*

эпо́ха—*epoch; period*

соста́вить эпо́ху—*represent a landmark*

Изобрете́ние а́томной эне́ргии соста́вило эпо́ху в исто́рии челове́чества. *The invention of atomic energy represents a landmark in the history of mankind.*

эстафе́та—*relay race; baton*

передава́ть эстафе́ту—*pass on the torch*

В своё вре́мя оте́ц основа́л фи́рму, а на ста́рости лет он переда́л эстафе́ту сы́ну. *Way back it was the father who founded the firm, and now that he is old, he has passed on the torch to his son.*

Ю

ю́бка—*skirt*

бе́гать за ю́бкой—*chase a skirt*

У Фёдора привы́чка бе́гать за вся́кой ю́бкой в на́шем го́роде. *It's Fedor's habit to chase after every skirt in town.*

держа́ться за ю́бку—*hang on to one's (a woman's) apron strings*

Мой сосе́д Арка́дий де́ржится за ю́бку свое́й жены́. *My neighbor Arkady hangs on to his wife's apron strings.*

Я

я́блоко—*apple*

я́блоко от я́блони недалеко́ па́дает—*like father, like son; a chip off the old block*

Оте́ц был во́ром, и сын уже́ шага́ет по престу́пной доро́жке: я́блоко от я́блони недалеко́ па́дает. *The father was a thief—and his son's on the best way to becoming a criminal. Like father like son.*

яблоку нéгде упáсть—*no room to turn around; can't drop even a needle*

Зал ожидáния так пóлон нарóду, что яблоку нéгде упáсть. *The waiting room is so full of people that you can't even drop a needle.*

язы́к—*tongue; language*

быть óстрым на язы́к—*have a sharp tongue*

Егó все боя́тся, он óстрый на язы́к. *Everyone is afraid of him, he's got such a sharp tongue.*

держáть язы́к за зубáми—*hold one's tongue; keep things to oneself*

Не волнýйтесь, Ивáн умéет держáть язы́к за зубáми. *Don't worry, Ivan knows how to hold his tongue.*

найти́ óбщий язы́к—*find common ground*

Стóроны нашли́ óбщий язы́к и вскóре подписáли контрáкт. *The negotiating partners found a common ground and signed the contract in a short time.*

укороти́ть язы́к—*silence someone*

Своими замечáниями Сáша укороти́л Петрý язы́к. *Sasha silenced Peter with his remarks.*

язы́к без костéй—*loose tongue*

Хоть бы промолчáл! У негó язы́к без костéй. *I wish he'd shut up! He's got a loose tongue.*

язы́к проглóтишь—*it makes your mouth water*

Лéна так вкýсно готóвит, что язы́к проглóтишь. *Lena is such a great cook that it makes your mouth water.*

язы́к чéшется сказáть—*be anxious* (or *itching) to say* (or *to speak)*

У Олéга язы́к чéшется вы́сказать своё мнéние. *Oleg is itching to voice his opinion.*

яйцó—*egg*

вы́еденного яйцá не стóит—*not to be worth a damn*

Наш догово́р не сто́ит вы́еденного яйца́. *Our contract isn't worth a damn.*

я́ма—*pit*

возду́шная я́ма—*air pocket*

Во вре́мя полёта мы попа́ли в возду́шную я́му. *We hit an air pocket during flight.*

самому́ себе́ я́му рыть—*fall into one's own trap*

Нача́льник рыл я́му само́му себе́, когда́ обвиня́л подчинённых. *The boss fell in his own trap when he blamed his employees.*

я́рость—*fury; rage*

быть вне себя́ от я́рости—*be beside oneself with rage*

Узна́в об изме́не му́жа, А́нна была́ вне себя́ от я́рости. *Anna was beside herself with rage when she found out that her husband was cheating on her.*

я́сный—*clear*

ясне́е я́сного—*as clear as daylight*

Слу́шая слова́ Бори́са, ста́ло ясне́е я́сного, что он Ма́шу не лю́бит. *It became clear as daylight upon hearing Boris's words that he didn't love Masha.*

я́щик—*drawer; case; box*

откла́дывать в до́лгий я́щик—*put off* (or *shelve*) *indefinitely*

Напра́сно ждать отве́та, е́сли заявле́ние откла́дывали в до́лгий я́щик. *It's unnecessary to wait for an answer if the petition has been indefinitely shelved.*

писа́ть в я́щик—SEE: **писа́ть на стол**

сыгра́ть в я́щик—*kick the bucket; turn up one's heels; cash in one's chips*

«Бо́льше не пей незнако́мых лека́рств, так мо́жно и в я́щик сыгра́ть»—говори́ли друзья́ Васи́лию. *"Don't take any unknown medicine—that's a way to kick the bucket," Vasily's friends told him.*

Russian Pronunciation Guide (Указáтель произношéния рýсского языкá)

Russian Alphabet	Approximate Pronunciation
А, а	like the phoneme /a/ in English ***father***, but also as represented by the [o] spelling as in ***Bob, got, college*** and ***pot***.
Б, б	like the phoneme /b/ in English; ***Bob, between, beat,*** etc. At the end of a word the Russian б /b/ is pronounced like a /p/, i.e., voicelessly.
В, в	like the English /v/ phoneme as in ***victory, valley, Vincent***, etc. At the end of word a Russian в /v/ is pronounced like an /f/, i.e., voicelessly.
Г, г	like the English /g/ phoneme in the words ***goose, gather, go, get***; never as in ***ginger, jittery***, etc. At the end of a word the Russian г /g/ is pronounced like a /k/, i.e., voicelessly.
Д, д	like the English phoneme /d/ in the words ***do, did, dad, dumb***; for further examples of "palatalized /dj/" similar to rapidly spoken English *did you* /dija/ see below. At the end of a word a Russian д /d/ is pronounced like a /t/, i.e., voicelessly.
Е, е	like the English /e/ phoneme in ***let, get and set*** preceeded by a /y/ as in *yes,* representable as a double-bodied sound /ye/. When /e/ or /ye/ is not stressed, Russians pronounce it as /i/ or /yi/; thus видите is not pronounced vjidjetje but as vjidjitji.
Ё, ё	Corresponds to the English /o/ phoneme preceeded by a /y/-glide. Always stressed, it occurs in names such as *Хрущев* and *Горбачев,* which are pronounced in Russian /khrushch**o**ff/ and /garbach**o**ff/, not /khrushchev/ and /gorbachev/.
Ж, ж	This corresponds to the English phoneme /z/ in the words *pleasure, leisure, measure, garage,* and the French loan word *soup de jour.*

Russian Alphabet	Approximate Pronunciation
З, з	like the English /z/ phoneme in the words ***z**oo, **z**any, **z**ebra, Su**z**ie*, etc.
И, и	like the English [ee] spelling in *s**ee**m, m**ee**t, f**ee**l,* but without the typical English habit of adding a /y/-like off-glide. On the contrary, this Russian sounds BEGINS with a /y/-like glide.
Й, й	This corresponds to the English /y/ phoneme, as in *bo**y**, to**y**, co**y***, etc.
К, к	Corresponding to English /k/ as in **c**ool, ***C**alvin, **c**at, **K**im, loo**k*** and *s**k**ill,* the Russian /k/ is never aspirated or "puffed with an extra {h}" at the beginning of words as in English.
Л, л	A basic equivalent of English /l/, as in ***L**uke, **l**ook, **l**amb, b**l**ame, **l**itt**l**e,* etc.; this sound has as many different values as does its English cousin. When followed by the soft sign ь, it is pronounced as *l* + *y* in rapidly spoken *wi**ll ya**?* or *Wi**lli**am.*
М, м	This corresponds to the English /m/ phoneme as in ***m**other, **m**inute, **m**ilk, **m**ouse,* etc., except that if followed by и, е, ю, or я it it pronounced like ***me**ow, **mu**te, **mu**le.*
Н, н	Basically like the English /n/ phoneme as in ***n**o, **N**ancy, **n**ight*, etc., except that if followed by the vowels и, е, ю, or я it is pronounced "palatalized," i.e., followed by a /y/ as in English *canyon, onion, opinion.*
О, о	There is no exact equivalent in American English, which is always a double-bodied "diphthongal" /ow/, rhyming with ***though, so, go, woe.*** The Russian /o/, when accented, sounds like /uo/ as in d**augh**ter, c**o**ffee, and b**ough**t. When a Russian /o/ is not accented, it turns into an /a/. In the word много, with two /o/s, the stress is on the first; thus Russians say /mn**o**ga/, more precisely [mn**uo**ga].

Russian Alphabet	Approximate Pronunciation
П, п	A close equivalent of the English /p/ phoneme, like /k/, this sound, too, is never aspirated word-initially as in English ***pill***, but pronounced without the escaping air as in ***spill***. When followed by the "soft vowels" и, е, ю, or я it is pronounced like *p* + *y* as in ***puke***, ***computer***.
Р, р	Corresponding to English /r/, this is a strong apical trill (rolling) as in Scottish English or Spanish *perro*, *carro*, and never the "murmured" sound of American English ***bird***, ***Burton***, ***murmur***.
С, с	A close correspondent of the English /s/ phoneme as in ***sit***, ***sister***, ***seem***, ***so***, etc., Russian с can be followed by the "soft vowels" и, е, ю, or я, in which case it resembles *s* + *y* in rapidly spoken English as in *miss you*, or the British pronunciation of ***issue***.
Т, т	The Russian т corresponds to the English /t/ phoneme with the following exceptions: it is never aspirated word-initially (similar to /k/ and /p/); imitate the /t/ of ***still*** not of ***till***. When followed by the "soft vowels" и, е, ю, and я, the Russian /t/ is palatalized, i.e, sounds like *t* + *y* in rapidly spoken English ***hit you***, ***meet you***, short of becoming the /c/ written [ch] of ***Charlie***.
У, у	Corresponding to the English /u/ phoneme of ***pool***, ***fool***, ***Sue***, ***shoe***, ***who***, and ***knew***, the Russian /u/ is "shorter" inasmuch as it is not followed by the /w/-glide typical of English. Russian /u/ never sounds like the English vowel in ***bull***, ***pull***, ***look***, ***soot***, etc.
Ф, ф	Corresponds to the English /f/ phoneme as in ***Fred***, ***food***, ***Phillip***, ***from***, etc. When followed by the "soft vowels" и, е, ю, and я, Russian /f/ sounds like English *f* + *y* in ***feud***, ***few***, ***fume***.
Х, х	There is no corresponding English sound; writing [kh] is but a rough approximation. Practice saying ***Howard***, ***Harry*** and ***Harriet*** as if gargling; the sound should be between /k/ and /h/; technically known as a "velar fricative."

Russian Alphabet	Approximate Pronunciation
Ц, ц	There is no single English sound corresponding to this Russian phoneme. The closest we can get to it is by thinking of [ts] as in *cats*. The word ***tsetse*** (a type of fly in Africa) is a good approximation. Very close to German /z/ as in ***Zimmer, Ziege, zwei;*** Italian *zio, zucchini,* etc.
Ч, ч	Corresponds to the English /ch/ sound as in ***Charlie, choose, chicken.***
Ш, ш	Corresponds to the English /sh/ sound as in ***she, shoe, Sheryll, wish, sugar, sure.***
Щ, щ	There being no English phoneme equivalent, one writes [shch], as if saying in rapid speech ***fresh chicken, fresh cheese, rush Charlie.***
Ъ, ъ	Known as the "hard sign," this symbol has no sound value, but indicates that the consonant in front of it is not to be palatalized, i.e., must not be followed by the /y/.
Ы, ы	Corresponds roughly to the "dark /l/" sound of rapidly and casually spoken American English *milk*, the second vowel of *rented*, or the /l/ of a "deep southern accent."
Ь, ь	Known as the "soft sign," this symbol indicates that the consonant immediately in front of it has to be palatalized, i.e., "softened" by the /y/. Typical after /t/ and /d/, which then are pronounced like *t* + *y* as in colloquial ***get you*** and *d* + *y* as in British ***due, dew.***
Э, э	Known as the "hard [e]," this sound, quite similar to English /e/ in let's get set, is never preceeded by the /y/-glide. *Этажерка* is thus /etazherka/ "bookcase, shelves."
Ю, ю	Comparable to *y* + *u* in English, as in ***you*** or ***ewe***, except that the /u/ does not round off in a /w/-like off-glide. (See remarks on /u/ above.)
Я, я	The last letter of the Russian alphabet corresponds to *y* + *a* in English as in ***yard, Yarborough***, or German *ja* "yes." It is the only Russian letter that is a self-contained word, meaning "I."

Further Remarks

Whenever Russian /o/ is unaccented, it sounds like an [a]. When Russian /e/ is unaccented, it sounds like [i]. When an /a/ is unaccented, it becomes like the English "murmured vowel," the last sound of *sofa*. It is therefore essential that students should pay particular attention to the placement of stress in Russian. A stressed /o/ — quite unlike English — does not round off in /ow/, but rather it starts with an /u/-like sound. Russian /u/ is between English /U/ as in ***bull, pull, full*** and */uw/* as in ***pool, fool, Luke***. Russian /i/ is between English *feel* and *fill*, closer in quality to the former and closer in duration to the latter.

Сокраще́ния, при́нятые в Росси́и
Abbreviations — Russian-English

Отсу́тствие сокраще́ний на ру́сском и́ли на англи́йском языке́ ука́зывает на их ра́зное примене́ние в да́нных языка́х.

Сокраще́ние	Значе́ние	Эквивале́нт, при́нятый в США	Сокраще́ние, при́нятое в США
		А	
	Ассоциа́ция автомобили́стов Аме́рики	American Automobile Association	AAA
АО	автоно́мная о́бласть	autonomous region	
АПН	Аге́нтство печа́ти «Но́вости»	Novosti Press Agency	APN
АТС	автомати́ческая телефо́нная ста́нция	automatic telephone exchange	
АЭС	а́томная электро́станция	atomic power station	
а/я	абонеме́нтный я́щик	(Post Office) Box	P.O.Box
		Б	
б.	бы́вший	former, ex-, one-time	
БАМ	Байка́ло-Аму́рская магистра́ль	Baikal-Amur Railway	
Б. дом	Бе́лый дом	White House	
Би-Би-Си	Брита́нская те́ле- и радиовеща́тельная корпора́ция	British Broadcasting Corporation	BBC
БТР	бронетранспортёр	armored personnel carrier	APC
б-р	бульва́р	boulevard	blvd.

Сокращéние	Значéние	Эквивалéнт, принятый в США	Сокращéние, принятое в США
бух.	бухгáлтер	bookkeeper; accountant	
		В	
В	востóк	east	E
в.	век	century	C
ВВС	воéнно-воздýшные сúлы	Air Force	AF
ВИЧ	вúрус иммунодефицúта человéка	human immuno-deficiency virus	HIV
ВМК	внутримáточный контрацептив	intrauterine (contraceptive) device	IUD
ВМФ	воéнно-морскóй флот	Navy	
ВНП	валовóй национáльный продýкт	gross national product	GNP
ВОЗ	Всемúрная Организáция Здравоохранéния	World Health Organization	WHO
Вт	ватт	watt	W
втуз	вы́сшее технúческое учéбное заведéние	college; university	
вуз	вы́сшее учéбное заведéние	college; university	
		Г	
г	грамм	gram	g; gr
г.	1. год 2. горá 3. гóрод 4. господúн	1. year 2. mountain 3. city; town 4. Mister	(2) mt. (4) Mr.

Сокра-щéние	Значéние	Эквивалéнт, прíнятый в США	Сокращé-ние, прíнятое в США
га	гектáр	hectare	ha
ГАИ	госудáрственная автомобíльная инспéкция	state motor vehicle inspection	
ГАТТ	Генерáльное соглашéние о тарíфах и торгóвле	General Agreement on Tariffs and Trade	GATT
гг.	1. гóды 2. городá 3. господá	1. years 2. cities; towns 3. Messrs; Mr. and Mrs.	(3)Messrs; Mr. and Mrs.
г-жа	миз; госпожá	Miss; Mistress	Ms.
г-жа	госпожá	Mistress	Mrs.
г-н	господíн	Mr.; Master	Mr.
ГУМ	госудáрственный универсáльный магазíн	state department store	GUM
ГЭС	гидро-электростáнция	hydroelectric power station	
		Д	
д.	дом	house	
ДЗУ	долговрéменное запоминáющее устрóйство	read-only memory	ROM
ДНК	дезоксирибо-нуклеíновая кислотá	deoxyribonucleic acid	DNA
до н.э.	до нáшей э́ры	before Christ	B.C.
д-р	1. дóктор 2. дирéктор	1. doctor 2. director	(1) Dr.

Сокра-щéние	Значéние	Эквивалéнт, прíнятый в США	Сокращé-ние, прíнятое в США
		Е	
ЕАСТ	Европéйская Ассоциáция Свобóдной Торгóвли	European Free Trade Association	EFTA
ЕВС	Европéйская валю́тная систéма	European monetary system	EMS
ЕКЮ	услóвная дéнежная единíца стран Европéйс-кого Союза	European Currency Unit	ECU
ЕП	Европарлáмент	European Parliament	EP
ЕС	Европéйский Сою́з (Евросою́з)	European Union	EU
ЕЭС	Европéйское экономíческое сообщество	European Economic Community	EEC
		Ж	
ж.	Жéнская (убóрная)	Ladies (lavatory)	
ж.д.	желéзная дорóга	railroad	RR
ЖКИ	жидко-кристаллíческий индикáтор	liquid-crystal display	LCD
ЖЭК	жилíщно-эксплуатациóнная контóра	housing office	

Сокращéние	Значéние	Эквивалéнт, прúнятый в США	Сокращéние, прúнятое в США
		З	
З	зáпад	west	W
ЗАГС	(отдéл) зáписи áктов граждáнского состоя́ния	registry office	
ЗУПВ	запоминáющее устрóйство с произвóльной вы́боркой	random-access memory	RAM
		И	
им.	úмени	named after	
ИРА	Ирлáндская республикáнская áрмия	Irish Republican Army	IRA
и т.д.	и так дáлее	and so on; et cetera	etc.
		К	
°К	грáдусов по Кéльвину	degrees Kelvin	K
к; кг	килó	kilo(s); kilogram(s)	kg
кв.	квартúра	apartment	apt.
КГБ	Комитéт Государственной Безопáсности	State Security Committee	KGB
КЛА	космúческий летáтельный аппарáт	spacecraft; space vehicle	
км	киломéтр	kilometer	km
КНДР	Корéйская Нарóдно-Демократúческая Респу́блика	People's Democratic Republic of Korea	

Сокращéние	Значéние	Эквивалéнт, прúнятый в США	Сокращéние, прúнятое в США
К°	компáния	Company	Co.
КП	Коммунистúческая пáртия	Communist Party	
КПСС	Коммунистúческая пáртия Совéтского Сою́за	Communist Party of the Soviet Union	CPSU
		Л	
л	литр	liter(s)	l
ЛСД	диэтиламúд лизергúновой кислоты́	lysergic acid diethylamide	LSD
л-т	лейтенáнт	lieutenant	Lt
		М	
М	1. метрó 2. Мужскáя (убóрная)	1. Subway; Underground 2. Gents; Gentlemen (lavatory)	
М.	Москвá	Moscow	
м	метр	meter(s)	m
м.	минýта	minute	min.
МБ	Междунарóдный Банк	World Bank	WB
Мб	мегабáйт	megabyte	Mb
м.б.	мóжет быть	maybe; perhaps	
МБР	межконтинентáльная баллистúческая ракéта	intercontinental ballistic missile	ICBM
МВД	Министéрство внýтренних дел	Ministry of Internal Affairs	
МВТ	Министéрство внéшней торгóвли	Ministry of Foreign Trade	

Сокращéние	Значéние	Эквивалéнт, при́нятый в США	Сокращéние, при́нятое в США
МВФ	Междунарóдный валю́тный фонд	International Monetary Fund	IMF
мг	миллигрáмм	milligram(s)	mg
м.г.	мину́вшего гóда	last year	
МГУ	Москóвский госудáрственный университéт	Moscow State University	
МИГ; миг	Микоя́н и Гурéвич	MiG (aircraft)	MiG
МИД	Министéрство инострáнных дел	Ministry of Foreign Affairs	
МТС	машиннотрáкторная стáнция	machinery and tractor station	
МФА	междунарóдный фонети́ческий алфави́т	International Phonetic Alphabet	IPA
МХАТ	Москóвский худóжественный академи́ческий теáтр	Moscow Arts Theater	
		Н	
наб.	нáбережная	embankment	
напр.	напримéр	for example	e.g.
НАТО	Организáция Сéверо-атланти́ческого договóра	North Atlantic Treaty Organization	NATO
НИИ-	нау́чно-исслéдовательский институ́т	research institute	
НЛО	неопóзнанный летáющий объéкт	unidentified flying object	UFO

Сокра-щéние	Значéние	Эквивалéнт, при́нятый в США	Сокращé-ние, при́нятое в США
НТР	нау́чно-техни́ческая револю́ция	scientific and technological revolution	
н.э.	нáшей э́ры	Anno Domini	A.D.
		О	
о.; о-в	óстров	island; isle	I
ОВИР	отдéл виз и регистрáций	visa and registration department	
о-во	óбщество	Society; Company	Soc.; Co.
ООН	Организáция Объединённых Нáций	United Nations Organization	UN
ООП	Организáция освобождéния Палести́ны	Palestine Liberation Organization	PLO
ОПЕК	Организáция стран-экспортёров нéфти	Organization of Petroleum-Exporting Countries	OPEC
ОСВ	ограничéние стратеги́ческих вооружéний	Strategic Arms Limitation Talks	SALT
ОССВ	ограничéние и сокращéние стратеги́ческих вооружéний	Strategic Arms Reduction Talks	START
		П	
ПЗУ	постоя́нное запоминáющее устрóйство	read-only memory	ROM
ПК	персонáльный компью́тер	personal computer	PC
пл.	плóщадь	Square	Sq.

Сокра-щéние	Значéние	Эквивалéнт, при́нятый в США	Сокращé-ние, при́нятое в США
пр.	проспéкт; авеню́	Avenue	Av(e).
продмаг	продовóльственный магази́н	food store	
		Р	
р.	1. рекá 2. рубль	1. River 2. ruble(s)	(1)R (2) r.
ред.	редáктор	editor	Ed.
РТС	ремóнтно-техни́ческая стáнция	repairs and engineering station	
		С	
с	сéвер	north	N
св.	святой; Сан(кт)-	Saint	St.
СЕАТО	Организáция договóра Ю́го-Востóчной А́зии	Southeast Asia Treaty Organization	SEATO
с.г.; с/г	сегó гóда	of this year	
секр.	секретáрь	Secretary	secy.
СКВ	свобóдно конверти́руемая валю́та	hard currency; freely convertible currency	
см.	смотри́	see; refer to; (quod vide)	q.v.
см. на об.	смотри́ на оборóте	please turn over	
СПБ;СПб	Санкт-Петербу́рг	St. Petersburg	
ср.	сравни́те	compare	cf.
ССР	Совéтская социалисти́ческая Респу́блика	Soviet Socialist Republic	
СССР	Сою́з Совéтских Социалисти́ческих Респу́блик	Union of Soviet Socialist Republics	USSR

Сокра-щéние	Значéние	Эквивалéнт, прúнятый в США	Сокращé-ние, прúнятое в США
ст. ложка	столóвая лóжка; (по столóвой лóжке)	tablespoon(ful)	tbs.
стр.	странúца; странúцы	page; pages	p.; pp.
США	Соединённые Штáты Амéрики	United States of America	USA
		Т	
т	тонна	ton(s)	t.
т.	1. товáрищ 2. том	1. Comrade 2. volume	(2) vol.
так наз.	так назывáемый	so-called	
ТАСС	Телегрáфное агéнтство Совéтского Союза	Telegraph Agency of the Soviet Union	TASS
т.е.	тó есть	that is	i.e.
тел.	телефóн	telephone	tel.
т. обр.	такúм óбразом	so that	
тoo.	товарúщество с ограничéнной ответственностью	limited liability company	Ltd.
тт.	1. товáрищи 2. томá	1. Comrades 2. volumes	(2)vols.
		У	
Т	«учéбная» (на машúне)	learner	L
ул.	ýлица	street	St.

Сокращéние	Значéние	Эквивалéнт, прйнятый в США	Сокращéние, прйнятое в США
		Ф	
°Ф	фаренгéйт	Fahrenheit	F
ФАО	Продовóльственная и сельскохозя́йственная организáция Объединённых Нáций	Food and Agriculture Organization of the United Nations	FAO
ФБР	Федерáльное бюрó расследований	Federal Bureau of Investigation	FBI
ФРГ	Федератйвная Респýблика Гермáнии	Federal Republic of Germany	FRG
		Ц	
Ц	Цéльсия	Celsius	C
ЦК	Центрáльный Комитéт	Central Committee	
ЦП	центрáльный процéссор	central processing unit	CPU
ЦРУ	Центрáльное развéдывательное управлéние	Central Intelligence Agency	CIA
ЦУМ	центрáльный универсáльный магазйн	Central Department Store	
		Ч	
ч.	час	hour; o'clock	hr.

Сокра-щéние	Значéние	Эквивалéнт, прúнятый в США	Сокращé-ние, прúнятое в США
		Ю	
ю	юг	south	S
ЮНЕСКО	Организáция Объединённых Нáций по вопрóсам образовáния, наýки и культýры	United Nations Educational, Scientific and Cultural Organization	UNESCO
ЮНИСЕФ	Дéтский фонд Организáции Объединённых Нáций	United Nations International Children's Emergency Fund	UNICEF

Abbreviations — English-Russian
Сокраще́ния, при́нятые в США

Russian or English equivalents are missing for some of these abbreviations; this reflects the fact that usage is not the same in the two languages.

Abbreviation	Meaning	Russian Equivalent	Russian Abbreviation
		A	
AAA	American Automobile Association	Ассоциа́ция автомобили́стов Аме́рики	
ABC	alphabet	алфави́т	
ACV	air-cushion vehicle	аппара́т на возду́шной поду́шке	
A.D.	Anno Domini	на́шей э́ры	н.э.
ad lib	ad libitum; at will	ско́лько уго́дно	
AIDS	acquired immune deficiency syndrome	синдро́м приобретённого иммýнного дефици́та	СПИД
a.m.	ante meridiem; before noon	у́тро; у́тром	
APC	armored personnel carrier	бронетранспортёр	БТР
APN	Novosti Press Agency	Аге́нтство печа́ти «Но́вости»	АПН
apt.	apartment	кварти́ра	кв.
a.s.a.p.	as soon as possible	как мо́жно скоре́е	
Av(e).	avenue	проспе́кт; авеню́	пр.
AWOL	absent without official leave	в самово́льной отлу́чке	
		B	
B.A.	Bachelor of Arts	бакала́вр гуманита́рных нау́к	
BBC	British Broadcasting Corporation	Брита́нская те́ле- и радиовеща́тельная корпора́ция	Би-Би-Си

Abbre-viation	Meaning	Russian Equivalent	Russian Abbrevi-ation
B.C.	before Christ	до на́шей э́ры	до н.э.
B.Ed.	Bachelor of Education	бакала́вр педагоги́-ческих нау́к	
B.Litt.	Bachelor of Letters	бакала́вр литерату́ры	
bldg.	building	зда́ние	
blvd.	boulevard	бульва́р	б-р
Br.	British	брита́нский	
bros.	brothers	бра́тья	
B.S.	Bachelor of Science	бакала́вр (есте́ст-венных) нау́к	
		C	
C	Celsius	Це́льсия	Ц
C	century	век	в.
Can.	Canada	Кана́да	
CD	compact disc	компа́кт-диск	
cf.	compare	сравни́те	ср.
CIA	Central Intelligence Agency	центра́льное разве́дывательное управле́ние	ЦРУ
CID	Criminal Investigation Department	отде́л уголо́вного ро́зыска	
Co.	company	компа́ния	К° ; о-во
c/o	care of	по а́дресу	
COD	cash on delivery	упла́та при поста́вке	
Corp.	Corporation	корпора́ция	
CPSU	Communist Party of the Soviet Union	Коммунисти́ческая Па́ртия Сове́тского Сою́за	КПСС
CPU	central processing unit	центра́льный проце́ссор	ЦП
CSE	Certificate of Secondary Education	аттеста́т о сре́днем образова́нии	

Abbreviation	Meaning	Russian Equivalent	Russian Abbreviation
		D	
dc	direct current	постоя́нный ток	
dept.	department	отде́л	
dist.	district	райо́н; о́круг	
DJ	disc jockey	ди́ск-жоке́й	
D.Litt.	Doctor of Letters	до́ктор литерату́ры	
DNA	deoxyribonucleic acid	дезоксирибонуклей-новая кислота́	ДНК
Dr.	1. doctor 2. drive	1.до́ктор 2.подъездна́я доро́га	(1) д-р
DTP	desktop publishing	насто́льная полигра́фия	
		E	
E	east	восто́к	В
ECU	European Currency Unit	усло́вная де́нежная едини́ца стран Европе́йского Сою́за	ЕКЮ
Ed.	editor	реда́ктор	ред.
EEC	European Economic Community	Европе́йское эконо-ми́ческое соо́бщество	ЕЭС
EFTA	European Free Trade Association	Европе́йская ассоциа́ция свобо́дной торго́вли	
e.g.	for example *(exempli gratia)*	наприме́р	напр.
EMS	European Monetary System	Европе́йская валю́тная систе́ма	ЕВС
encl.	enclosure	приложе́ние	прил.
Eng.	England; English	А́нглия; англи́йский	
ESP	extrasensory perception	экстрасенсо́рика	
Esq.	Esquire	господи́н	г-н
EP	European Parliament	Европарла́мент	ЕП
EU	European Union	Европе́йский Сою́з (Евросою́з)	ЕС

Abbre-viation	Meaning	Russian Equivalent	Russian Abbrevi-ation
		F	
F	Fahrenheit	фаренге́йт	°Ф
FAO	Food and Agriculture Organization of the United Nations	Продово́льственная и сельскохозя́йственная организа́ция Объединённых На́ций	ФАО
FBI	Federal Bureau of Investigation	Федера́льное бюро́ рассле́дований	ФБР
fed.	federal	федерати́вный	
fem.	feminine	же́нский	
FRG	Federal Republic of Germany	Федерати́вная Респу́блика Герма́нии	ФРГ
		G	
g.	gram(s)	грамм	гм
GATT	General Agreement on Tariffs and Trade	Генера́льное соглаше́ние по тари́фам и торго́вле	ГАТТ
GNP	gross national product	валово́й национа́льный проду́кт	ВНП
	Gents; Gentlemen	мужска́я (убо́рная)	М
govt.	government	прави́тельство	
GP	General Practitioner	врач о́бщей пра́ктики	
GPO	General Post Office	главпочта́мт	
GUM	state department store	госуда́рственный универса́льный магази́н	ГУМ
Gr. Brit.	Great Britain	Великобрита́ния	
gro. wt.	gross weight	вес бру́тто	
		H	
H-bomb	hydrogen bomb	водоро́дная бо́мба	
HQ	headquarters	штаб-кварти́ра	
hr.	hour	час	ч.

Abbre-viation	Meaning	Russian Equivalent	Russian Abbrevi-ation
HIV	human immuno-deficiency virus	ви́рус иммунодефици́та челове́ка	ВИЧ
		I	
id.	the same *(idem)*	то́т же	
ICBM	intercontinental ballistic missile	межконтинента́льная баллисти́ческая раке́та	МБР
ID	identity card	удостове́рение ли́чности	
i.e.	that is (*id est*)	то́ есть	т.е.
IMF	International Monetary Fund	Междунаро́дный валю́тный фонд	МВФ
IOU	I owe you	долгова́я распи́ска	
IPA	International Phonetic Alphabet	Междунаро́дный фонети́ческий алфави́т	
IQ	intelligence quotient	коэффицие́нт у́мственного разви́тия	
IRA	Irish Republican Army	Ирла́ндская респуб-лика́нская а́рмия	ИРА
ISBN	international standard book number	междунаро́дный станда́ртный кни́жный но́мер	
IUD	intrauterine device	внутрима́точный контрацепти́в	ВМК
		J	
JC	Jesus Christ	Иису́с Христо́с	
jr.	junior	мла́дший	
		K	
K	degrees Kelvin	гра́дусов по Ке́львину	°K
kg	kilogram	кило́	к; кг

Abbre-viation	Meaning	Russian Equivalent	Russian Abbrevi-ation
KGB	State Security Committee	Комите́т госуда́рственной безопа́сности	КГБ
km	kilometer	киломе́тр	км
KO	knockout	нока́ут	
		L	
L	learner	«уче́бная» (на маши́не)	У
l	liter(s)	литр	л
LCD	liquid-crystal display	жи́дко-кристал-ли́ческий индика́тор	ЖКИ
Lt	lieutenant	лейтена́нт	л-т
LSD	lysergic acid diethylamide	диэтилами́д лизерги́новой кислоты́	ЛСД
Ltd.	limited liability company	това́рищество с ограни́ченной отве́тственностью	too.
		M	
m	meter(s)	метр	м
MA	Master of Arts	ма́гистр гумани-та́рных нау́к	
Mb	megabyte(s)	мегаба́йт	Мб
MD	1. Doctor of Medicine 2. Managing Director	1. до́ктор медици́ны 2. дире́ктор-распоряди́тель	д-р
mg	milligram(s)	миллигра́м	мг
MiG	(aircraft) MiG	Микоя́н и Гуре́вич	МИГ; миг
min	minute	мину́та	м
MP	Member of Parliament	член парла́мента	
Mr.; Messrs.	Mister; Misters	господи́н; господа́	г-н; гг.
Mrs.	Mistress	госпожа́	г-жа

Abbreviation	Meaning	Russian Equivalent	Russian Abbreviation
MS	manuscript	ру́копись	
Ms.	Miss; Mistress	миз; госпожа́	г-жа
MS	Master of Science	маги́стр (есте́ственных) нау́к	
Mt.	Mount	гора́	г
		N	
N	North	се́вер	С
NASA	National Aeronautics and Space Administration	Национа́льное управле́ние по аэрона́втике и иссле́дованию косми́ческого простра́нства	НАСА
nat.; natl.	national	национа́льный	
NATO	North Atlantic Treaty Organization	Организа́ция Се́веро-атланти́ческого догово́ра	НАТО
NT	New Testament	Но́вый заве́т	
n. wt.	net weight	чи́стый вес; вес не́тто	
		O	
0	null	ноль	0
OK	okay; all right	«до́бро»	
OPEC	Organization of Petroleum-Exporting Countries	Организа́ция стран-экспортёров не́фти	ОПЕК
OT	Old Testament	Ве́тхий заве́т	
oz	ounce	у́нция	
		P	
p.a.	per annum	в год	
PC	1. police constable 2. personal computer	полице́йский персона́льный компью́тер	ПК
p.d.q.	pretty damn quick	поживе́е; «как из пу́шки»	
PE	physical education	физкульту́ра	

Abbre-viation	Meaning	Russian Equivalent	Russian Abbrevi-ation
p.; pp.	page; pages	страни́ца; страни́цы	стр.
Ph.D.	Doctor of Philosophy	сте́пень кандида́та нау́к	
PLO	Palestine Liberation Organization	Организа́ция освобожде́ния Палести́ны	ООП
p.m.	post meridiem	пополу́дни	
PO	Post Office	по́чта	
POW	prisoner of war	военнопле́нный	
PR	public relations	взаимоотноше́ние с клиенту́рой	
Prof.	Professor	профе́ссор	
P.S.	postcript	припи́ска (к письму́); постскри́птум	
PTO	please turn over	смотри́ на оборо́те	см. на об.
publ.	publisher	изда́тель	изд.
		Q	
QED	which was to be demonstrated *(quod erat demonstrandum)*	что и тре́бовалось доказа́ть	
QT	to do something on the quiet	сде́лать по-ти́хому	
q.v.	see *(quod vide)*	смотри́; (та́м-то)	см.
		R	
RC	Roman Catholic	като́лик	
RAM	random-access memory	запомина́ющее устро́йство с произво́льной вы́боркой	ЗУПВ
Rd.	road	доро́га	
ref.	reference	сно́ска; ссы́лка	
Rep.	1. representative 2. Republican	1. представи́тель 2. член Республика́нской па́ртии	
Rev.	Reverend	его́ преподо́бие	

Abbre-viation	Meaning	Russian Equivalent	Russian Abbrevi-ation
ROM	read-only memory	долговре́менное запомина́ющее устро́йство	ДЗУ
RR	railroad	желе́зная доро́га	ж.д.
RSVP	please answer *(répondez s'il vous plaît)*	бу́дьте любе́зны отве́тить	
		S	
S	south	юг	
SA	South America	Ю́жная Аме́рика	ю
SALT	Strategic Arms Limitation Talks	перегово́ры по ограниче́нию стратеги́ческих вооруже́ний	ОСВ
SEATO	Southeast Asia Treaty Organization	Организа́ция догово́ра Ю́го-Восто́чной А́зии	СЕАТО
secy.	secretary	секрета́рь	секр.
Soc.	Society	о́бщество	о-во
SOS	save our souls	(ра́дио) сигна́л бе́дствия	
Sq.	Square	пло́щадь	пл.
St.	1. street; 2. Saint	1. ули́ца 2. свято́й; Сан(кт)-	1. ул.; 2. св.
START	Strategic Arms Reduction Talks	перегово́ры о сокраще́нии стратеги́ческих вооруже́ний	ОССВ
		T	
t	ton(s)	то́нна	т
TASS	Telegraph Agency of the Soviet Union	Телегра́фное аге́нтство Сове́тского Сою́за	ТАСС
tbs.	tablespoon(ful)	столо́вая ло́жка; (по столо́вой ло́жке)	ст. ложка

Abbreviation	Meaning	Russian Equivalent	Russian Abbreviation
tel.	telephone	телефо́н	тел.
transp.	transport	тра́нспорт	
TV	television	телеви́зор	
		U	
U.; Univ.	university	университе́т	
UFO	unidentified flying object	неопо́знанный лета́ющий объе́кт	НЛО
U.K.	United Kingdom	Соединённое Короле́вство (Великобрита́нии и Се́верной Ирла́ндии)	
U.N.; UN	United Nations (Organization)	Организа́ция Объединённых На́ций	ООН
UNESCO	United Nations Educational, Scientific and Cultural Organization	Организа́ция Объединённых На́ций по вопро́сам образова́ния, нау́ки и культу́ры	ЮНЕСКО
UNICEF	United Nations International Children's Emergency Fund	Де́тский фонд Организа́ции Объединённых На́ций	ЮНИСЕФ
USA	United States of America	Соединённые Шта́ты Аме́рики	США
USA	United States Army	Арми́я Соединённых Шта́тов Аме́рики	
USSR	Union of Soviet Socialist Republics	Сою́з Сове́тских Социалисти́ческих Респу́блик	СССР
		V	
V	volt(s)	вольт	В
VCR	video cassette recorder	видеомагнитофо́н	
VD	venereal disease	венери́ческая боле́знь	

Abbre-viation	Meaning	Russian Equivalent	Russian Abbrevi-ation
VDU	visual display unit	дисплéй	
VIP	very important person	высокопостáвленное лицó	
Ven.	Venerable	преподóбный	
vol.	volume	том	т.
vols.	volumes	томá	тт.
VP	Vice President	вúце-президéнт	
vs.	versus, against	прóтив	
		W	
W	watt	ватт	Вт
WB	World Bank	Междунарóдный Банк	МБ
WC	water closet; toilet	убóрная	
WHO	World Health Organization	Всемúрная Организáция Здравоохранéния	ВОЗ
wk.	week	недéля	
wt.	weight	вес	
		X	
Xmas	Christmas	Рождествó	
		Y	
yd.	yard	ярд	
YMCA	Young Men's Christian Association	Христиáнский сoюз молодых людéй	
yr.	year; years	год; гóды	г.; гг.
YWCA	Young Women's Christian Association	Христиáнский сoюз жéнской молодёжи	
		Z	
Z	Zone	зóна	

Ве́са и ме́ры (Weights and Measures)

Ста́рые ру́сские веса́ и ме́ры нахо́дятся в ско́бках. The old Russian weights and measures are in parentheses.

Веса́ и ме́ры, при́нятые в Росси́и		Measures used in Russia	
Веса́ (Weight)			
грамм	0,03 у́нции	gram	0.03 ounce
и́ли	15,43 гра́на	or	15.43 grains
килогра́мм	2,20 фу́нта	kilogram	2.20 pounds
то́нна	2204,60 фу́нта	ton	2204.60 pounds
(фунт)	0,90 фу́нта	(funt)	0.90 pound
(пуд)	36,07 фу́нта	(pood)	36.07 pounds
Ме́ры длины́ (Length)			
киломе́тр	0,62 ми́ли	kilometer	0.62 mile
метр	39,37 дю́йма	meter	39.37 inches
сантиме́тр	0,39 дю́йма	centimeter	0.39 inch
миллиме́тр	0,03 дю́йма	millimeter	0.03 inch
(верста́)	0,66 ми́ли	(verst)	0.66 mile
(са́жень)	7,00 фу́тов	(sazhen)	7.00 feet
(фут)	1,00 фут	(foot)	1.00 foot
(арши́н)	28,00 дю́ймов	(arshin)	28.00 inches
(вершо́к)	1,75 дю́йма	(vershok)	1.75 inches
(дюйм)	1,00 дюйм	(inch)	1.00 inch
Ме́ры ёмкости (Capacity)			
литр	1,05 ква́рты жи́дкости	liter	1.05 fluid quart
и́ли	0,26 галло́на	or	0.26 gallon
и́ли	33,81 у́нции жи́дкости	or	33.81 fluid ounces

Ме́ры объёма (Volume)

куби́ческий метр	35,31	куби́ческих фу́тов	cubic meter	35.31 cubic feet
и́ли	1,30	куби́ческих я́рдов	or	1.30 cubic yards
куби́ческий сантиме́тр	0,06	куби́ческого дю́йма	cubic centimeter	0.06 cubic inch

Квадра́тные ме́ры (Area)

квадра́тный киломе́тр	0,38	квадра́тной ми́ли	square kilometer	0.38 square mile
гекта́р	2,47	а́кра	hectare	2.47 acres
квадра́тный метр	10,76	квадра́тных фу́тов	square meter	10.76 square feet
и́ли	1,19	квадра́тных я́рдов	or	1.19 square yards
квадра́тный сантиме́тр	0,15	квадра́тного дю́йма	square centimeter	0.15 square inch
(десяти́на)	2,70	а́кра	(desyatina)	2.70 acres

Weights and Measures
(Ве́са и ме́ры)

US Measures		Веса́ и ме́ры, при́нятые в США	
Weights (веса́)			
grain	0.06 gram	гран	0,06 гра́мма
ounce	28.35 gram	у́нция	28,35 гра́мма
pound	0.45 kilogram	фунт	0,45 килогра́мма
ton	907.18 kilogram	то́нна	970,18 килогра́мма
Linear (ме́ры длины́)			
mile	1.60 kilometer	ми́ля	1,60 киломе́тра
knot	1.85 kilometer/hour	у́зел	1,85 киломе́тра в час
yard	0.91 meter	ярд	0,91 ме́тра
foot	0.30 meter	фут	0,30 ме́тра
inch	2.54 centimeter	дюйм	2,54 сантиме́тра
Capacity (ме́ры ёмкости)			
fluid quart	0.94 liter	ква́рта жи́дкости	0,94 ли́тра
dry quart	1.10 liters	ква́рта сыпу́чих тел	1,10 ли́тра
gallon	3.78 liters	галло́н	3,78 ли́тра
bushel	35.24 liters	бу́шель	35,24 ли́тра
Volume (ме́ры объёма)			
cubic inch	16.38 cubic centimeters	куби́ческий дюйм	16,38 куби́ческих сантиме́тров
cubic foot	0.02 cubic meter	куби́ческий фут	0,02 куби́ческого ме́тра
cubic yard	0.76 cubic meter	куби́ческий ярд	0,76 куби́ческого ме́тра

Area (квадра́тные ме́ры)

acre	0.40	hectare	акр	0,40	гекта́ра
square mile	259.00	hectares	квадра́тная ми́ля	259,00	гекта́ров
square yard	0.83	square meter	квадра́тный ярд	0,83	ква́дратного ме́тра
square foot	929.03	square centimeters	квадра́тный фут	929,03	квадра́тных сантиме́тров
square inch	6.54	square centimeters	квадра́тный дюйм	6,54	квадра́тных сантиме́тров

Index

В

Д

Е

Ж

З

И

Й

К

Л

M

О

Р

С

У

Ф

Х

Ц

Ч

Notes

Notes

Notes

Notes